Illinois
Politics

Illinois Politics

A Citizen's Guide

JAMES D. NOWLAN,
SAMUEL K. GOVE, AND
RICHARD J. WINKEL JR.

Published in collaboration with the Institute of Government
and Public Affairs at the University of Illinois

UNIVERSITY OF ILLINOIS PRESS
Urbana and Chicago

Library of Congress Cataloging-in-Publication Data
Nowlan, James Dunlap, 1941–
Illinois politics : a citizen's guide / James D. Nowlan,
Samuel K. Gove, and Richard J. Winkel, Jr.
p.   cm.
Includes bibliographical references and index.
ISBN 978-0-252-07702-9 (pbk. : alk. paper)
1. Illinois—Politics and government. I. Gove, Samuel K.
II. Winkel, Richard. III. Title.
JK5716.N68   2010
320.4773—dc22   2009038147

Contents

• • • • • • • • • • • • •

Preface

• • • • • • • • • • • • •

This book is a substantial revision of a 1996 work by Gove and Nowlan, *Illinois Politics and Government: The Expanding Metropolitan Frontier* (University of Nebraska Press). The authors of the present book are an academic (Gove), a practical politician (Winkel), and a hybrid of the two types (Nowlan). Our goal is to provide the reader with a systematic overview of the way practical politics operates in and affects Illinois state government.

The earlier work emphasized, first, an individualistic Illinois political culture in which self-interest dominates and political corruption is tolerated and, second, a rapidly expanding metropolitan area that would likely come to dominate Illinois politics and government.

With regard to at least two matters, speculative observations that we made in 1996 appear to have been in error. In the earlier book, we declared that efforts to reduce political corruption had apparently met with some success and that in the new century the political "landscape will have tilted more sharply toward the expanding metropolitan frontier."

We now find it hard to make the case that corruption has abated, given the conviction in 2006 of Illinois governor George Ryan, the continuing successful prosecution of Chicago officials and businessmen, and, of course, the unprecedented legislative impeachment, conviction, and removal from office in 2009 of Governor Rod Blagojevich.

Nor has the political landscape tilted toward the suburbs, with the possible exception of increased population. Indeed, the political tilt appears to be toward the City of Chicago, though it has but half the population of the suburban collar that surrounds the city. At the time we were writing the 1996 book, Republicans controlled both chambers of the Illinois General Assembly, the executive mansion had been a GOP residence for two decades, and suburban Republicans dominated their party.

Since 1996, however, political observers and presidential candidates have concluded that Illinois has become a solidly "blue," or Democratic, state. In both 2000 and 2004, the Republican presidential campaigns early conceded the Illinois electoral vote outcome to the Democrats, bypassing the state to focus their efforts on "battleground" states. More important to Illinois politics, in 2009 all statewide offices as well as the two top posts in the legislature were held by Chicago Democrats. For additional reasons we develop in the chapters that follow, the suburbs have been unable to take political advantage of their geopolitical region's numerical superiority.

In the present work we revisit the theme of political culture and increase the focus on political corruption. We also reflect a bit on the state's "averageness." Over coffee one day in 2008, the authors lamented that for many if not most state lawmakers, being average among the states in our rankings on education, health care, and other indicators appeared to be acceptable, good enough. Coincidentally, in the following week, the Associated Press named Illinois "the most average state" in the nation on the basis of state rankings on twenty-one indicators such as demographics, educational achievement, and economic mix.[1]

We are not able to offer any profound observations about what it means, underneath, to be average. And, of course, statewide averages mask a wide range of outcomes within a state, from education outcomes to infant mortality rates. Nevertheless, in several places in the text, we identify this averageness and in the concluding chapter speculate on what it might mean for the state and its future.

The text includes chapters about the primary institutional branches of Illinois state government. We also present a chapter on education, arguably the single most important function for state government and its school districts. In addition, we devote a chapter to "following the money," that is, spending and taxing in Illinois, a topic important to a state that has been struggling to maintain its support for state services. Indeed, over the years the state has often been spending to meet current operating demands with dollars that, many think, should be saved to meet obligations to future state pensioners.

We encourage readers to feel free to communicate observations that might inform and improve a subsequent edition of this book, should there be one. We can be reached through the Institute of Government and Public Affairs Web site at www.igpa.uillinois.edu.

Acknowledgments

● ● ● ● ● ● ● ● ● ● ● ● ● ●

The authors owe a significant debt of gratitude to Kent Redfield and Zachary Stamp. Their meticulous reading of a draft of the manuscript generated numerous corrections, suggestions, and interpretations that improved the final product markedly. We are also indebted to Kent for writing the chapter about elections, which he is best qualified to do.

No authoritative book about Illinois politics can be produced without the sage counsel of Paul Green, Rich Miller, and Dick Simpson, each of whom made important contributions to the book.

Others who provided observations that improved our product included Katie Anselment, Jim Broadway, Andrew Flach, Ron Michaelson, Jim Reed, Ben Schwarm, Deanna Sullivan, David Tretter, and Mark Warnsing.

Kim Osmond of the Institute of Government and Public Affairs at the University of Illinois gathered the several drafts from the authors and produced the final manuscript in her typically efficient, capable, and pleasant manner.

The authors are affiliated with the Institute of Government and Public Affairs, and Samuel K. Gove is a former director of the institute. We want to thank institute director Robert F. Rich and all of our colleagues at the institute for their cogent observations about Illinois politics and government and for their camaraderie over the years.

Finally, we appreciate the thoughtful guidance provided by University of Illinois Press director Willis Regier, who encouraged us from the book's inception through every stage of production. In addition, we acknowledge the excellent copyediting by Jane Zanichkowsky, which made this book much more readable, and capable project oversight by Angela Burton of the University of Illinois Press.

Any errors of fact or interpretation reside with the authors.

Illinois
Politics

1.

Illinois in Perspective

● ● ● ● ● ● ● ● ● ● ● ● ●

Since its earliest days, Illinois has been captive to a political culture that treats government as just another marketplace in which to do business. In turn, this marketplace has provided a fertile setting for corruption, which has flourished. As we move into the second decade of the twenty-first century, glimmers of reform emanate from assertive good-government groups, and more ethical behavior may be forthcoming in reaction to a series of successful, nonpartisan prosecutions by a forceful, dogged U.S. attorney in Chicago.

The state is also characterized by its diversity. At the center of the nation, Illinois is sometimes referred to as a microcosm of the country. In 2007, for example, the Associated Press, in more prosaic terms, named Illinois "the most average state" in the nation, based on how closely the states matched national levels with regard to twenty-one demographic and economic factors. According to the AP, "Illinois' racial composition matches the nation's better than any other state. Education levels are similar, as are the mix of industry and the percentage of immigrants."[1]

Average, maybe, but, as we hope readers will conclude by the end of this book, anything but typical; that is, Illinois is a truly distinctive state in cultural and political terms.

This chapter provides a cultural, demographic, and economic framework in which to understand Illinois. Subsequent chapters view the state's government and politics from within this framework and in the context of the major institutions of government.

We begin with a brief introduction to the topic of political culture, which, we believe, is central to the understanding of the distinctive cast of Illinois politics.

Daniel Elazar was the leading student of political culture. Elazar has identified three primary strains of political culture among the groups that settled the American states: traditionalistic, moralistic, and individualistic.[2] For the traditionalistic culture, government's function is positive but is limited to securing the continued maintenance of the existing social order and its dominating elites. The moralistic orientation tends to view government as a positive instrument for promoting public good, with honesty and commitment to public service as strong values. The individualistic strain sees the democratic order as just another marketplace where individuals and groups may improve themselves socially and economically; ideology—and, in particular, an ideology of the common good or public interest—is of little concern, and because of the government-as-market orientation, profiting from government activity is tolerated.[3]

All three cultures still exist in Illinois, but the values of individualism are dominant, according to Elazar. "Politics in Illinois," he writes, "came early to be centered on personal influence, patronage, distribution of federal and later state benefits, and the availability of economic gain of those who were professionally committed to politics as their 'business.'"[4] Or, as politicians as well as interest groups and regional interests in the state have been known to ask, "Where's mine?"

In addition to the individualistic political culture, Illinois can be understood better, we believe, using demographic and economic perspectives. The slow growth of the population, for example, masks a pulsing of people outward from Chicago to an ever-widening suburban growth ring. The decades-long movement of population from Chicago and the inner rings of the metropolitan area to bigger homes and more space on the outer rings has now brought the Democratic Party's influence and electoral clout to a region long dominated by Republicans.

The state's economy, though huge, has generally been growing more slowly than that of the nation since World War II. While still a bit wealthier than the nation as a whole, the Illinois economy no longer yields tax revenue sufficient to meet either the wants of its residents or the spending habits of its elected officials. Before turning to each of these conditions, however, we offer some historical perspective.

The "Tall State," as it was called in a 1960s tourism campaign, stretches almost four hundred miles from its northern limit at the Wisconsin line to its southern tip at Cairo (pronounced "kay'-ro"), nestled between Kentucky and Missouri. The northernmost latitude is on a line with Portsmouth, New Hampshire, and at Cairo, its latitude is close to that of Portsmouth, Virginia.

The state's diversity is due in great measure to U.S. territorial delegate Nathaniel Pope, who in 1818 succeeded in passing an amendment to the Illinois Enabling Act that moved the new state's northern boundary forty-one miles to the north. This area of eight thousand square miles—mostly empty at the time—today encompasses metropolitan Chicago and almost 80 percent of the state's population; without it, Illinois would never have become the powerhouse that it is.[5]

Settlement of the state was facilitated by natural factors, ingenuity, and human achievements. The Ohio River offered a convenient super-waterway, and the state's generally level topography made the prairie relatively easy to traverse on foot. The opening of the Erie Canal in New York in 1825 facilitated the flow of Yankees and European immigrants via the Great Lakes. The early development of Illinois as a railroad center helped disperse the newly arrived throughout the state; later, the main line of the Illinois Central Railroad, running from New Orleans, would bring tens of thousands of blacks to jobs in Chicago.

The platting, or dividing, of Illinois into townships of thirty-six uniform parcels of one-mile squares, as decreed by the U.S. Congress in the Northwest Ordinances of 1785 and 1787, was designed to transfer public lands efficiently into private hands.[6] This it did. Each mile square represented a "section" of land of 640 acres. Township roads were laid out along the sections. The township plats made it simple to survey and sell virgin land with a minimum of confusion and dispute. Even today, for the airplane traveler crossing Illinois, a geometric checkerboard pattern passes below.

There was a hunger to develop this rich flatland, but, first, transportation infrastructure was needed to get the settlers in and the bounty of the fields to market. When Abraham Lincoln and Stephen A. Douglas served as state lawmakers in the 1830s, the legislature embarked on an ambitious scheme of "internal improvements," but the dreamed-of network of wood-plank roads, canals, and railroads collapsed under the weight of poor planning, a weak national economy, and a lack of both capital and engineering capacity.[7] Lincoln and Douglas later became U.S. congressmen and revived the idea, this time convincing the U.S. government to assist by providing huge land grants for private investors. In 1851 the federal government offered 3.75 million acres of railroad right-of-way and adjoining land to investors in the Illinois Central Railroad. Within five years, 705 miles of track had been laid from Cairo to Galena, with a spur to Chicago. The Illinois Central became the longest railway in the world and the nation's largest private venture to date.

Railroads served as the interstate highways of the nineteenth century. If a town was on a rail line, it generally prospered; if not, the town was often abandoned. Railroad trackage in Illinois increased from 111 miles in 1850 to 2,800 miles in 1860 to 7,000 miles by 1875. In part because of its railroad grid, Illinois was the fastest-growing territory in the world by the middle of the nineteenth century.[8] The thirty-six million acres of land in Illinois were enough for about a quarter-million quarter-section (160-acre) farms. One-fourth of those farms had been taken by 1850 and nearly all by 1875. Three in four farms were within five miles of a railroad, and only 5 percent were more than ten miles distant.[9]

Early Triumph for the "Modernizers"

In the free-for-all environment of the state's early days, no one culture held sway. This northern state had been settled first by southerners, primarily poor, land-hungry northern British and Scots-Irish pioneers from the uplands of Virginia and the Carolinas and from Tennessee and Kentucky.[10] James Simeone describes the first settlers as the "white folks" who saw the West (Illinois Territory) as a place of opportunity and feared the reestablishment of an economic aristocracy by English and old Virginia families.[11]

A second surge came in the 1830s via the new Erie Canal, primarily from New England and the Middle Atlantic states. These Yankees, who mostly settled in the central and northern parts of Illinois, generally brought more assets with them and put down roots into richer farmland than did those farther south.

These settlement patterns set the stage for a struggle between the "white folks" in southern Illinois and the "modernizers," primarily Yankees, in the north.[12] The genius of the modernizers, according to Richard Jensen, lay in a combination of values: faith in reason, a drive for middle-class status, equal rights, and the sense of having a mission to transform the world in their image. Education was their remedy, efficiency their ideal.

Everyone in Illinois recognized the difference between modernizers and white folks, or "traditionalists," as Jensen identifies them, although nobody used those words. Each group thought the other peculiar. Fast-talking Yankee peddlers were distrusted—one county even set a prohibitive fifty-dollar-per-quarter license fee for clock peddlers. One Yankee woman was amused by the drinking, horse trading, and quaint, slow drawl of the southerners. She talked with one who allowed that "it's a right smart thing to be able to read when you want to" but who didn't figure that books and the sciences would "do a man as much good as handy use of the rifle."[13]

Strong commitment to education was the hallmark of the modernizers. By 1883 the northern part of the state provided its children with one-third more days of schooling than did the schools in "Egypt," as deep southern Illinois was called, with its towns of Cairo, Karnak, and Thebes.[14] Jensen quotes a nineteenth-century governor on the values in northern Illinois: "Is a school house, a bridge, or a church to be built, a road to be made, a school or minister to be maintained, or taxes to be paid? The northern man is never to be found wanting."[15]

By 1860 the Yankee modernizers dominated northern Illinois politics, while traditionalists held sway in the south. Central Illinois became the uncertain political battleground. With Lincoln's election and the Civil War, the modernists triumphed and, through the Republican Party, controlled Illinois politics almost continuously for the following seventy years. (In order to emphasize that generalizations about traditionalists and modernizers are just that, we note that Lincoln the modernizer came from southern traditionalist roots while Stephen A. Douglas, who represented the traditionalist viewpoint in the 1860 presidential election, came from upstate New York.)

Chicago and the Great Midwest

In a compelling synthesis of the organic relationship between a great city and the vast prairie that envelops it, William Cronon explains that neither Chicago nor the rich countryside of the Midwest would have developed its great wealth if not for the symbiosis between the two: the urban center contributing creativity, energy, and capital and the farmers and small towns providing ambition, intelligence, and the harvest from incredibly fecund soils.[16] Plentiful water and easy waterborne transportation provided further economic stimulus. The Wabash, Ohio, and Mississippi Rivers formed Illinois's natural boundaries, while the Illinois River traversed the middle, positioning the state at the heart of the young nation's economic expansion.[17]

At the southern tip of Lake Michigan, Chicago sat astride the boundary between East and West. Chicago's meatpackers, grain merchants, and manufacturers showed extraordinary drive and creativity, not to mention a knack for attracting capital. The railroads were eager to carry their goods, and these capitalists put the Midwest's natural resources to use to create an unprecedented hive of economic development by the end of the 1800s.

Almost all the Chicago capitalists were Yankees such as the meatpackers Philip Swift and Gustavus Armour. These two men and their collaborators systematized the market in animal flesh. Building on the adage that "the hog is regarded as the most compact form in which the Indian corn crop . . . can be transported to market," they created hog slaughtering lines that were the forerunners of the assembly line.[18] Cattle were standardized as grade no. 1,

2, or 3. Rail cars were refrigerated so that dressed beef from Chicago could be marketed in the East.

According to Cronon, the overarching genius of Swift and Armour lay in the immense, impersonal, hierarchical organizations they created, operated by an army of managers and workers who would outlive and carry on after the founders. By 1880 Chicago had more than seventy-five thousand industrial workers, the largest such labor force west of the Appalachians.[19] To quote the muckraker Frank Norris: "The Great Grey City, brooking no rival, imposed its dominion upon a reach of country larger than many a kingdom of the Old World."[20]

By 1890, Chicago, with more than one million residents, was the nation's second-largest city. It promoted itself in 1893 by presenting the World's Columbian Exposition to twenty-seven million visitors. From a one-square-mile tract of marshes and scrub pines on the south side of Chicago arose a fairy city that hosted the exhibits of forty-six nations, a single exposition building said to seat three hundred thousand persons, and an amusement park ride built by George Ferris that could carry forty persons in each of thirty-six cars on a 250-foot-high revolving wheel.[21] Visitors were equally impressed by the real-world development a few miles up the lakefront in the city center. At twenty-one stories, the Masonic temple was the world's tallest building, a so-called skyscraper.

There was a tension between the fairy city of the exposition and the real city that surrounded it, a tension that persists to this day. Rural visitors from "downstate" (the portion of Illinois outside of Chicago and its suburban ring) were agog at the artificial White City but "afeared" of the perceived dangers and tumult of Chicago. Many Chicagoans, in fact, had already become eager for the tranquility of the country. In 1868 the urban planner Frederick Law Olmsted designed Riverside, west of Chicago, as a new community where families could enjoy the country while the breadwinner could take the train to his job downtown. Skyscraper and suburb created each other, said Cronon, and the railroad made both possible.[22]

By 1930 Chicago had 3.4 million inhabitants—almost half the state's total— and was the fourth-largest city in the world and the second-largest (after New York) in the United States. By 1945 Chicago's population peaked at 3.6 million, as the suburban era began in earnest. Auto ownership doubled between 1945 and the early 1950s, and expressways were being built, foreshadowing suburban growth. According to Jensen, "Comfort, security, and the promise of continued progress . . . made the suburban era a time of placid complacency."[23]

With Chicago leading the way and many downstate communities still thriving with mixed industrial and agricultural economies, Illinois was a relatively strong state through most of the twentieth century. But driven as it was by commercial achievement and with a succession of local and state-wide leaders who worked closely with and profited from business interests, Illinois became a place where the wealth of opportunity was matched only by the ruthlessness of those pursuing it.

The writer Nelson Algren, in his prose poem "Chicago: City on the Make," identified two key characteristics of the culture that came to dominate Illinois. First, leadership and success were highly prized, and, second, if the success involved a bit of shady dealing, so be it. "If he can get away with it I give the man credit," Algren said of a safe-blower. The same culture has always looked askance at weakness, brooking no sympathy for a woman reduced to prostitution or a jobless man numbing himself with beer. Warned Algren: "Wise up, Jim: it's a joint where the bulls and the foxes live well and the lambs wind up head-down from the hook."[24]

Downshift in the Economy

Though average, perhaps, among the states according to many indicators, Illinois has throughout its history been significantly wealthier than the nation as a whole. This has made it easier to provide decent schools and good public universities than has been the case for poorer states, even if the poorer states tax their citizens more heavily than does Illinois. The state continues to have a big economy; its gross state product in 2006 stood at $590 billion, which would make it about the sixteenth-largest economy in the world, just below the economies of Australia, Brazil, and Russia.[25] Since World War II, however, Illinois has experienced a gradual yet persistent slowing in its rate of growth relative to the nation's, which creates problems for elected officials who would like to fulfill the high expectations of citizens but find that their revenue stream cannot always keep up.

In 1949 average per capita personal income in Illinois was about 122 percent of the amount for the nation as a whole; in 1973 it had slipped to 114 percent, by 1992 it had fallen to just 109 percent, and by 2004 it stood at 104 percent of the national average.[26]

Since 1990 the growth rate of the Illinois economy has fallen behind those of the United States and the rest of the Midwest. On a scale with a starting point of 100 in 1990, the U.S. economy reached 124 by 2006 and that of the Midwest (minus Illinois) reached 117, while Illinois reached only 113.[27] Illinois has been lagging the United States in job growth as well. Since 1990 the state has not been able to match the nation in employment growth in any of ten sectors, from construction to trade, transportation, and utilities.[28] And job loss in the manufacturing sector has been more severe than for the United States. Following a loss of 200,000 jobs in 2000–2001 in the Illinois economy, as of June 2008 Illinois still had 65,900 fewer jobs than it did at its peak in November 2000—and this was before the recession of 2008. And the job growth has come in sectors that pay less on average than the manufacturing jobs they replaced.[29]

Prosperity continues to elude much of rural Illinois. During the 1980s jobs and wealth declined in rural western Illinois for the first time since the Great Depression. In 2004 the highest rate of poverty was not in Cook County, where Chicago is located (15.2 percent) but in Alexander County, along the Ohio River (23.8 percent), Pulaski County (20.7 percent), and Jackson County (20.2 percent), all in southern Illinois.[30] One measure of the economic desperation in small communities is their willingness to pursue jobs that would have been shunned in better times. In the 1960s a corrections department official would have been tarred, feathered, and run out of town if he had proposed building a prison in a community. By the 1980s downstate communities were literally begging to be the sites for new prisons to hold Illinois's burgeoning inmate population.

Division by Demographics

"Illinois stands at the geo-historical center of the United States," declares Daniel Elazar, "crossed by the great waves of migration that spread settlements across the country in the late eighteenth and nineteenth centuries from the middle states, the South, and New England, reinforced by the great migrational streams from Europe in the nineteenth century and of African Americans, Latinos, and Asians in the twentieth."[31]

Because of this diversity, people writing about Illinois have long called the state a microcosm of the United States, as if to enhance the importance of what is written about the Prairie State. The diversity is real and deep. For example, the classic "southern" movie *In the Heat of the Night,* featuring Sidney Poitier and Rod Steiger, was filmed almost entirely in the Illinois towns of Sparta and Chester because the moviemakers wanted a southern feel in an area that was close to a major airport, that in St. Louis. And Sparta and Chester are not even in deep southern Illinois!

At the other end of the state, on the Chicago Transit Authority train to O'Hare Airport a rider often hears more Spanish and Polish than English spoken by the passengers in this great entrepot city for immigrants.

If politics in Illinois is a business, votes are the currency, and since its earliest days Illinois politics has been shaped by the demographics of the voting public. In 1858 senatorial candidate Abraham Lincoln gave most of his campaign speeches in central Illinois (and only one in Chicago), from Danville in the east to Carthage and Dallas City in the west. This made sense because nearly half of the state's population lived in the central third of the state.[32] The sympathies of voters in northern Illinois were clearly with the new Republican Party, and those of voters in southern Illinois were strongly with the Democrats. Central Illinois was mixed, and either party could win elections. In contrast, statewide candidates in 1992 devoted great effort to garnering coverage by the television stations based in Chicago, which reach two-thirds of all the households in Illinois. Candidates spent little, if any, time in Danville, Carthage, or Dallas City.

The demographic profile of Illinois has been shifting, often dramatically, since the 1840s, when immigrants fleeing famine or turmoil in Ireland, Germany, and the Scandinavian countries began to reach the state. For the whole of the nineteenth century, Germans made up the largest immigrant group in St. Louis as well as in Chicago and Illinois as a whole. By 1860 nearly one-half of Chicago's burgeoning population was foreign-born.

A decade later, the sources of immigration had shifted to Italy and Eastern Europe; they came in great numbers until quotas went into effect in 1927. Poles began pouring into Chicago around the turn of the century, and by 1920 they numbered almost five hundred thousand.[33]

The first blacks were brought to the Illinois Territory as slaves. The state's first six governors were all slave owners at one time, and several had registered black servants while in office.[34] The Northwest Ordinance of 1787 had banned slavery, but it had failed to ban its surrogate, registered servitude. The white folks in southern Illinois generally favored slavery and forced a compromise in the 1818 Constitution that maintained the status quo for French slaves and indentured servants brought in during the territorial period.[35] Any future introduction of slavery was prohibited, with the exception that slaves could be used to mine salt at the salt springs near Shawneetown until 1825. The adoption in 1824 of a "black code" effectively prevented free blacks from settling in the state.[36]

Major settlement by blacks did not begin until after the Civil War, and even then it grew slowly. In 1871 Chicago's black neighborhood was three blocks wide and fifteen blocks long, with about twenty-five hundred residents.[37] But when, during World War I, severe labor shortages hampered production in Chicago factories, a large-scale migration from the South began. Between 1910 and 1920, about fifty thousand blacks rode north on the Illinois Central Railroad and crowded into the expanding Black Belt, triggering the first of many waves of white flight. (Segregation was not limited to Chicago; even after World War II, black state legislators were denied access to restaurants and hotel rooms, including rooms at the Abraham Lincoln Hotel, in Lincoln's home town of Springfield.) The expansion of the south-side Black Belt and, after another surge of migration during World War II, the growth of the west-side ghetto proved politically important; the concentrated voting power resulted in the 1928 election of a Republican black congressman, former Chicago alderman Oscar DePriest, and, by 1983, the election of Harold Washington as Chicago's first black mayor.

Slow Growth Masks Diversity

The population of Illinois has grown to an estimated 12,901,000 in 2008, although growth has been slow in recent decades.[38] For example, between 2000 and 2008 the Illinois growth rate was 3.9 percent, whereas that for the nation was 8.0 percent. This slow growth cannot be attributed to a lack of migration into the state, especially by Latino and other foreign-born immigrants, which has been substantial. Persons of Latino heritage tripled in number in Illinois between 1980 and 2006 from 600,000 to more than 1.8 million. Asians showed even faster growth rates, quintupling their numbers from 1980 to 2006, when more than 525,000 dwelt in Illinois.

Instead, the growth has been slowed by a significant net out-migration of whites in recent decades. For example, an estimated net out-migration of 700,000–900,000 whites occurred in the 1970s alone, and this out-migration continues.[39] (*Net migration* is the difference between the total number moving into a state and the total number moving out in the same period.) Indeed, Illinois is importing residents from other countries and exporting them to other states, primarily to southern and Sunbelt states.

In 1950, one in thirteen residents of the state belonged to so-called minority groups; by 2006, the ratio was one in three, with African Americans representing 15.1 percent, Latinos 14.3 percent, and Asians 4.1 percent. The formerly all-white suburb of Cicero, near Chicago, is now 77 percent Latino, and the outlying cities of Aurora (population 162,000) and Elgin (97,000) in Kane County are both one-third Latino.[40]

Since the middle of the twentieth century, tectonic shifts in Illinoisans' choice of location have occurred. For example, in 1950 Chicago had a population of 3,620,962, but by 2006 that figure had declined to 2,869,121, or 22 percent of the total state population.[41] In the same period, suburban Chicago had grown from 17 percent to 44 percent of the state's populace.[42] Meanwhile, the remaining 95 of 102 counties, those known collectively as "downstate," had shrunk since 1950 from 42 percent of the state total to barely more than one-third.

From 2000 to 2006, the state's increase of 412,000 residents occurred almost wholly in the suburban collar of seven counties around Cook County and Chicago. Six hundred thousand persons migrated out of Cook County and Chicago in that period, mostly to the outlying suburban counties. Conventional wisdom holds that population growth in the suburbs is good for Republicans, and over the long term that may be so, yet initially the migration of Latinos to the suburbs has benefited Democrats. In 2006, Democrats picked up four state senate seats in suburban counties, three in territory that never before had been represented by a Democrat in the state senate.[43] Also in 2006, a once-strong Republican area elected Democrat Melissa Bean to the U.S. House of Representatives. In a special election and then in the general election of 2008, Democrat Bill Foster defeated Republican Jim Oberweis to replace Republican U.S. Congressman Dennis Hastert in a district drawn for the former Speaker of the House.

Generalizations and statistical trends tend to drain the color and texture from Illinois's rich mosaic of people from the world around. In the early 1970s, James D. Nowlan was a state representative from a rural district in northwestern Illinois. He recalls enjoying *bagna cauda* ("hot bath") dipping sauce and *sumpanella* (a flat, tortilla-like bread) with the Italian Americans in Dalzell and Ladd, watching preparations for pigeon races at the Flemish-American Club in Kewanee, and enjoying late-night music at the Latino-Americano Club in Rock Falls.[44] Later, as a statewide candidate, he helped celebrate the birthday of Santa Lucia (a Swedish holiday) in Galesburg in central Illinois, hoisted steins of beer with descendants of German immigrants in Belleville and Millstadt, east of St. Louis, watched bocce ball played by Italian Americans on the green along the commuter rail tracks in suburban Highwood (which in recent years has become heavily Latino), and marched with blacks in the Bud Billiken Day parade on the South Side of Chicago.[45]

The 2003 Chicago phone book listed 450 O'Connors, 130 Wisniewskis, 750 Gomezes, and 300 Wongs. In Chicago there are large communities of Filipinos, Asian Indians, Chinese, Koreans, Japanese, and Vietnamese.[46]

For ethnic whites in metropolitan Chicago, the melting pot metaphor applies fairly well. There are now more Irish, Italians, Germans, and Poles in the Chicago suburbs than in the city. Within the city, however, *mosaic*—with sharply etched lines separating the pieces—is a more apt term than *melting pot*. According to Gregory Squires and his coauthors, "In the city, race has come to be a far more significant characteristic for defining group membership and neighborhood residence than ethnicity."[47] Ten of the city's poorest fifteen neighborhoods are at least 94 percent African American.[48] In 2006 the Chicago area ranked fourth in the nation in African American–Caucasian school segregation; 47 percent of all public schools in Chicago are 90 percent African American and 30 percent are 100 percent African American.[49]

Population and Politics in Illinois's Three Regions

Caesar divided Gaul into three provinces, the better to govern it. Illinois political observers have divided the state into three regions, the better to understand it—Chicago, the suburban collar around the city, and the ninety-five downstate counties.

Chicago: The Biggest Player

We begin with the smallest yet arguably the most important "region," Chicago. In 1950 blacks composed 13.6 percent of the population of Chicago and Latinos, only 5 percent. In 2000 African Americans represented 36.8 percent and Latinos 26 percent. Chicago is today clearly a "majority minorities" city.

Immigrant groups have brought different political needs and skills to Illinois. The Irish, the Poles, and the Italians brought less capital and education—and received less social acceptance—than did the English and the Germans who generally preceded them. The former three ethnic groups found, however, that democratic institutions offered opportunities for success and acceptance that were often denied them in business and the professions.

The Irish have dominated Chicago politics since the Civil War and especially since the time of the Kelly-Nash machine of the 1930s. Most recently, Mayor Richard J. Daley and his son Mayor Richard M. Daley have been the most prominent representatives of Irish political power. Although they were always a distinct minority of the population in Illinois and in Chicago, Irish political leaders have been skilled at building coalitions, especially with Poles and Italians.[50]

On arriving in Chicago, the Poles seemed to find boss-directed patronage organizations attractive. The political bosses welcomed immigrants and helped them. "Seemingly anyone could become a boss in America," writes Edward Kantowicz, in contrast to the feudal nobility caste in Poland to which peasants had no access. "Thus American politics fulfilled economic, occupational and psychological functions in 'Polonia' (Poland in America)."[51]

For most participants, Chicago politics has been a full-time profession rather than a part-time civic activity. During the years of machine politics, many hundreds of people did strictly political work (or no city work at all), although their city paycheck might have been for street-cleaning or an obscure desk job. Former U.S. judge Abner Mikva found this out when, as a college student, he called on the local Democratic ward committeeman: "I came in and said I wanted to help. Dead silence. 'Who sent you?' the committeeman said. I said, 'Nobody.' He said, 'We don't want nobody nobody sent.' Then he said, 'We ain't got no jobs.' I said, 'I don't want a job.' He said, 'We don't want nobody that don't want a job. Where are you from, anyway?' I said, 'University of Chicago.' He said, 'We don't want nobody from the University of Chicago.'"[52] Mikva would later learn that patronage and insider contracts were frequently used tools that created webs of fierce political loyalty and rigid hierarchical management.

The Irish became skilled at sharing the rewards of power and soon came to master Chicago politics after working their way up from jobs as canal diggers and policemen. They honed the art under Mayors Edward J. Kelly and Patrick Nash from 1933 to 1947, by sharing first with other white ethnic groups and then with the city's growing black population. By 1940 Democratic ward committeeman William Dawson was the top black political boss in the white-dominated Cook County Democratic Party. He was among those who urged the party to drop Mayor Martin J. Kennelly in 1955 and replace him with new party chairman Richard J. Daley. Dawson delivered five wards in the primary to put Daley over the top. Daley's majority of 125,000 votes over Democrat-turned-Republican Robert Merriam in the subsequent general election came largely from margins provided in Dawson's ward and four other black wards.[53]

Daley became legendary during more than two decades as both chairman of the Cook County Democratic Central Committee (1953–76) and mayor (1955–76). He skillfully gathered immense political power over patronage, nominations for office, and policy making in local, state, and federal government. Anyone who wanted one of the thirty thousand patronage jobs or hundreds of elective offices that he controlled had to go through the local Democratic ward committeeman and the mayor's office. In return, loyalty to the mayor and the Democratic Party was obligatory.

His son Richard M. Daley won his sixth four-year term as mayor of Chicago in 2007 with 71 percent of the vote and carried all fifty wards in a three-way race. He wields political power almost as great as his father. Having eschewed the role of party leader, Daley draws power from money and the ability to award contracts for business with the city. Chicago's tax increment financing districts alone generate more than a half-billion dollars per year, and the mayor directs the spending of that money with contractors who "appreciate" the mayor with large campaign contributions. Daley also has the power to appoint aldermen and -women to fill vacancies on the City Council. One observer estimated that he had appointed more than thirty of the fifty members of the council, often after finding a good job for the person departing the council. "If I had to identify the ten most powerful people in Chicago," says the veteran political analyst Paul Green, "I would say Daley, Daley, Daley, and at No. 10 it might still be Daley."[54] Others farther down on Green's list would be Speaker Michael Madigan, Congressman Jesse Jackson Jr., and businessman Pat Ryan, who heads the City's Olympic bid committee. With the 2008 election of Senator Barack Obama to the presidency, we should add the Chicagoans Obama and his chief of staff, Rahm Emanuel.

The political columnist and popular political blogger Rich Miller agrees: "Daley can get anything done he wants to."[55] In almost two decades in office, Daley has exercised his veto in the city council only once; the council failed to override it. And in a controversial 2008 violation of the almost sacred principle that an alderman dictates zoning issues in his or her ward, the mayor succeeded in winning strong council support for a plan to move a major children's museum into Millennium Park, along the city's lakefront.

Chicago is still the biggest player in Illinois politics. If its population decline were the whole story, the political balance would have long since shifted to suburbia, but that has not been the case. The primary reason is that Illinois has over the course of the past four decades shifted from a highly competitive state balanced between Republicans and Democrats to a state that leans strongly Democratic—and Chicago continues to be the dominant player in the Illinois Democratic Party. As of 2009, all elected statewide officials as well as the speaker of the house and the president of the senate resided in Chicago.[56]

As for party identification, a 2007 survey found that 50.1 percent of Illinois voters called themselves Democrats but only 33.3 percent identified as Republicans, with 16.6 percent identifying as independents. In Chicago the figures were 75.6 percent Democratic and 8.4 percent Republican.[57]

Suburban Growth but Fragmented Power

Metropolitan Chicago as defined by the U.S. Census Bureau in 2000 was a nine-million-person megalopolis stretching from the business parks and hamlets of southern Wisconsin to the steel mills of Gary, Indiana. The bulging center of this "consolidated metropolitan statistical area" remains Chicago with its collar counties. But as homes and businesses spiral outward, residents of the Rockford and Kankakee regions (to the northwest and south of Chicago, respectively) have begun to wonder when their open spaces will be absorbed by what we have termed the "metropolitan frontier."

The hallmarks of the expanding metro frontier are independence, space, a sense of security, lack of congestion, cleaner air, and a "back-to-the-country" appeal. For first-time home buyers, who make up half of the suburban market, the largest and most affordable lots are found on the fringe of the region.[58] The outward trek generally moves along the interstate highway corridors that radiate from Chicago almost as neatly as bicycle spokes: I-57, I-55, I-88, I-90, and I-94.

Huntley, McHenry County, has evolved from farm town to boom town. From a population of a little more than 2,000 in 1990 the community reached 22,000 in 2006, with a two-thousand-home subdivision still to be built. Naperville, in the center of the region, had only 5,000 residents after World War II but 138,000 in 2003. Farther south in Will County, the quiet, attractive town of Frankfort saw its population double in the 1980s to 7,844 and jump to 13,000 by 2004.

While Chicago and Cook County declined slightly in population between 2000 and 2006, the other six suburban Illinois counties grew substantially in the period. The population of Will County increased by 33 percent, and Kendall's jumped by 61.7 percent.[59] The six and one-half suburban counties (Lake, McHenry, DuPage, Kane, Will, and Kendall Counties plus suburban Cook County) now have about double Chicago's nearly three million residents.

Though still predominantly white and homogeneous, suburbia is rapidly diversifying racially and ethnically, and growth of the Latino population is especially dramatic. All the suburban counties have a population that is at least 10 percent Latino, and Kane County was 28 percent Latino in 2006.

Suburban blacks and Latinos tend, however, to be concentrated. As suburbanites with the means to do so reach farther out on the collar to fulfill their dream of a single-family home with a spacious yard, Latinos often move behind them into the aging suburbs adjacent to Chicago and to older industrial cities farther out, such as Aurora and Elgin in Kane County. In 1990 Cicero, which abuts Chicago's West Side, was 37 percent Latino; in 2003 the figure had climbed to 77 percent. Aurora and Elgin had populations that were 23 percent and 19 percent Latino, respectively, in 1990; by 2003, each was one-third Latino.

Low-income blacks are concentrated near Chicago in communities such as Maywood on the west, where they make up 83 percent of the population, and Chicago Heights and Ford Heights on the south. Middle-class blacks bypass those poor suburbs for Hazel Crest and Country Club Hills, farther south. "Blacks are moving for the same reasons as white families—better schools, less crime, more space," according to the political observer Paul Green. The suburban settlement appears to be perpetuating the same patterns of segregation that separated poor blacks, middle-class blacks, and whites in Chicago. "The south suburbs will become an extension of the old south side of Chicago," avers Green.[60]

This concentration makes it easier for Democrats to craft suburban legislative districts in which their candidates, often minorities now, can win.

The suburbs appear to be even more diverse in religious terms than in racial terms. One major survey found that Catholics outnumber Protestants in the collar region.[61] Nineteen parishes in the suburbs offer masses in Polish.[62] The telephone directory for north-central DuPage County listed five Catholic churches, five Baptist, three Methodist, and three Episcopal, as well as the Hindu Society, the Chinese Gospel Church, the Muslim Society, and the Korean Church of Western Chicagoland, among others.

With the emergence of the suburbs and their demands for a fair share of resources, the politics of redistribution may dominate state politics in the coming years. As we detail below, the collar counties have been contributing more than they have received back from state government. This should be expected because there is more wealth per capita in the collar counties than in the other regions. Nevertheless, the questions of how state tax dollars are distributed for schools, highways, mass transit, and local governments—and how effectively the regions spend those dollars—are coming to dominate the political agenda. Now that the collar counties form the largest of the three regions in terms of not only wealth but also population and political representation, the region has tried to flex its political muscle, primarily through the Republican Party in the state legislature, which is controlled by Democrats.

Erosion of Downstate

The first region of the state to rise to power historically is the weakest player on the field today. In the twenty-first century much of the downstate region is struggling to regain economic and political health. Boasting only three cities of more than one hundred thousand people, downstate's checkerboard landscape is dotted with eight hundred mostly small towns such as South Beloit (population 4,072), on the Wisconsin line, and, four hundred miles to the south, Cairo (population 4,846), south of Paducah, Kentucky. The poverty rate in Alexander County, home of Cairo, was 23.8 percent in 2004, higher than the 21.3 percent rate of Chicago and more than twice that of the state average of 11.9 percent.[63]

In between is the desperately poor, isolated black community of East St. Louis, and cutting diagonally across rich farmland from the St. Louis area toward Chicago, along old Route 66, is a string of nearly all-white market towns, among them Litchfield, Lincoln, and Pontiac. Indeed, there is little sense that there is a single downstate, other than as a geographic identifier.

The increasing concentrations of population, wealth, and media in Chicago and the collar counties have drained downstate of the influence and prominence it enjoyed in an earlier era. Even Springfield is less visible. Politicians must go to Chicago if they want major television coverage because the Chicago stations do not staff the Capitol pressroom. Meetings of statewide public advisory councils are more likely to take place in the futuristic State of Illinois Center in the Loop than in Springfield, simply because members, including downstaters, often find it more convenient to meet in or near Chicago. On election in 2002, Governor Rod Blagojevich announced that he would continue to reside in Chicago rather than occupy the executive mansion in Springfield, striking a psychological blow to the capital and to downstate generally.

Simply put, downstate has been shrinking relative to the collar county region in population, political strength, economic wealth, and media visibility. Big chunks of Illinois farmland are being transformed into new subdivisions around metro Chicago and St. Louis. The growth envelops small towns where the Main Street coffee shop regulars never dreamed they would one day become part of the suburban ring and, by extension, of the suburban power bloc.

Regional Conflict

For all the variety within each region and the policy values shared by the regions, there are important economic distinctions in the twenty-first century that provide powerful political justification for perceiving and acting on regional differences. The contrasts in wealth generate periodic calls from each one for its fair share of the state's largesse. This has become a serious issue that divides the regions. In 1987 a research unit of the state legislature looked at where state taxes came from and how state spending for selected major programs was distributed by region.[64] The collar counties paid 46 percent of the taxes but received only 27 percent of state spending. Downstate was the big net beneficiary, paying 33 percent of taxes while receiving 47 percent of spending. Chicago paid 21 percent of the taxes and received 25 percent of the spending. (The research has not been updated, reportedly because of political fallout from the 1987 report.)

The formula for allocating state aid to local schools provides a good illustration. Collar county legislators argue that their voters are already paying much more than other regions in state taxes (true) and getting much less back (also

INTO THE SUNSET

Fig. 1.1. Cartoon by Bill Campbell (Courtesy of Carl Sandburg College)

true). According to long-time observer Kent D. Redfield, school politics pits the suburbs against the downstate schools, with many suburban lawmakers resisting an income tax–property tax swap because their suburbs would be net losers and downstate residents would be net gainers.[65] Downstate and Chicago legislators retort that their schoolchildren are getting less financial support per pupil from all sources than are the suburban children (also true, generally speaking). At the heart of the problem is a school funding structure based on local property taxes rather than on major state financial aid, which could even out differences between rich and poor communities to a significant extent.

The inability of the regions to forge a solution prompted former state school superintendent Ted Sanders to lament, "Education reform has been 'slip-slidin' away into the quicksand of politics and provincialism."[66]

In the 1960s, when the University of Illinois created a major new campus in Chicago, downstate leaders insisted, successfully, on a new campus in Edwardsville for Southern Illinois University. More recently, in 2007, the

An Illinois Legislator, As Seen By...

A Chicagoan...   ...A Downstater

Fig. 1.2. Cartoon by Bill Campbell (Courtesy of Carl Sandburg College)

Downstate Democratic Caucus in the Illinois legislature declared that there would be no state budget until rate relief was provided for Ameren electric utility customers (Ameren is a central and southern Illinois company). And that's the way it worked out, with Ameren customers winning about $1 billion in rate relief.

In 2009, Chicago Democratic state senators tried to reverse the historic road fund split of 55 percent for downstate and 45 percent for the Chicago region. "That split is closer to the collective heart of downstate politics than anything else," observed Rich Miller.[67] Downstate senators from both parties rebuffed the challenge to the split, but the issue will be back. Single regions are, however, not always able to achieve their objectives. For example, in 2007–8, when Chicago and suburban leaders pushed for new taxation for regional mass transit, downstate lawmakers demanded, unsuccessfully, a highway and schools construction program intended largely for downstate.

In summary, regional political differences result largely from self-interest, differences in wealth, and strong perceptions that the other regions are out for themselves, not primarily from sharp cultural or attitudinal differences among the regions. Political struggle and conflict across the regions of Illinois will continue. As the historian Robert M. Sutton put it: "The public interest in Illinois today is a kind of common denominator hammered out by the interplay of these powerful regional forces."[68]

Corruption: A Tradition in Illinois

Corruption has been a constant companion of Illinois and Chicago governments throughout their history.[69] By the 1890s, declares Robert J. Schoenberg, "Chicago routinized corruption as never before—politicians, police, prosecutors, defense bar, judiciary, citizenry and lawbreakers became so bound by ties of graft, bribery and intimidation that honesty appeared eccentric."[70] During the 1890s traction magnate Charles T. Yerkes paid bribes of up to $50,000 each to Chicago aldermen in return for particularly favorable franchises. Yerkes simply bought most of the sixty-eight members of the City Council. He set market prices for council favors: $100 for a saloon license, $500 to restore a license that had been revoked for cause.[71] The $200-per-year job of alderman became worth $25,000, often more, to the boodling lawmakers (those participating in graft).

Yerkes also tried, with some success, to buy the state legislature. The bribery was so blatant that a reporter for the *Chicago Evening Journal* was inadvertently offered money for his "vote." Sitting in the seat of a member of the house before the day's session got under way, the journalist was mistaken for that member by a near-sighted old state senator. "The lawmaker sat down beside me," recalled the reporter, "and opened with the explicit statement he would pay $2,500 for my vote on the traction bill. He quickly discovered his mistake, and there was much scurrying in the ranks of the grafters."[72]

In the first decade of the twentieth century, supporters of Congressman William J. Lorimer created a national sensation when they apparently paid a total of $100,000 in bribes to as many as forty state lawmakers in Springfield to elect Lorimer to the United States Senate.[73] Sums of up to $2,500 per bribed lawmaker were split between pre-vote payments and then disbursed from a post-session "jackpot" of payments from the major interest groups to lawmakers who had voted in favor of their interests. At the time, a new Model T Ford cost $850. In 1912 Lorimer was expelled from the U.S. Senate on the grounds that he would not have been elected absent the bribery. The scandal generated renewed interest in passage of the Seventeenth Amendment to the U.S. Constitution, adopted in 1913, which provides for popular election of senators.

By the time Al Capone came to town a few years later, one alderman declared, "Chicago is unique. It is the only completely corrupt city in America."[74] In such an environment and with much of the citizenry thirsty for the beer and spirits prohibited by the Eighteenth Amendment to the U.S. Constitution, "a Capone became not just logical but inevitable."[75] Capone and his gangs gained power through the corruption already in place and through willing accomplices in government and the citizenry. During the reigns of Mayor William Hale (Big Bill) Thompson and of the supportive Capone, Police Chief Charles Fitzmorris himself admitted that about half his force of six thousand officers was involved in bootlegging—not simply as solicitors and recipients of bribes, but actively pushing booze.[76]

As Kenneth Alsop observes, writing of Chicago: "But, after the start of Prohibition, who was the crook? Millions of people who regarded themselves as upright, law-respecting . . . began . . . to cheat and lie, and entered into routine conspiracy with the underworld."[77] As Capone once put it: "Nobody's on the legit. . . . Your brother or your father gets in a jam. What do you do? Do you sit back and let him go over the road, without trying to help him? You'd be a yellow dog if you did. Nobody's legit when it comes down to cases."[78]

Corruption was so pervasive in the Capone era that observers at the time said that even honest politicians "had to make compromises with evil, in their judgment, in order to create a greater good."[79] The system, as it had developed, made them do it.

Little has changed, apparently. Scott Fawell was a senior aide to former governor George Ryan. Convicted of corruption as part of the Ryan scandal, Fawell reportedly once said that in Illinois "you gotta be incredibly corrupt before anybody notices." In his case, somebody noticed.

Corruption is difficult to quantify; it takes place in the interstices of society's web. One measure lies in convictions for "public corruption," which are compiled by the public integrity section of the U.S. Department of Justice. From 1996 to 2005, the U.S. Attorney's Office for the Northern District of Illinois (the Chicago region) logged 453 convictions, more than the 371 in New Jersey and the 219 in eastern Louisiana, areas often grouped with Illinois as being the most corrupt in the country.[80]

The Illinois convictions included a first in 2003—the Governor George Ryan Campaign Committee was convicted on racketeering charges. In 2006 Ryan himself was convicted on all twenty-four counts with which he was charged, including racketeering, mail fraud, filing false tax returns, and lying to investigators. During the same period, Chicago politicians, including the city clerk, were convicted of various charges ranging from bribery to violation of a court decree forbidding patronage. Indeed, three of the past six governors (Otto Kerner, Dan Walker, and George Ryan) have been convicted of wrongdoing by federal courts, although Walker's "white collar" misdeeds were not related to his service in public office.

Rod Blagojevich, proclaiming that there would be "no more business as usual" in Illinois government, became governor in 2003 on a reform platform. In 2008, however, a top fundraiser and advisor to Blagojevich named Antoin (Tony) Rezko was convicted of corruption in what U.S. Attorney Patrick Fitzgerald called "a pay-to-play scheme on steroids" (requirement of major campaign contributions in return for favors by the administration).[81] Prosecutors accused Rezko of "trying to collect nearly $6 million in kickbacks from government deals and trying to shake down a Hollywood producer for $1.5 million in campaign contributions to Blagojevich."[82]

In December 2008 federal agents arrested Blagojevich for having been heard on a wiretap allegedly trying to sell the appointment of a successor to the U.S. Senate seat previously held by President Barack Obama. Fitzgerald said that the governor's actions forced his office to intervene. "Gov. Blagojevich has been arrested in the middle of what we can only describe as a political corruption crime spree," he stated, adding that Blagojevich's "conduct would make Abraham Lincoln roll over in his grave." Robert Grant, special agent in charge of the FBI's Chicago office, said of Illinois, "If it isn't the most corrupt state in the United States, it's certainly one hell of a competitor. Even the most cynical agents in our office were shocked."[83]

With the arrest fueling legislative charges that Blagojevich had abused the power of his office, the Illinois house in January 2009 impeached the governor. The state senate then convicted Blagojevich by a unanimous 59-0 vote, removing him from office. As this book went to press, Blagojevich was awaiting trial on federal charges of corruption in office.

In 2006 the *Chicago Tribune* ran an editorial titled "Corruption on parade" concerning the level of corruption manifest in the state: "But as you plow through the daily digest of indictments, not-guilty pleas, convictions, the occasional acquittal, sentencings and look-whose-heading-off-to-prison stories, it's possible to lose the big picture. This is a unique time in Illinois. . . . Illinois produces enough guilty pleas for these kinds of crimes to establish that this state's problem is close to unique."[84]

In a major 2006 speech, the president of the Illinois Chamber of Commerce, a veteran observer of state politics, challenged citizens to address the corruption issue: "Illinois must confront and resolve its reputation as a political cesspool. Investigations, indictments and political corruption trials dominate the daily media and appear unending, no matter which political party is in power. The impression that heavy-handed politicians who tolerate pay-to-play contracting, job-buying, political shakedowns, kickbacks, intimidation, retribution, and regulatory populism at the expense of free markets suggests the fifth largest U.S. state is as corrupt as the proverbial banana republic."[85]

Illinois residents are, indeed, against corruption, at least in the abstract. In the 2007 Illinois Policy Survey conducted by Northern Illinois University, 90 percent of respondents said that corruption is a somewhat serious or very serious problem in state government.[86] Yet how do citizens behave when faced with their own governmental problems? At the beginning of each course in American politics that he teaches at the University of Illinois at Urbana-Champaign, James D. Nowlan conducts an exercise with his students, generally seniors who are headed for law school.

In summary, the exercise asks students what advice they would give an older brother who has been charged with driving under the influence of alcohol. The older brother must have a car for his first job after college and would lose his license if convicted of the charge; he has a desperate need for his job. A wily lawyer has told the older brother that he knows his way around the court system and can get the charge dismissed, but it will take $1,000 in cash in addition to his fee. Should the older brother reject the offer or "go for it"?

Nowlan has conducted the exercise with about thirty students in each of seven courses. Two-thirds of all these students said: Go for it. In one class, nineteen of twenty-three gave this response. The main reasons given for the student responses: the brother was in a desperate situation and, anyway, everyone else who can goes for it.

The culture of corruption in Illinois will not be changed easily.

2.

Power, Parties, Groups, and the Media

• • • • • • • • • • • • •

Politics in Illinois is about the struggle for power and influence, which allow one to make or block change in public policy and to control governmental administration. This chapter illustrates the application of power and influence inside government and then assesses the roles of the primary institutions that affect, from the outside, what goes on inside—political party organizations, interest groups, and the media.

Politics is a serious game in which the players apply their respective bundles of power and influence as skillfully as they know how in order to achieve their objectives. Power is the application of coercion, threats, control, even force to cause someone to do something he or she would not have done otherwise, to stimulate, as Bertrand Russell said, "the production of intended effects."[1] Influence is a subtler form of power centered on persuasion. The person who is influenced acts freely, unlike the victim of a power play. Power is wielded when a legislative leader coerces another legislator to cast a vote that the lawmaker was not planning to cast. Influence is displayed when a lobbyist provides persuasive information to convince a governor to veto a bill that the governor had been planning to sign.[2]

Power comes in many forms. Formal powers of elected officials include the vote of a legislator and the appointment power of a legislative leader. The governor has multiple veto powers, jobs and contracts to award, and the perquisites of the office such as invitations to the executive mansion and use of state airplanes. Informal powers can be wielded not only by elected officials but also by others on the political stage. These powers are money, organizations, charisma, specialized knowledge, media coverage, coalition-building skills, and creativity.

Illinois is not unique, of course, in the way power and influence are used, but without question the state has produced some masters of the art. We begin with a portrait of one of those masters.

Madigan's Genius for Concentrating Power

In 1969 Michael J. Madigan served in the Old State Capitol as a delegate to the Illinois Constitutional Convention. In 1970 he was elected to the Illinois house, where he has served continuously since. During this period Madigan has also been the Democratic committeeman of Chicago's thirteenth ward and in recent years has been chair of the Illinois Democratic Party. On the side he has also developed a reportedly lucrative Chicago law practice that focuses on property tax appeals work.

As house minority leader in 1981, Madigan combined luck and skill to craft a redistricting map that was extremely favorable to Democratic candidates. If the legislature failed to enact a plan, the 1970 Constitution provided for a complicated redistricting process. A balanced bipartisan commission was appointed; if the commission failed to agree on a map, a Republican or Democratic name was picked from a hat. The Democrats were lucky enough to win the draw in 1981 and, making use of new computer software, "drew districts that were more Democratic than even legislators living in them thought possible."[3] As a result, throughout the 1980s and early 1990s, Democrats enjoyed comfortable majorities in the house.

Madigan was elected speaker of the house in 1983 and held that office until 1994, when Republicans won a majority of house seats for two years only. He was reelected speaker in 1997 and has served in the post through 2009. During the 1983–94 period, Madigan methodically enhanced the powers of the speaker. He did this by centralizing power in the house within the speaker's office, developing fundraising committees whose war chests outstrip those of other legislative leaders, using his campaign funds to help elect and reelect Democrats in contested races, and convincing powerful interest groups that the speaker is the key to passage or defeat of their legislation.

Madigan controls all staff assignments for his party in the house, including staff for committees. He further increased his influence in legislative committees by changing rules to allow him to substitute committee members sympathetic to him for those less so, even for a single vote in committee. Once

Madigan became speaker in 1983, he gradually took control of the scheduling of bills for floor votes, which until that time generally had been called according to their order on the legislative calendar. Later in the 1980s, Madigan adopted new rules that gave the leader control over floor amendments as well.

His two campaign committees (one in his name, the other in that of the Democratic Party of Illinois) spent $5.7 million in the election cycle of July 2005 to December 2006. Madigan spent much of it on behalf of fellow house Democrats from the suburbs and downstate who needed—and were grateful for—his help. For example, in 2006 incumbent Illinois house Democrat Naomi Jakobsson of Urbana received half of the $217,000 raised in the July–December 2006 period from the Democratic Party of Illinois in her lightly contested race, which she won by a 2-1 margin.[4]

In hotly contested races, Madigan has poured in hundreds of thousands of dollars. Southern Illinois house incumbent Kurt Granberg received $250,000 in contributions from the Democratic Party of Illinois in his successful $700,000 race for reelection in 2006. And that isn't all. Madigan can guide interest groups to contribute more than they might have otherwise to particular candidates in tight races. Granberg was reelected by a razor-thin margin of 126 votes in 33,000 votes cast.

Once elected, new members continue to receive help. Madigan arranges for staff assistance with legislation that would make them look good at home, and, when Madigan has a comfortable majority, new members are generally excused from casting tough votes on controversial legislation. "He is more than willing to feed those guys and burp them," said one lobbyist. "The majority are willing to let him do that. He's made the water nice and warm."[5]

Many Springfield lobbyists and Democratic legislators have become willing participants in a Madigan-engineered system that some compare to one-stop shopping. Well aware that Madigan controls the fate of house legislation, lobbyists often contribute directly to one of the speaker's funds or seek his advice as to which Democratic incumbents need help the most. Using a classic "you scratch my back and I'll scratch yours" argument, Chicago personal injury lawyer Philip H. Corboy in 1986 wrote a "give until it hurts" letter to members of the Illinois Trial Lawyers Association. "Mr. Madigan uses the money obtained at his reception for assisting all Democratic legislators throughout the state," Corboy wrote. "Obviously, allegiances to him are then acquired from those that he himself has helped. . . . We must be in a position to help him so that he can retain his majority vote in the House and so that he in turn has a rapport with his legislative constituency."[6]

The result of all this has been a major shift of power from individual members to the speaker of the house (and to the senate president, for that matter) from 1980 to 2008.

Madigan's power was illustrated dramatically one day in May 1989. For three years Governor James R. Thompson had unsuccessfully sought an increase in the state income tax. Various proposals had been debated extensively, but Madigan had always blocked a vote. This was to the relief of many members of his party, who were unenthusiastic about voting for an increase, although they were under significant pressure from education groups to do so.

On May 17, 1989, to the astonishment of everyone, Madigan introduced, debated, and passed from the house a temporary two-year increase in the state income tax—all in one day. Half of the revenues would go to education and half to local governments. The Illinois Municipal League had not been asking for an increase, but it was clear that new Chicago mayor Richard M. Daley needed the financial help. The Madigan proposal was subsequently adopted in the Senate and signed by the governor.

Nevertheless, Madigan faced limits. In 2007 and 2008 he battled with Governor Rod Blagojevich and Senate President Emil Jones, who were aligned; the ultimate budgets reflected few of Madigan's priorities. Blagojevich did not get his revenue increases, nor did Emil Jones get his income tax increase for education. None of these people works in a vacuum. They are affected in various ways by outside influences and by power brokers who use their own bundles of power to affect decisions and outcomes. Other key players, discussed in the remainder of this chapter, are the party organizations, interest groups and their lobbyists, and the media.

Decline of Party Organizations

The Democratic Party of Illinois held its first nominating convention in 1835 and came to dominate the opposing Whig Party for the next two decades.[7] By 1856 Abraham Lincoln and many fellow Whigs had defected to join other anti-Democrats in forming the Republican Party. It became the state's leading party, with few lapses, until 1932. The tables turned again during the Depression, when Chicago Democrats formed a generally unified organization that made their party dominant in Chicago and highly competitive statewide. By 2009, the party had become dominant across the state.

Party organizations were originally developed to help like-minded political activists elect their partisans to government office in hopes of influencing, even controlling, government processes. Originally party organizations were informal, unregulated entities. Slowly statutes were adopted, primarily by the states, to regulate these organizations. The most important activity became that of nominating candidates to contest general elections.

A formal party organization chart in Illinois has the shape of a pyramid. At the base of each party organization is a precinct committeeman for each of the state's nearly twelve thousand precincts, each representing about five hundred voters. For all counties except Cook, precinct committeemen are elected every two years by those who vote in the party's primary nominating election. In Cook County, party voters elect thirty township committeemen outside Chicago and fifty ward committeemen in the city. Each ward and township committeeman theoretically appoints a captain to keep in touch with voters in each and every precinct, but where parties have little public support, such as the GOP in the city and the Democratic Party in many suburbs, these slots often go unfilled.

After each primary election, precinct committeemen elect a chairman from their ranks. They "vote their strength," each casting for chairman the total number of votes cast in their respective precincts in the primary. In Cook County, the township and ward committeemen elect the county chairman, using the same voting system.

Above the county chairs on the organizational chart are the state central committeemen, one for each of the state's nineteen congressional districts. In 1989 the Republican Party was successful in passing legislation that gives each party the option of either continuing to elect state central committeemen at the party's primary election or to elect them by a weighted vote of the precinct committeemen based on party turnout in the respective precincts (township and ward committeemen in Cook County). In theory, election by the precinct committeemen would link the base of the party pyramid with the crown and conceivably infuse the top with whatever influence exists at the county level. Since 1990, Republicans have used the option of electing state central committeemen by weighted vote of precinct committeemen, whereas Democrats continue with election by primary voters.

That the organization is statewide implies that power peaks at the top of the hierarchy, but in practice party power has traditionally been strongest at the county level. State chairmen have generally wielded little influence. Political party power varies greatly from locale to locale and can change over time. It depends on the local political culture, individual leadership, the resources available to a party organization, and the party's effectiveness in influencing nominations. The Cook County Democratic Central Committee was once the model of the strong party machine. It had access to huge resources in the form of party workers, money, and campaign savvy, and it used them skillfully to dominate the nomination process.

A Downstate Mini-Machine

The legendary skills of Chicago's politicians might give a false impression that strong political organizations have been the sole preserve of the urban Democrats. Not so. Getting out the vote is a result of cultural attitudes toward leadership and patrons, and here and there downstate Republicans learned the tricks as well. According to James Nowlan, for example:

> In my first try for office in 1966 I sought a Republican nomination for the Illinois house from a rural district. Heeding the abundant advice given by old-timers, I paid a call on Louis Falletti, owner of a popular tavern and precinct committeeman for the small community of Italian Americans in and around the village of Dalzell in Bureau County, whose forebears had come to mine coal.
>
> Lou Falletti, a courtly gentleman, received me graciously. But he told me bluntly he already had two candidates and I wasn't one of them. Furthermore, I would not get a single vote in his precinct, Falletti said confidently. I left the Falletti home, adjacent to the tavern, vowing to prove him wrong. I spent more time and money in the precinct than planned, walking door-to-door to introduce myself, even hanging around the popular Italian bakery to say "Hi" to residents.
>
> I proved Lou Falletti wrong. Of 562 votes cast among six candidates for the two nominations, I received 10 votes. Falletti's candidates garnered 539 votes between them. Two years later I ran again. Falletti's candidates were not running this time, so he backed me in a four-way hotly contested race. I captured nearly all the votes in Dalzell this second time, and was elected. Whenever Lou wanted help finding a job or doing a favor for one of his constituents, I busted my tail trying to get what Lou wanted!

According to Illinois parties specialist Kent Redfield, the best places to look for signs of strength or weakness in parties are in the traditional functions of recruiting and influencing nominations, running election campaigns, raising money, getting voters to the polls, and providing voters with cues about how to vote.[8] Although the two major parties have often been competitive statewide, one party or the other has tended to dominate in local areas. As a result, a party organization's power lies in its ability to control or heavily influence party nominations. That is, if a party organization dominates access to nomination and then election, officeholders tend to do what party organization leaders want.

The influence of party organizations over elections has been eroding since about the turn of the twentieth century. In 1889 Illinois adopted the Australian secret ballot. In place of ballots distributed by the respective parties, the Australian ballot put all parties and candidates onto a single ballot, which was cast secretly. It allowed voters, for the first time, to split their general election votes among candidates of more than one party.

The primary election, adopted in the early 1900s in Illinois, replaced the convention as the parties' nominating mechanism. Primary elections allowed party voters to challenge party-endorsed candidates for nomination. By the 1960s, the influence of party organizations in primary elections began to wane. Patronage jobs for party loyalists had been declining in number as a result of expanded civil service protections and court decrees that prohibited partisan hiring and firing. Thus party leaders had fewer resources with which to reward active precinct workers. In 1997 Illinois enacted legislation that prohibited use of the party "straight ballot," in which a voter could vote once at the top of the ballot for all Republican or Democratic candidates. This change also tended to weaken the party organization in its capacity to ensure voting only for its own candidates.

Another factor was the growing influence of television, which allowed candidates to appeal directly to voters and diminished the need to depend on party organizations to carry candidates' messages to the voters. The use of television also caused sharp increases in the costs of campaigns, costs that exceeded the resources of most party organizations. As a result, candidates began to raise most of their own campaign funds, further reducing their link to party organizations. Finally, consultants emerged who specialized in campaign management, media, and fundraising. Candidates can now "rent" their own campaign organizations without the need to rely on the skills of party organizations.

As a result, the formal political party organizations provided for by statute, such as the Illinois Republican State Central Committee and the Democratic Central Committee of McLean County, have often become little more than enthusiastic boosters of the party label. There are still exceptions to be found. Certain wards in Cook County, the St. Clair County Democrats, and the Sangamon (Springfield) and DuPage (suburban) GOP organizations can affect nominations. For the most part, however, candidates achieve success on their own and thus have little obligation to the formal party organizations whose banners they carry. In contrast, the political party *inside* government, such as that inside the Illinois General Assembly, is very strong, as shown by the account of Madigan above and as discussed in chapter 5.

The lack of party organization influence was clear in 1990 in the Nineteenth Congressional District in eastern Illinois. That year every one of the eighteen GOP county chairmen in the congressional district endorsed the same candidate for the party nomination to the U.S. House, yet their candidate lost at the party primary election.[9]

In the era of Richard J. Daley, statewide aspirants went hat in hand to party leaders to seek endorsement—and dutifully dropped out if they didn't receive it. In 1994, for the first time in memory, the Democratic state party avoided making any endorsements. "Why fool each other?" said Democratic Party chairman Gary LaPaille. "We know these people are going to run regardless of what happened in this room. . . . In the old days if you weren't endorsed that sent a pretty strong signal that you wouldn't have the money or the political support to wage a primary campaign. Today, it makes no difference."[10]

Indeed, in 2006 the Democratic Party of Illinois (DPI) endorsed Paul Mangieri for state treasurer, the only open contest on the statewide ballot. Nevertheless, Mangieri lost decisively to Alexi Giannoulias, who enjoyed the personal endorsement of popular U.S. senator Barack Obama.[11] Some would say that DPI chair and house speaker Michael Madigan had little interest in this race by the unknown and unfunded downstater Mangieri against a well-funded candidate who had strong connections to the supportive Greek communities of Illinois. Nevertheless, the outcome shows that the imprimatur of the state party organization alone counts for little. On the other hand, in 2002 state chairman Madigan put the resources and staff of the DPI behind his daughter Lisa in her successful and hard-fought primary and general elections for attorney general.

Observes Redfield: "Participation in party activities is declining at all levels. The public is dissatisfied with party politics. The state parties have almost no role in the recruitment of candidates for statewide office and little impact on those statewide campaigns. The electoral power of Illinois legislative leaders is growing. Both office seekers and officeholders generally act independently of their party organizations at all levels."[12] The only hope for increased power among state party units, it seems, is to continue to expand their financial bases and spend the money on behalf of candidates. After 2007, however, most state and local party organizations in Illinois would have to be classified as weak.

The Rise of Interest Groups

As political parties have declined in influence, interest groups have aggressively sought to fill the vacuum. They have done this by helping candidates, especially incumbents, meet the escalating costs of campaigns and by providing campaign managers and other election resources to candidates for state office and the legislature, roles that were once the preserve of party organizations.

In 2007, 1,726 companies and entities registered with the Illinois Secretary of State as having representation from 2,200 lobbyists.[13] Registered groups range from the Illinois State Acupuncture Association to Zion Township in Lake County. Business interests dominated the field, but labor, education, professional, and social service organizations are also heavily represented.

The power of a group can be measured by the intensity of membership feeling, wealth, group prestige, and membership numbers, roughly in that order of importance. The Illinois Rifle Association represents only a few thousand members, yet the members have such intense, focused feelings about their single issue that their influence in the legislature surpasses that of much larger groups.

Groups with large memberships include the Illinois AFL-CIO union affiliates (with one million member families in 2008), and the Illinois Farm Bureau (with eighty thousand farm families in 2008). The Illinois State Medical Society (ISMS) claims a decidedly smaller membership of thirteen thousand, few of whom are active politically. But the physicians contribute generously to the society's political action committee. Because physicians represent a prestigious elite, the society organizes its members to serve as individual contacts with lawmakers; often these contacts are the lawmakers' own personal physicians—an effective and highly personal approach to influencing government.

The Illinois Education Association (IEA) represents an almost perfect fulfillment of the elements of influence. The IEA has a large membership from across the downstate region and the suburbs, a lot of money for contributions, and articulate members who will work elections and who are visible and generally respected professionals in their communities. The IEA has an effective professional lobbying team and a "white hat" issue, for who can oppose educating children? As a result, it is always mentioned in the first breath when lawmakers are asked to name the most important interest groups.

Interest groups draw on many of the informal elements of power. They not only provide valuable information to policy makers but also give a sense of the intensity of feeling that groups—and supposedly their members—have toward an issue. Interest groups routinely report back to their members on the favorable and unfavorable votes cast by legislators. The "Legislative Ratings" from the Illinois State Chamber of Commerce Political Action Committee are typical. The ratings display the percentage of favorable votes cast by a legislator concerning issues of interest, and they help determine endorsements and campaign contributions to be made by the group's political action committee. Such rating systems are common among interest groups, and legislators often try to maintain high ratings with groups that are important to them.

Money speaks volumes for interest groups. As opposed to the national government, where corporations are prohibited from contributing and interest group contributions are limited to $10,000 per campaign cycle, no contribution limitations existed in Illinois prior to 2009. In 2009 the legislature enacted limits of $5,000 per individual per year and $10,000 for corporations and labor unions. Higher limits were imposed for contributions to multicandidate and noncandidate committees.[14] Reform groups consider the legislation weak and full of loopholes. For example, it specifically excludes from limitation in-kind contributions, which legislative leaders use to fund the television commercials, direct mail, and campaign management of their legislative candidates.

Critics of large contributions to governors call the practice "pay-to-play," that is, contribute in order to receive state business contracts and favorable policies. In the 2007–8 session of the Illinois General Assembly, House Bill 1 as amended prohibited business owners with more than $50,000 in state contracts from making contributions to the statewide elected officials awarding the contracts. The bill passed the house 116-0, became stalled in the state senate, was ultimately enacted by the General Assembly, and was signed by Governor Blagojevich in 2008.

When legislators are asked to name the most influential interest groups in the General Assembly, they tend to list those that are also the largest contributors to legislative campaigns. Teachers' unions (the Illinois Federation of Teachers, the IEA, and the Chicago Teachers Union) topped the list of biggest spenders in the 2006 general election, at a total of $5 million. The Illinois State Medical Society, the Illinois Hospital Association, the state Chamber of Commerce, realtors, trial lawyers, and several labor unions are also among the top spenders in Illinois campaigns.[15] These are also the groups that lawmakers consider to have the most power and influence in the General Assembly.[16]

In his first campaign for governor in 2002, Rod Blagojevich raised $26 million. Labor groups topped the list with $3.5 million, followed by finance, insurance, and real estate interests ($2.4 million), lawyers ($2.1 million), construction and engineering interests ($1.9 million), general business interests ($1.6 million), and health care interests ($1.3 million).[17] All of these groups have intense interests in doing business with the state of Illinois and in the laws and rules promulgated by state government.

Gauging Interest Group Strength

In 1981 the political scientist Sarah McCally Morehouse classified Illinois as a state with "moderately strong" interest groups.[18] In 1999 Clive Thomas and Ronald Hrebenar categorized them as "dominant/complementary," that is, the interest groups are very strong yet face limitations because of the capacities of the governor and legislative leaders.[19] The influential interest groups are provided with seats at the table at which public policy issues are bargained. Governors regularly convene task forces on major issues, and appointments to these panels appear to be meticulously balanced among the most influential interest groups.

Interest groups are more effective at protecting a benefit won earlier than at achieving a major change. It has always been easier to beat a bill in the legislature than to pass one. The IEA has been able to protect teacher tenure laws but has been less successful in getting the legislature to pass tax increases for education. And the time-honored practice of asking competing interest groups to work out an "agreed bill" tends to result in modest change from the status quo, not in dramatic victory for one side or in total defeat for the other.

Because of the perception in the 1980s of the increased power of the legislative leaders and the governor, many interest groups have been concentrating their campaign contributions on legislative leaders and gubernatorial candidates and not on individual legislators. This increases the likelihood that the groups will be consulted closely by several if not all of the five leaders during their negotiations concerning issues of importance to the groups.

As Redfield observes: "Being a significant player in the financing of legislative elections insures that you have a seat at the table when issues are raised, defined, and decided. It will be impossible to craft a state response to whatever new federal health care program is enacted that does not take into account the interests of public and private labor unions, large corporations and interest groups representing organized health care professionals and facilities. These groups may not be able to dictate the exact terms of the response, but they will be able to exercise a veto."[20]

Information Applied Artfully: Lobbyists

Lobbying is the art of getting the right information to the right person in the right format and at the right time. Good lobbyists have intimate knowledge of the political process and a keen sense of the information delivery game.

In addition, the premier lobbyists have access when they need it to the governor, his staff, legislative leaders, and their top staff.

A sage observer of both Illinois and Iowa politics said that when you want something in Iowa, you go in the front door, but when you want something in Illinois, you go in the side door. Getting in the side door takes access paid for by campaign contributions, personal relationships, or, ideally, both.

Although money and campaign services might grease the wheel, information is often a key ingredient in gaining or losing a vote on a legislative proposal. Lobbyists are the primary conduits of this information, sharing it with legislators and staff, the governor's office, other interest groups, and anyone else who can have some impact on policy making. Lobbyists are strategists, tacticians, builders of coalitions among groups, experts, and communicators. They testify in committees, buttonhole lawmakers one-on-one, organize meetings between members of their groups and legislators, stage rallies and demonstrations, and try to put a favorable "spin" on media coverage of their issues.

Senior lobbyists develop political action strategies that dovetail with the needs and resources of their association or client, helping decide, for instance, whether contributions should be oriented to leadership or to candidates, be partisan or bipartisan, or favor incumbents or challengers. They also shape the way information is conveyed and, when possible, do a little horse-trading with other lobbyists to develop compatible strategies for related issues.

One organization of lobbyists is the Business and Industry Federation of Economic Concern, which meets weekly in Springfield when the legislature is in session. The thirty-plus members brief each other on the status of bills. Requests are sometimes made that a group or corporation join a coalition in support of or opposition to legislation. This federation holds a workshop before each primary election to evaluate legislative races. The workshops provide intelligence that is useful in allocating political action committee campaign contributions.

Many lobbyists are regular employees of corporations, unions, and trade associations. Others have their own lobby firms or work for law firms and contract their services to corporations and groups. Some lobbyists are known to have strong relationships with the Democratic house leadership or with Republican senators. Thus with regard to issues important to well-financed interests, several contract lobbyists will be hired to supplement the work of lobbyists employed by the organization.

Lobbyists come in all styles. Some are congenial fellows and women who are appreciated for putting on dinner parties following the day's session.

Others eschew the nightlife and are skilled at getting critical information, in the right format, to the right people, at just the right time.

Information and expertise are the keys to influence for Saul Morse—lobbyist, attorney, member of the state human rights commission, and paraplegic. Morse has worked for the Illinois Commerce Commission and as a Republican staffer in the senate. He has represented several major clients in Illinois, including the Illinois State Medical Society. Morse belies the stereotype of the influence-peddling lobbyist and emphasizes the educational aspects of the role. In 1989 the General Assembly passed a major revision of the Illinois Medical Practice Act. The 123-page bill was drafted entirely in Morse's office.

Whereas many lobbyists are employed full-time by one organization, "hired gun" lobbyists work on contract, sometimes for many clients. For example, the lobbying firm of Fletcher, Topol, O'Brien, and Kasper listed forty-four clients in 2008, from Apple, Inc., to the Illinois CPA Society, Northwestern Memorial Hospital, and UPS.[21]

Some contract lobbyists are specialists in composing and orchestrating the client's legislative plan of action, while others are known for their access to key legislative leaders or the governor. Many major lobbying initiatives involve the creation of coalitions of interests and the employment of several lobbyists from different firms, each with a special niche role to play in the overall execution of the lobbying plan. As lobbying becomes more special-ized, the numbers of organizations and businesses lobbying for themselves has dropped from 564 in 2001 to 313 in 2007. At the same time, the numbers of contract lobbyists has increased from 1,316 in 2001 to 1,754 in 2007.[22]

Power of the Media

Exposure in the media is a time-tested way to raise an issue or even start a political party. In the nineteenth century, many community newspapers were started primarily to promote the platforms of political parties. Present-day reminders include the *Quincy Herald-Whig,* the *Belleville News-Democrat,* and the *Belvidere Daily Republican.* The impetus for the Republican Party of Illinois came from newspaper editors when Paul Selby, editor of the *Morgan Journal* in Jacksonville, issued a formal call in 1856 for a conference of newspaper editors.[23] Twelve influential editors plus Abraham Lincoln, the only non-editor admitted to the gathering, met in Decatur and put together a platform that advocated full restoration of the 1820 Missouri Compromise, which limited the extension of slavery. This stimulated the call for a conven-tion to organize an Illinois Republican party.

Fig. 2.1. Cartoon by Bill Campbell (Courtesy of Carl Sandburg College)

Today the media influence politics and public policy in at least three direct ways: public and behind-the-scenes lobbying, editorial positions and
endorsements of candidates, and investigative and in-depth public policy
reporting. The Illinois Press Association lobbies openly to protect the state
requirement that legal advertising must appear in local newspapers. The Illinois Broadcasters' Association has worked for statutes that require public
bodies to hold open meetings. During the 1960s George Tagge, the political editor of the *Chicago Tribune,* used his press box privileges (the boxes
are adjacent to the house and senate floors) to lobby vigorously for a new
exhibition center in Chicago to be named after the *Tribune's* late publisher,
Colonel Robert McCormick. Called McCormick Place today, in the 1960s

it was referred to by state lawmakers as "Tagge's Temple." In part because of this strong-armed advocacy, a ranking from the 1980s of top interest groups in Illinois included the *Tribune*.[24]

Newspaper endorsements in Illinois have never been restricted to the editorial pages; often they have appeared in a subtler form in news stories. Heavy and generally positive coverage of the 1970 Constitutional Convention, for instance, helped soften up the voters for the constitution's eventual passage. Advertising can also play a role. In October 1978 the late columnist Mike Royko, then with the *Chicago Sun-Times,* wrote three columns that were highly critical of the Democratic challenger to U.S. Senator Charles H. Percy. With Royko's blessing, the Percy campaign spent $200,000 to enlarge and reprint two of the columns as separate full-page advertisements in every daily newspaper in Illinois. The columns and reprints generated great public comment and were considered highly significant by Percy's campaign managers in their candidate's come-from-behind victory.[25]

The supportive editorial is especially sought after in order to provide credibility to candidates as well as public issue campaigns. Shoestring advocacy groups and pinstriped corporate executives alike ask for and generally receive time with the editorial boards of the state's major newspapers, and if they state their case clearly and persuasively enough, an editorial may appear a few days later.

Politicians are less comfortable with the media's other political device, the investigative report. Though expensive, investigative reporting has been practiced with some vigor by many Chicago and downstate newspapers and some television stations, usually to uncover corruption or expose a dysfunctional bureaucracy. Television commentators Len O'Connor and Walter Jacobson spent years digging up and broadcasting embarrassing material about Chicago political shenanigans, for example, and the *Chicago Sun-Times* went so far as to open a tavern, the Mirage, in order to expose the kickbacks schemes and bribery of the city's various inspectors.

Perhaps because blatant corruption and freeloading on the job are not as common as in years past, more recent investigative reporting has taken on a more educational, almost academic, character. The *Chicago Tribune* in particular periodically assigns large teams of reporters, editors, and photographers to analyze in minute detail the social or economic ills of the city. A 1985 series titled "The American Millstone" described the sad and broken world of Chicago's so-called underclass.[26] It set off a firestorm of protest from black residents who felt the series was blaming the victims for their plight. Later work by *Tribune* teams chronicled the physical decay of Chicago's public schools, the troubled public housing system, and the wholesale killing of children on Chicago's streets. To a lesser extent, the *Sun-Times,* the *Daily Southtown,* the *Herald* (Arlington Heights), and the *Peoria Journal-Star* have done similar work, though they lack the financial resources to duplicate the exhaustive coverage of the *Tribune.*

Investigative reporting provides political mileage in a circular way. To show the value of their own work, media outlets are typically generous with airtime and news space when a lawmaker announces a legislative proposal that responds to the investigation. The media benefit as well because national news associations that make awards for investigative work consider change in public policy as a criterion for a successful report.

With printed newspaper readership in sharp decline in recent years, and thus advertising revenue, nearly all daily newspapers have reduced their reportorial staff and newsroom budgets. As a result, we can expect less of this expensive investigative reporting. Though it is too soon to say, internet bloggers and whistleblowers may in some ways provide a substitute for investigative reporting.

Both the media and politicians are in "the eyeball business"; that is, the more eyeballs reached by papers the greater the advertising revenue. For politicos, the more eyeballs reached in a positive way, the greater the visibility and credibility of candidates for office. Elected officials are clearly sensitive to the media, and most are fully aware that media space, time, and comment—positive and negative—are powerful elements in Illinois politics. But one aspect of media influence overshadows all others by far in its influence on political strategies: television. Until about 1960, candidates for statewide office charted their campaigns according to a map of the 102 counties of Illinois. Although the counties varied dramatically in population, candidates felt an obligation to proclaim that they had campaigned in all of them. Candidates would often travel in small caravans and be met at county lines by caravans from the receiving county.

In those days, there was no substitute for personal campaigning, either by the candidate or by party workers. Today, there is. What television lacks in the personal touch, it makes up in its ability to present the candidate to literally everybody in the state and to do so with controlled, polished messages.[27]

Ten television markets serve Illinois, as shown figure 2.2. Virtually all households have one or more television sets, and the average one is on for nine hours per day. As a result, television can and does bring candidates to almost every voter in the state, via paid advertisements and news broadcasts.

Because of this reach, candidates now consider campaigning in every county counterproductive. Instead, schedules are arranged to visit the cities that have network-affiliated television stations. Schedulers try to find or

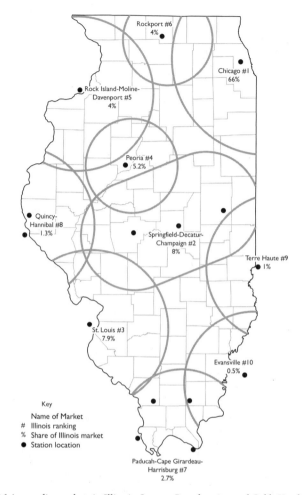

Fig. 2.2. Major media markets in Illinois. Source: *Broadcasting and Cable Yearbook 1994* (New Providence, N.J.: Bowker, 1994). The percentage figure for each market represents the portion of Illinois households considered to be in each market area of dominant influence. These percentage calculations are assigned on a county basis with no provision for overlapping market signals. The rounded market boundaries are for illustration purposes only. They provide a rough approximation of market signal reach.

create events that will be attractive to station assignment editors. The criteria are convenience, so that little crew time is needed; visual appeal, because the television medium craves an interesting, lively background; and shortness and simplicity, because most television news stories are one hundred words or less in length, and the crews need to move on to cover other stories.

Though there is limited direct evidence to prove television's power to affect voters, a study of a 1982 statewide campaign confirmed that it can have a strong impact.[28] In the Republican primary election for state treasurer, candidate John Dailey spent more than $150,000 for television ads in the five media markets in northern Illinois and nothing in the five markets that serve southern Illinois. His opponent, Robert Blair, a former speaker of the house in Illinois, had much less to spend in his campaign and spent nothing on television. Endorsements by county Republican party organizations were split about evenly between the two candidates.

Dailey won the primary. He carried nearly all the counties in which he ran television ads, and he lost most of those in which he did not use television. Dailey consistently fared better in counties where his advertising aired than in those where it did not. Television helped him fare well even in counties whose Republican organizations had endorsed his opponent. He did poorly, despite county party backing, in areas where he did not advertise on television.

The problem for candidates—and perhaps for voters—is that television is expensive and tends to benefit those who have money to spend, while hurting those without big campaign treasuries. In 2006 Governor Rod Blagojevich spent $18.1 million on television for 22,109 spots, most of the money on negative ads that attacked his opponent, state treasurer and state GOP chair Judy Baar Topinka, who was able to spend "only" $4.6 million to defend herself via 4,638 spots, unsuccessfully.[29]

Because political party organizations lack the capacity to raise significant money for the many candidates running under party banners, candidates must raise their own funds. This situation has enhanced the power of the individuals and interest groups that are able to make large contributions. Fueled by this money, television has largely replaced the party organization as the primary conduit of messages from candidates to the voters.

The internet does not yet appear to have had a major impact on state and local campaigns and political parties in Illinois, as it did in the 2008 campaign of President Barack Obama. This may say more about the lack of compelling appeal in Illinois candidates than about the potential of the relatively new medium. For example, Obama has been able to utilize the internet effectively to develop a base of about three million contributors. At the state legislative level, Daniel Biss (D-Evanston) reported raising $100,000 over the internet by July 1, 2008, in his unsuccessful campaign that year against Representative Elizabeth Coulson (R-Glenview). As Rich Miller noted: "That's just unheard of for a legislative candidate."[30]

Nevertheless, most candidates as well as the political parties have Web sites, which are effective tools for communicating quickly with whatever databases of supporters that the political committees have been able to create. For example, the Champaign County Republican Central Committee maintains an active site that is used to communicate, rally volunteers, and raise money. The site proved valuable in quickly raising several thousand dollars in 2007 for an unexpected need.

By far the most effective and influential Web site used to communicate about Illinois politics is Rich Miller's CapitolFax, a "must-read" subscription fax and email service that carries extensive "inside dope" on Illinois politics to an audience estimated at several thousand. Miller's Capitol Fax Blog also provides links to several other Illinois political sites with smaller audiences. The Miller blog had 1.7 million page views in June 2008. Miller also writes a syndicated column that appears in scores of papers and reaches, by one estimate, up to one million readers each week.[31]

As a result, the faxed and emailed daily report, the blog, and the column represent a force to be reckoned with. Reporters at other papers ask for play for their stories on Miller's blog and are among those feeding him inside information. "The blog," says Miller, "has become a living, breathing thing. It can change instantaneously and we keep it alive."[32]

That money is central to power and influence in Illinois should come as no surprise. Money drives campaign strategies, nurtures legislative leaders' power, and provides inordinate support to the governor, whichever party is in power. All of this is consistent with the individualistic political culture of Illinois, where government and politics compose a marketplace in which participants exchange credits and debits as they pursue their goals. In chapter 3, Kent Redfield looks at the dynamics of campaigns and elections in Illinois, details where most of the money is spent, and develops the discussion of the roles of political parties, groups, and legislative leaders in elections.

3.

Elections

Kent D. Redfield

• • • • • • • • • • • • • •

Although presidential elections continue to take place every four years in the United States, it has become increasingly more difficult to find any evidence of those campaigns in Illinois. Since the 1992 presidential election Illinois has been considered a Democratic (blue) state, with Republican presidential candidates making only brief stopovers there. After the 2008 election Democrats held all of the statewide elected offices, controlled both chambers of the legislature, held both U.S. Senate seats, and increased their edge in the state's seats in the U.S. House of Representatives to 12-7. It is easy to think of Illinois as a lost cause for Republican candidates for public office. But if you look at color-coded county maps for recent statewide elections, you find a large area of Republican red surrounding Cook County and extending north, west, and south throughout the state, interrupted by a few blue counties, primarily in deep southern Illinois and in the Metro East area across the Mississippi River from St. Louis. DuPage County has just as good a record over the course of the past fifty years of shutting out Democratic candidates for state and local office as its neighbor, Cook County, has for shutting out Republican candidates. And when Rod Blagojevich was elected in 2002, he became Illinois's first Democratic governor since Dan Walker was elected in 1972. So what is the reality when it comes to elections in Illinois? How blue is the state? The simple answer is, it's pretty blue, but the true picture is much more complex.

Beyond the question of partisan outcomes, Illinois elections clearly reflect and reinforce the way the state's great economic and cultural diversity, its regional, partisan, and racial fault lines, and its pragmatic, individualistic, often corrupt political culture shape its politics. The mix varies, but demographics, region, race, organized interests, campaign contributions, political parties, political leaders, political culture, election laws, and campaign finance laws all impact elections in Illinois.

Election Laws and Participation

In the game of politics, the formal rules are starting points that set parameters and establish advantages and disadvantages for competing interests. As the nation learned in 2000 during the post-election battle in Florida over the outcome of the presidential race, elections in the United States are administered by local government units under the direction of state law. Federal statutes and the United States Constitution set down some basic rules and processes, but states have great leeway in determining who has access to the ballot and access to the polls. The same is true for administrative questions including concerns about the counting of voters. State legislatures, state election officials, and local government officials decide what political parties are on the ballot, when one can register to vote, and how one's ballot will be counted and verified.

The current election calendar in Illinois divides elections into two groups: general elections, which take place in the even-numbered years, and consolidated elections, which take place in the odd-numbered years. In even-numbered years, partisan elections for federal, state, and local offices are held. The party primaries for these offices have historically been held in March along with elections of local political party officials. Illinois's March primary was one of the earlier general primaries. Many states hold their nonpresidential primaries later in the year. In 2007 the Illinois Election Code was amended to set the first Tuesday in February as the date for the primary in even-numbered years. The hope was that this change would give Illinois a more significant role in presidential primaries. The general elections take place in November. Elections for president, Congress, governor and other constitutional offices, the legislature, judges, county boards and offices, and township officials all take place in the even-numbered years. The election of the governor and the other constitutional officers takes place in the even-numbered year that occurs between presidential elections. In odd-numbered years, consolidated elections are held in the spring for municipal government and special districts and for school districts. Most but not all of the consolidated elections are nonpartisan.[1]

When the citizens of Illinois go to the polls they are faced with long ballots because of the large number of elected offices in the state. Chapter 8 deals with the rich tradition of local government in Illinois. As a result of that tradition, a voter in a general election could be faced with choices between candidates for county board, countywide offices, township offices, and three levels of judicial office in addition to choices between candidates for federal office, statewide office, and the state legislature. In a spring nonpartisan general election the voters could be asked to choose between candidates for mayor, alderman, school board, park district board, library district board, convention center board, fire protection district trustee, or community college board. The large number of elected officials and units of government in Illinois can be viewed as evidence of a commitment to democratic participation and control. But the persistence of this system also clearly serves the interests of politicians and local and state parties by providing a multitude of means for them to build political power and engage in patronage in jobs and governmental contracts.

Eligibility requirements for holding public office in Illinois are set out in the state constitution as to age and residency.[2] Eligible candidates gain access to the ballot by collecting signatures on nomination petitions. In partisan elections, Illinois's election laws favor candidates who declare themselves to be members of an officially recognized state political party. The laws work to the disadvantage of candidates who want to run as independents and groups that want to establish new parties. Independent candidates in partisan elections face much higher thresholds for signatures on nominating petitions, and groups seeking party status face significant organizational requirements. In nonpartisan elections candidates run without party labels, and the rules for ballot access apply equally to all candidates.[3]

The Green Party joined the Republican and Democratic Parties as an officially recognized state party after the 2006 election by fielding a full slate of candidates for statewide office and having its candidate for governor receive more than 5 percent of votes cast. If the Green Party does not maintain that level of success in statewide elections in 2010, it will lose its official party status and have to reestablish itself in order for its candidates to have access to the primary and general election ballots in 2012 as Green Party candidates.

In terms of participation, Illinois is not a particularly voter-friendly state. It does not have same-day voter registration as do six other states. Voters must register twenty-eight days before a general election and twenty-nine days before a primary election. Although it does not require party registration prior to voting, voters who participate in a partisan primary election must publicly choose the party primary in which they want to vote. An official record of those who participate in a party primary is available to local and state party officials and candidates. Illinois has adopted modest forms of late registration and early voting to supplement the traditional absentee voting

Fig. 3.1. Cartoon by Bill Campbell (Courtesy of Carl Sandburg College)

process, but there have been no serious moves to allow widespread voting by mail. In contrast, a large portion of the votes in Oregon and Washington are cast by mail prior to Election Day.

The prevailing attitude among those in political power in Illinois has been that participation in elections is generally encouraged, but increasing participation is not valued more than retaining the partisan and strategic advantages of the status quo. More attention is usually paid to the partisan impact of changes in voting laws than to the policy content. Allowing same-day registration and allowing voting by mail would increase participation, but these practices would

THERE'S JUST SOMETHING ABOUT HALLOWEEN THAT STIMULATES MY...

... IMAGINATION.

Fig. 3.2. Cartoon by Bill Campbell (Courtesy of Carl Sandburg College)

also make participation more unpredictable and less manageable from the perspective of a candidate or a political party. When the legislature considered extending the hours that the polls are open and making voter registration available at the Department of Motor Vehicles, the discussion that preceded their approval focused as much on the potential for one party to gain an advantage over the other as it did on the potential for increased participation. Given the clear evidence that requiring voters to show official identification at the polling place tends to suppress participation by groups that tend to vote Democratic (racial minorities, immigrants, and the poor), it is not surprising that the issue has not gained any traction in the Illinois legislature, which has been controlled by the Democratic Party since 2002.[4]

Reasonable thresholds and organizational requirements are necessary to ensure that ballots do not become overcrowded with frivolous candidates. Reasonable rules for voter registration and participation are necessary to ensure the integrity of the voting process. But the rules in Illinois were written by those holding political power, who are primarily interested in protecting the status quo. When the General Assembly organizes committees every two years, the election committees in the house and the senate always have memberships that are completely loyal to their legislative leaders and their respective political parties. There are never any surprises during roll calls on bills in the legislature's election committees. Designing a system that favors broad, easy ballot access for candidates and new political parties in Illinois would not be difficult, but implementing it in Illinois would fly in the face of the dominant political culture.

Regulating Campaign Finance

In adopting laws to deal with the role of money in politics, states tend to follow one of two models. Some states, such as Wisconsin and Minnesota, have adopted systems of limits and prohibitions, seeking to restrain or eliminate the role of money by means of regulation. An alternative is to rely solely on disclosure and reporting to provide restraint and self-regulation. Illinois is the poster child for this type of "sunshine" approach. Illinois places no limits or prohibitions on who can contribute, how much they can contribute, or to whom they can contribute. Most states and the federal government prohibit campaign contributions from non-individuals (businesses, corporations, and unions acting as corporate entities). Not Illinois. Most states and the federal government place limits on how much individuals can contribute and specifically ban certain individuals with conflicts of interest (such as those with government contracts) from contributing. Not Illinois. Since the beginning of the post-Watergate era in American politics in 1975, Illinois has had one of the least restrictive sets of campaign finance laws in the country.[5]

Illinois's campaign finance law both reflects and reinforces the dominant political culture in the state. One of the key precepts of individualistic, marketplace politics is that participants should be free to gather as many resources as their skills allow and to use those resources to their fullest strategic advantage. In Illinois, money is just one more resource that individuals and groups can use to win the political game. Political candidates and political parties are free to raise as much as they can from anyone they can and to use the money for anything except an expenditure that would personally benefit a candidate financially. One cannot use campaign contributions to buy a house or send one's children to college, but almost everything else is on the table. An important element of the lack of limits on spending campaign contributions in Illinois is the ability of politicians to use their political committees to raise money and then transfer that money to another candidate or spend it on behalf of another candidate without limit. This means that a legislative leader can transfer money that he or she has raised directly to a legislative candidate's political committee or spend money on television or direct mail advertising in support of a legislative candidate.

A modest bill was enacted into law in the fall of 2008 after a legislative overview of a gubernatorial veto. This law prohibits individuals and companies with governmental contracts worth more than $50,000 from making campaign contributions to the public officials who control those contracts. Although outlawing such a blatant conflict of interest may seem obvious to observers outside the state, it is the first time in modern Illinois history that a specific type of campaign contribution has been made illegal. The importance of the new law is not merely the specific change it makes but the fact that it represents a fundamental shift in the logic and values of the Illinois campaign finance system. It is also the first significant change in that system in more than a decade.[6]

In contrast to this approach to regulating campaign contributions, Illinois has one of the best reporting and disclosure systems of any state in the country. The political committees of candidates, parties, and interest groups are required to file comprehensive reports of campaign contributions and expenditures every six months. They are also required to file a contribution report thirty days before an election and then file reports of large contributions within two days of receiving them during the thirty days prior to an election. By law, the vast majority of those reports must be filed electronically, making them instantly available on the Web site of the State Board of Elections. Although the development of such a progressive system does not square with the general political culture in Illinois, its genesis is in the desire to avoid contribution limits. When the first extensive effort to adopt contribution limits was undertaken in the mid-1990s, the legislature's response was to assert the "sunshine" argument that complete reporting and public disclosure were the only things needed in order for the system to be self-regulating. Legislation was adopted requiring that the campaign finance reports be made available on the Web. This took place at a time when most members of the legislature had little appreciation for the potential of the internet to provide public access to public records. Before the law took effect, the staff of the State Board of Elections convinced the legislature that electronic filing would be necessary to avoid an administrative nightmare. The law was amended to require that reports of amounts over a certain dollar threshold be filed in electronic form, using software developed by the State Board of Elections.

Election Districts for the State Legislature and Congress

As discussed in chapter 5, legislative districts, from which the state's voters elect members of the U.S. House of Representatives and the members of the Illinois legislature, are drawn by the state legislature every ten years. According to the principle of "one man, one vote," established by a series of U.S. Supreme Court decisions handed down in the early 1960s, legislative districts must be adjusted to reflect changes in population so that each district contains approximately the same number of voters. In addition, the federal courts have ruled that minority populations cannot be discriminated against. They have also ruled, however, that race cannot be the sole purpose for drawing the boundaries of a legislative district absent a historical pattern of discrimination. State constitutions can add more criteria for drawing legislative districts. The Illinois constitution requires that they be substantially equal in population and compact and contiguous. It provides no criteria for the drawing of congressional districts.[7]

The U.S. Supreme Court has not limited the ability of state legislatures to draw legislative maps that favor the electoral chances of a particular party. Whoever controls the redistricting process can significantly affect the partisan makeup of the legislature that results. The example of the placement of Champaign and Urbana presented in chapter 5 clearly makes this point. Although there are limits, a change in control of the redistricting process can dramatically reshape the outcome of legislative elections.

There are 59 senate districts and 118 house districts in Illinois. These numbers are set by the state constitution and do not change every ten years. The number of congressional districts in Illinois is determined by federal law. Illinois has had 19 congressional districts since the 2001 redistricting. Because the total number of seats in the U.S. House of Representatives is set by the federal law and then divided among the states according to population, the number of congressional districts can change every ten years as a result of increases or decreases in the state's population. Illinois lost one seat in 1990 and in 2000 as the nation's population grew and shifted south and west, while Illinois's population increased only slightly. The prospects are good that Illinois will lose another seat after the federal census of 2010. Having to draw a new map that eliminates an existing seat in Congress complicates an already difficult task.

Congressional maps in Illinois are created by the state legislature. If the state legislature fails to act, it falls to the federal courts to approve a new map. The current congressional map is the result of an agreement among nineteen of the twenty congressmen holding office in 2001. Faced with the loss of one seat, a deal was reached to force an incumbent downstate Democrat to run against an incumbent downstate Republican in a district that favored the Republican. Once that agreement was reached, the other districts were drawn to maximize the reelection prospects of the other eighteen incumbents. The resulting map was approved by the state legislature without change. The map was intended to protect incumbents rather than maximize the election prospects of one party. For the first three elections it generally worked as planned. But, as discussed below, the combination of the retirements of Republican congressmen, national political trends, and shifting political demographics produced a high degree of competition in Illinois congressional elections in 2006 and 2008.

The process for creating legislative districts for the Illinois legislature is set out in the state constitution. Prior to July 1 of the year following the new census, a new map can be created by the legislature and signed into law by the governor. If one party controls both chambers of the legislature and the governor's office, such an agreement should be possible. Each time the process has taken place in the past four decades, however, control of the process has been split between the Democrats and the Republicans and no agreement has been reached prior to July 1. Once that deadline passes, an eight-member redistricting commission is established in which the governor plays no role. The commission has four Democrats and four Republicans who are appointed by the four legislative leaders. If the commission is unable to reach an agreement by August 10, a ninth member is chosen by lot from a Republican and a Democratic nominee selected by the Illinois Supreme Court. The commission, with one party holding a 5-4 advantage, then has until October 5 to file a final map with the secretary of state.[8]

The logic of this process is that if control of state government is split between parties, the process forces the initial eight-member commission to compromise before the ninth member is appointed. The assumption was that the political parties would reach an agreement rather than risk having the outcome of the redistricting process decided by the luck of the draw. The process produced a compromise in 1971, but stalemates in 1981, 1991, and 2001 resulted in draws to choose the ninth member. Democrats won the draw and controlled the process in 1981 and 2001, and Republicans won control in 1991.

Control of the redistricting process is a significant advantage for a political party, but the drawing of legislative maps is far from an exact science. The Democrats have won control of the state senate in each election held according to the 1981 and 2001 Democratic maps, whereas the Republicans won control over the state senate in each election held with the 1991 Republican map. Drawing the map does not ensure success. The Republicans were able to win control of the house only one time (1994) with the 1991 Republican map. The success of the house Democrats in 1996, 1998, and 2000 with a Republican map and the failure of the senate Democrats to duplicate that success show that the quality of the candidates and the strength of campaigns do make a difference in spite of the advantages created by having control over the map-drawing process.

The Role of State and Local Political Parties in Illinois Elections

As discussed in chapter 2, political parties at the state and local levels once dominated Illinois elections. Parties recruited candidates, controlled primaries, financed campaigns, delivered the party faithful at the polls, and provided an organizational structure for governing once elected officials took office. The strength of the state political parties came from strong county party organizations, typified by the Cook County Democrats and the DuPage County Republicans. Until 1972 state political parties controlled their primaries and provided indispensable support for their candidates in the general election in coordination with local party organizations.[9]

The same dynamic existed at the county level. Apart from Cook and DuPage Counties, strong downstate party organizations controlled local politics. The Sangamon County Republicans did so with the assistance of Republicans who controlled state government during the 1980s and 1990s, and the Madison County and St. Clair County Democrats dominated elections in the Metro East area. Governor George Ryan was a product of the Kankakee County Republican party organization; Governor Jim Edgar's political roots were in a strong Republican organization in Coles County. As we saw in chapter 2, the new reality in Illinois is that county party organizations are much weaker than they were twenty or thirty years ago, and the state parties are only shadows of their former selves.

The recent record of both parties in recruiting candidates and controlling their primaries for statewide office has been mixed. The failure of the party-endorsed candidate for state treasurer to defeat a self-recruited and self-financed candidate in the 2004 Democratic primary was noted in chapter 2. The Democratic primary elections for governor in 1994, 1998, and 2002 were also wide-open, multicandidate contests. In 1994 and 1998 the winners had very limited financial resources and little momentum going into the fall elections, which they lost to Republican candidates who had no serious primary opposition. In 2002 the winner of the Democratic primary was able to build on his success in spite of a very expensive primary and defeat the Republican candidate, who won an expensive, contentious primary but carried the mantle of a scandal-plagued Republican state party.

The recent record of the state Republican Party has been worse. The time between 1976 and 2002 was marked by an orderly succession from Governor James Thompson (1976–90) to Governor Jim Edgar (1990–98) to Governor George Ryan (1998–2002) and largely uncontested primaries for other constitutional offices. In contrast, wide-open, multicandidate gubernatorial primaries in 2002 and 2006 resulted in bruising, hugely expensive contests that put the winning Republican candidates at a serious disadvantage going into the general elections, which they both lost. After the withdrawal of the winner of the Republican primary for the U.S. Senate seat in 2004, the state central committee chose Alan Keyes, a controversial conservative who was not an Illinois resident, to run against Barack Obama. Keyes suffered the worst defeat of a major-party candidate in Illinois history. In 2008 the candidate endorsed by the state Republican Party for the U.S. Senate won the primary but lost the general election by more than two million votes.[10]

The Role of Interest Groups in Illinois Elections

Interest groups participate in elections by endorsing candidates, making campaign contributions, and providing direct organizational support to campaigns. A group that does all three of these things very well is the Illinois Education Association. Their endorsement provides a seal of approval for a candidate as a friend and supporter of education. Their political action committee contributed $6.9 million to candidates for statewide office and the state legislature in three recent election cycles (2001–2, 2003–4, 2005–6). With more than one hundred thousand members located throughout the state and a long history of directly working campaigns, they can provide expertise and staff to a campaign. In addition, the Illinois Federation of Teachers/Chicago Teachers Union, the Service Employees International Union, and the Illinois State Medical Society were the most heavily involved with political campaigns in these three election cycles. Groups such as these also contribute to safe incumbents and legislative leaders, but they are distinguished by their focus on support for candidates in contested elections. Other prominent election-oriented interest groups include the American Federation of State, County, and Municipal Employees; the Illinois Trial Lawyers Association; the Illinois Association of Realtors; and the Illinois Manufacturers Association.

Not all interest groups make endorsements or work campaigns, however. And not all gifts from interest groups to candidates are about elections. Some groups make contributions almost exclusively to incumbents and play little or no direct role in political campaigns. Their goal is creating access to power, not shaping the outcome of elections. For example, in the past two decades, tobacco companies have made significant campaign contributions in Illinois.

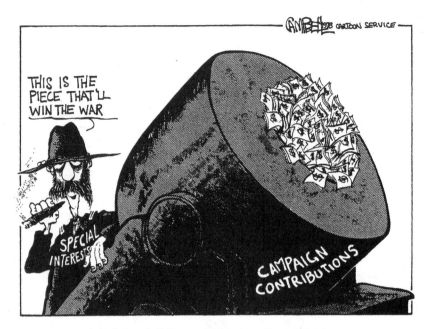

Fig. 3.3. Cartoon by Bill Campbell (Courtesy of Carl Sandburg College)

These gifts have gone overwhelmingly to incumbent governors, legislative leaders, legislators, and constitutional officers. They were intended not to influence elections but to create relationships in which meetings took place and phone calls were returned as the legislature and state agencies dealt with issues involving state regulation and taxation of tobacco in Illinois. Other interest groups that make significant contributions aimed primarily at creating access are the Associated Beer Distributors of Illinois, AT&T, Comcast, and gambling interests such as the Duchossois family and its companies.

Although most interest groups either combine election and access strategies or only pursue access strategies, a few groups pursue only election strategies. The primary example is Personal PAC, a pro-choice group. The vast majority of their contributions go to candidates in contested elections who are pro-choice. They are rarely involved in direct lobbying in Springfield. Groups who focus their contribution strategy exclusively on electing friends to public office are rare.

Illinois's campaign finance laws are a major reason why large interest group contributions play such a significant role in contrast to the role of gifts from individuals. At the federal level there are contribution limits, and non-individuals are prohibited from contributing. Of necessity, federal candidates focus on building networks of individual donors. In Illinois, companies, associations, and unions can contribute without limit. As a result, contributions of one hundred thousand dollars or more to a candidate for governor from a single source are not unusual. The same is true for contributions of twenty thousand dollars or more from a single source to a candidate for the legislature. There is no reason to spend time generating 100 one-thousand-dollar contributions from individuals if you can get a check for a hundred thousand dollars from one company or interest group.

Table 3.1 ranks the twenty biggest campaign contributors in the 2005–6 election cycle and the 2007–8 election cycle. The office of governor and other statewide offices were on the ballot in 2006. With one exception, the groups and contributions shown in table 3.1 are typical of recent election cycles. The exception is a national business group that provided financing for a single candidate for a state appellate court seat in 2006.

Statewide Voting Patterns in Illinois

In the 2006 general election only 48.6 percent of the registered voters in Illinois cast ballots (see table 3.2). Not all those eligible to vote were registered at the time of the election. The Illinois State Board of Elections estimates that approximately 77 percent of the eligible voters were registered prior to the 2006 election. This translates into approximately 37 percent of the eligible voters actually participating. In the presidential election two years earlier, the turnout of registered voters was 71.4 percent, which represented 56 percent of the eligible voters. These numbers are consistent with recent presidential and nonpresidential elections in Illinois, with participation in the former elections always being significantly higher than in the latter. Illinois's rates of registration and participation are close to the national averages. Unofficial results from the 2008 general election indicate a slight increase in participation relative to the 2004, another presidential election year.

At the level of presidential politics, Illinois is Democratic blue. The last Republican presidential candidate to carry the state was George H. W. Bush in 1988. Yet from 1978 to 2002 Illinois had Republican governors. After the 1994 general election all six of the constitutional officers were Republicans, and there were Republican majorities in both chambers of the legislature. Only eight years later, the 2002 election put Democrats in control of all of state government. Has Illinois gone from a competitive state to a Democratic-leaning state to a dominant Democratic state?

A political consultant sizing up Illinois for the 2008 presidential election would have seen a state that the Democratic candidates for president carried

Table 3.1. Contributions to statewide, legislative, and appellate court candidates

Top 20 contributors, 2005–6		Top 20 contributors, 2007–8	
$2,363,000	Illinois Federation of Teachers/Chicago Teachers Union	$1,708,000	Illinois Education Association/Illinois PAC for Education
$2,198,000	Illinois Education Association/Illinois PAC for Education	$1,248,000	Illinois Federation of Teachers/Chicago Teachers Union
$1,875,000	U.S. Chamber of Commerce	$1,201,000	Illinois State Medical Society
$1,741,000	SEIU Illinois Council PAC	$1,173,000	Associated Beer Distributors of Illinois*
$1,621,000	Illinois State Medical Society	$1,163,000	Health Care Council of Illinois
$1,391,000	Illinois Hospital Association	$1,083,000	AFSCME Council 31
$1,160,000	AT&T PAC*	$944,000	AT&T PAC*
$994,000	Associated Beer Distributors of Illinois*	$898,000	Illinois Hospital Association
$938,000	Illinois Pipe Trades PAC	$760,000	Illinois Association of Realtors RPAC
$849,000	Duchossois Co. & Family*	$720,000	Duchossois Co. & Family*
$803,000	Local 150 Operating Engineers	$718,000	Exelon PAC*
$754,000	Illinois Association of Realtors RPAC	$708,000	Illinois Pipe Trades PAC
$754,000	Illinois Laborers' Legislative Committee	$685,000	Ameren*
$591,000	Family Taxpayers Network	$634,000	Illinois Trial Lawyers Association
$576,000	AFSCME Council 31	$627,000	Illinois Laborers' Legislative Committee
$554,000	Illinois Trial Lawyers Association	$613,000	Comcast Cable*
$548,000	Comcast Cable*	$612,000	Associated Firefighters of Illinois
$542,000	Associated Firefighters of Illinois	$584,000	Personal PAC
$523,000	Cable TV & Communications Association of Illinois*	$523,000	Altria–Philip Morris*
$512,000	Illinois Chamber of Commerce	$456,000	Credit Union PAC*

Source: Sunshine Project/Illinois Campaign for Political Reform (www.ilcampaign.com) from primary data from the Illinois State Board of Elections (www.elections.state.il.us).
*The contributions were access-oriented rather than elections-oriented.

easily in 2000 and 2004, a state where more voters identify themselves as Democrats than as Republicans, where the Democratic party organizations and voter base (particularly within the City of Chicago and among African American voters) are unified and reliable, and where the Republican party organizations and voter base are ideologically fragmented. Because a state's electoral votes are awarded on a winner-take-all basis, it is not surprising that Illinois has been conceded to the Democrats in recent presidential elections. True to form, the Democratic presidential candidate carried Illinois by more

Table 3.2. Voting turnout and registration

	Registered voters casting ballots	Eligible voters casting ballots	Estimated voting-age population registered to vote
1998	52%	40%	76%
2000*	69%	54%	78%
2002	52%	39%	75%
2004*	71%	56%	79%
2006	49%	37%	77%

Data source: Illinois State Board of Elections (www.elections.state.il.us).
*Presidential election year.

than 1.3 million votes in 2008. Given the right mix of candidates and issues, Illinois could be in play in a presidential election. But for the time being, the results of presidential elections in Illinois will be a foregone conclusion as Republican candidates direct their campaigns at states that are considered more competitive.

For a candidate running for governor or some other constitutional office or the U.S. Senate, the strategic considerations are more complex. Table 3.3 shows the portion of the total vote, cast by region, for the six statewide elections between 1998 and 2008. During that time, roughly 20 percent of the statewide vote came from Chicago, 19 percent from suburban Cook County, 23 percent from the five collar counties (DuPage, Lake, Kane, McHenry, and Will), and 38 percent from downstate.

Writing in 1978, the political scientists Peter W. Colby and Paul Michael Green asserted that the old conception that Illinois elections were contests between Chicago and rest of the state was outdated. Instead, they concluded, the Democratic margin of the vote in the City of Chicago and the Republican margin of the vote in suburban Cook and the collar counties tended to balance each other out. Statewide elections were won by winning in the complex and competitive downstate region made up of the remaining ninety-six counties.[11] Writing twenty-five years later, Green sees a new reality in statewide elections. Noting that Rod Blagojevich in 2002 was the first Democratic candidate to carry suburban Cook County in modern times and that he won a plurality of the vote in Lake and Will Counties in 2006, Green now contends that success in nonpresidential statewide elections requires the kind of candidate that can win in politically competitive suburban Cook County.[12] By implication, a Republican candidate would also win with sufficiently strong margins in the suburban counties and downstate to offset the Democratic vote in Chicago, and a Democratic candidate who can carry suburban Cook would be able to cut into the Republican vote in the collar counties and still achieve an overwhelming majority in Chicago. Green

Table 3.3. Percentage of total votes cast in Illinois general elections by region

Year	Chicago	Suburban Cook County	Collar counties	Downstate	Total vote turnout (%)
1998	21.3	19.2	19.7	39.8	3,541,000 (52.4)
2000*	20.9	19.4	21.6	38.1	4,932,000 (69.2)
2002	19.9	19.1	21.5	39.4	3,651,000 (51.9)
2004*	19.9	19.2	23.0	37.9	5,350,000 (71.3)
2006	18.8	19.0	22.9	39.3	3,588,000 (48.6)
2008*	20.4	19.4	24.1	36.1	5,371,000 ——

Data sources: Sunshine Project/Illinois Campaign for Political Reform (www.ilcampaign.org), compiled from primary data from the Illinois State Board of Elections (www.elections.state.il.us) and unofficial 2008 results from the Associated Press.
*Presidential election year.

concludes that Chicago has become stable in population while voting even more strongly Democratic than in the past. In contrast, the downstate region is voting more strongly Republican but is shrinking in population. The new battlegrounds for statewide elections are the collar counties and suburban Cook County, all of which are gaining in population and becoming more competitive. Most significant, the voting trends in 2002 and 2006 indicate long-term trouble for the Republican Party in its efforts to win nonpresidential statewide elections.

Looking at the five races for governor (which occur in nonpresidential election years), we see that since 1990 (as presented in table 3.4), Democratic candidates have carried Chicago every time, and Republican candidates have carried the collar counties and downstate. They also won suburban Cook County and the governor's office in 1990, 1994, and 1998, whereas Democrats carried them in 2002 and 2006.

In five races for the U.S. Senate held between 1990 and 2008 (see table 3.4), Democrats carried Chicago each time. They also carried suburban Cook four in five times and downstate four in five times. Republican candidates won the collar counties two in five times. Democrats won four of these five elections.

In the presidential elections of 1992, 1996, 2000, 2004, and 2008 (see table 3.4), the Democratic candidate won each time. They carried Chicago and suburban Cook in each election. Democratic candidates also won the downstate region in 1992, 1996, and 2008, whereas Republican candidates won the region in 2000 and 2006. Republicans carried the collar counties in every election prior to that of 2008, which the Democrat carried for the first time in modern Illinois history. Even though this may reflect the fact that the Democratic candidate was from Illinois, it may also be a sign of a further weakening of Republican strength in the suburbs.

Table 3.4. Margins of victory by region, statewide elections

				Gubernatorial elections	
Year	Chicago	Suburban Cook County	Collar counties	Downstate	Winner (Margin)
1990	244,000 D	113,000 R	149,000 R	47,000 R	Edgar R (83,000)
1994	156,000 D	221,000 R	316,000 R	533,000 R	Edgar R (915,000)
1998	238,000 D	110,000 R	239,000 R	9,000 R	Ryan R (120,000)
2002	418,000 D	50,000 D	147,000 R	70,000 R	Blagojevich D (253,000)
2006	404,000 D	103,000 D	32,000 R	109,000 R	Blagojevich D (367,000)
				U.S. Senate elections	
Year	Chicago	Suburban Cook County	Collar counties	Downstate	Winner (Margin)
1996	538,000 D	126,000 D	58,000 R	48,000 D	Durbin D (655,000)
1998	407,000 D	13,000 R	164,000 R	328,000 R	Fitzgerald R (98,000)
2002	445,000 D	142,000 D	7,000 D	198,000 D	Durbin D (778,000)
2004	796,000 D	503,000 D	407,000 D	499,000 D	Obama D (2,206,000)
2008	385,000 D	483,000 D	304,000 D	465,000 D	Durbin D (2,037,000)
				Presidential elections	
Year	Chicago	Suburban Cook County	Collar counties	Downstate	Winner (Margin)
1992	593,000 D	51,000 D	108,000 R	187,000 D	Clinton D (719,000)
1996	559,000 D	132,000 D	44,000 R	108,000 D	Clinton D (754,000)
2000	601,000 D	141,000 D	97,000 R	76,000 R	Gore D (570,000)
2004	655,000 D	187,000 D	101,000 R	195,000 R	Kerry D (545,000)
2008	771,000 D	354,000 D	154,000 D	59,000 D	Obama D (1,336,000)

Data sources: Sunshine Project/Illinois Campaign for Political Reform (www.ilcampaign.org), compiled from primary data from the Illinois State Board of Elections (www. election.state.il.us) and unofficial 2008 results from the Associated Press.

The task for a Democratic candidate running statewide is to turn out the party base of voters in Chicago and in the pockets of Democratic strength downstate and to compete for swing voters in the suburbs. The task for a Republican candidate is to turn out the base downstate and in the suburbs while also competing for suburban swing voters. The current political demographics of the electorate in Illinois clearly favor Democratic candidates in statewide elections, but elections are always relational. The quality of the candidate and of the campaign can overcome the advantage with which any Democrat in a statewide race currently begins a campaign.

The political demographics of Illinois can also be seen in the difference in the primary vote by region in Democratic and Republican primaries (see table 3.5). On average, in the past four statewide primary elections 59 percent of the vote in a typical Democratic primary came from Chicago (37 percent) and Cook County (22 percent), about 15 percent came from the collar counties, and 26 percent from the downstate counties. In contrast, more than 52 percent of the Republican vote, on average, came from the collar counties (36 percent) and suburban Cook County (16 percent), 44 percent came from the downstate counties, and slightly less than 4 percent from Chicago. In a two-way race between a Democrat from Chicago and a Democrat from downstate or the suburbs, the Chicagoan should win the Democratic primary. Though it is less certain, a suburban Republican candidate should prevail in a two-way race with a candidate from downstate in a Republican primary. In multicandidate races, however, the outcomes tend to be much more unpredictable.

Participation in primary elections varies widely. Generally, turnout will be higher in nonpresidential elections in which candidates for statewide office are being selected. Turnout in 2008, when Barack Obama was on the Democratic ballot, was significantly higher than in recent presidential election years. Turnout in the Republican primary always significantly underrepresents the potential Republican vote in the general election. Because of the dominance of the Democratic Party in local politics in Chicago, there are often few candidates or choices for Republican voters beyond those at the top of the ticket. There is also reluctance among many Republican-leaning voters in Chicago to publicly identify themselves as Republicans. The result is a stark contrast between the number of Democratic and Republican ballots cast in the primary in Chicago; this overstates the advantage that Democrats hold statewide in party identification. The size of the margin between the two parties in recent primary elections signals another troubling trend for Republicans running in statewide elections in Illinois.

The Outcome of Statewide Elections

One of the electoral advantages of strong state political parties in Illinois was their ability to structure slates of statewide candidates in ways that usually produced no serious contests in the primary.[13] By providing a ladder of opportunity for ambitious candidates, balancing tickets in terms of regional, ethnic, and racial considerations, and discouraging independent candidates, this system gave candidates and the party a clear path to the general election. In the current era of self-recruitment and candidate-focused fundraising, primaries without an incumbent for statewide office (state and federal) follow two patterns. In the first, a strong candidate, usually a holder of a lower office, is able to scare off serious opposition and proceed to the general election without much trouble. For example, in 1990 Jim Edgar, the Republican secretary

Table 3.5. Votes cast in party primary elections, by region

		Democratic			
Year	Chicago (%)	Suburban Cook County (%)	Collar counties (%)	Downstate (%)	Votes cast
1998	40.2	17.4	8.5	33.9	1,036,000
2000*	46.3	16.1	8.6	21.5	917,000
2002	38.4	21.2	13.8	26.6	1,321,000
2004*	36.2	21.4	14.7	27.7	1,310,000
2006	39.6	23.8	14.2	23.4	944,000
2008*	31.3	21.7	19.4	27.6	2,060,000
		Republican			
Year	Chicago (%)	Suburban Cook County (%)	Collar counties (%)	Downstate (%)	Votes cast
2000*	3.6%	19.2	36.0	41.2	781,000
2002	3.6%	16.3	35.1	45.0	946,000
2004*	3.9%	17.6	35.8	42.7	703,000
2006	3.3%	15.1	37.8	43.8	736,000
2008*	4.8%	15.0	32.5	47.7	911,000

*Presidential election year.
Data source: Sunshine Project/Illinois Campaign for Political Reform (www.ilcampaign.org), compiled from primary data from Illinois State Board of Elections (www.elections.state.il.us).

of state, and Neil Hartigan, the Democratic attorney general, easily won their party's nomination for governor after Governor Jim Thompson chose not to run for reelection. In 1998 the Republican secretary of state, George Ryan, easily won his party's nomination for governor after Edgar chose not to run for reelection. In the second pattern, the lack of a clear favorite and of strong state party structures to moderate the process produces very contentious, hugely expensive multicandidate primaries that drain resources and make party unity in the general election more difficult. In 1994, 1998, and 2002 the Democratic gubernatorial primaries all had at least three serious contenders. There were three serious contenders in the 2002 Republican primary and four in the 2006 Republican primary race for the governor's office. Republican candidates spent $22.0 million in 2002 and $22.9 million in 2006 in the primary; Democratic candidates spent $14.5 million in the 2002 primary.

The campaigns of former governors Edgar and Ryan demonstrate the formula for a Republican victory in a statewide election in Illinois. Both were incumbent secretaries of state who ran largely unopposed in the primary. Edgar was a downstate politician with a base in Coles County, whereas Ryan was from Kankakee County. Edgar won in 1990 against the Chicagoan Hartigan. Edgar's victory came from a strong showing downstate and among Republicans and swing voters in the suburbs. Hartigan failed to win Chicago with the kind of margin needed to overcome Edgar's suburban and downstate strength. When Edgar chose not to seek reelection, Ryan won in 1998 against Glenn Poshard, a downstate Democrat, by competing downstate and winning swing voters in the suburbs while Poshard failed to win in Chicago by the margin needed to offset Ryan's broad appeal. Poshard was widely perceived as more conservative than Ryan with regard to key social issues, and Ryan's campaign used this issue to build his support among swing voters in the suburbs. At the same time, the vote totals in Chicago demonstrated a lack of enthusiasm for Poshard, who generated little support there beyond core Democratic voters. Ryan also had a significant monetary advantage over Poshard, who had to spend heavily in his primary race and then had trouble raising money for the general election.

The winning formula for a Democratic candidate in a statewide election can be seen in Governor Rod Blagojevich's victories in 2002 and 2006. Running in 2002 against the incumbent attorney general, Jim Ryan (who unfortunately shared the last name of the highly unpopular and soon-to-be disgraced incumbent, George Ryan), Blagojevich won Chicago by 418,000 votes but lost downstate by 60,000 votes. The key to his victory was his strong showing in suburban Cook County and the collar counties. He carried suburban Cook by 51,000 votes, while Ryan's margin in the collar counties was only 147,000 votes. In spite of low popularity ratings and nagging fiscal problems, Blagojevich's victory in 2006 over the incumbent Republican state treasurer, Judy Barr Topinka, followed the same pattern. With the Green Party candidate receiving 10.4 percent of the vote, Blagojevich won slightly less than half the total vote but scored strong majority victories in Chicago and suburban Cook County and plurality victories in the traditionally strongly Republican collar counties of Lake and Will. Topinka was unable to generate the level of support among swing voters in the collar counties and suburban Cook County needed for a Republican to win statewide office in Illinois.

A closer look at the results of the 2006 general election illustrates the fact that the heart of the base of the Democratic Party in Illinois is the vote in Chicago, and the heart of the Chicago vote is the group of wards with large African American majorities. In the 2006 general election, Blagojevich received more than 90 percent of the vote in sixteen of Chicago's fifty wards. Fifteen of those wards had large African American majorities; the other had a large Latino majority. Overall, Blagojevich received 77.4 percent of the Chicago vote. Though impressive, that percentage was the lowest for the statewide Democratic candidates in Chicago. Attorney General Lisa Madigan received an astounding 90 percent of the Chicago vote.

While suburban Cook and its five collar counties once formed the heart of the Republican Party base in Illinois, the results of the 2006 general election show a continuation of the troubling trend that appeared four years earlier. In 2002 Blagojevich won suburban Cook County by 51,000 votes and carried thirteen of its thirty townships. In 2006 he won suburban Cook by 104,000 votes and carried eighteen of the townships. In 2002 Blagojevich lost all five collar counties, but in 2006 in a three-way race he won two of the five. Though Topinka, the Republican candidate for governor, had a plurality in the collar counties in 2006, she received less than 50 percent of the total vote. Democrat Lisa Madigan carried all five of the collar counties in 2006. The results from the governor's race in downstate Illinois show more support for the Republican candidate in 2006 than in 2002, but the total margin of victory was not nearly enough to surmount the overwhelming Democratic vote in Chicago and the increasingly competitive situation in suburban Cook and the collar counties.[14]

Because Illinois has a large population, a sizeable land mass, and a diverse network of media markets, it has always been very expensive to mount a campaign for statewide office. Yet the jump in the cost of those campaigns in the 2002 and 2006 election cycles has been staggering. In 2002 the two losing Democratic primary candidates and the two losing Republican primary candidates spent $18.7 million in the aggregate. Rod Blagojevich spent a total of $23.4 million in the primary and the general election to win the office of governor. At the same time Jim Ryan spent a total of $15.8 million in his unsuccessful bid. The total cost of the campaigns for all of the candidates for governor in 2002 was a record $57.9 million, more than twice the previous high. The 2006 race broke that record. The three losing Republican primary candidates and the one losing Democratic primary candidate spent $20.8 million collectively. Blagojevich spent a total of $28.9 million to win reelection, and Topinka spent $10.7 million in her losing campaign. The total cost of the campaigns of all candidates for the governor's office in 2006 was $60.4 million.

Contests for the offices of secretary of state, attorney general, comptroller, and treasurer are not usually anywhere as expensive as races for the governor's office. But the potential is there. In 2002 the Republican and Democratic primaries in the state attorney general's race were strongly contested. The eventual winner, Lisa Madigan, spent a total of $10.8 million, while the Republican candidate, Joe Birkett, and the two losing candidates from the primary spent $8.9 million collectively. In total, $19.7 million was spent on the race.

In assessing the impact of money on statewide elections, it is important to note that having money and spending it wisely are two different things. The candidate who spent the most in the 2002 Republican primary in the governor's race, Lieutenant Governor Corinne Wood, finished third in the race, and the candidate who spent the most in the 2006 Republican gubernatorial primary, Ron Gidwitz, finished fourth. Candidates with money do not always win, but they almost always beat candidates without money. Rod Blagojevich's success in raising money played a huge role in his gaining the governor's office in 2002 and winning reelection in 2006. In 2002 his huge monetary advantage in the primary allowed him to campaign extensively in downstate counties, in contrast to his two opponents. His success in downstate counties provided the margin of his victory. In the general election he enjoyed an almost two-to-one advantage in spending over Jim Ryan, who spent almost half of the total money he raised for the campaign to win the primary. In 2006 Blagojevich outspent Topinka by more than three to one in the general election. He ran more than 22,109 ads costing $18.1 million between the primary and the general election, compared to the 4,638 ads Topinka ran at a cost of $4.6 million.[15] The main thrust of his campaign was to tie his opponent to disgraced former governor George Ryan and the budget problems that Blagojevich had inherited four years earlier. After more than seven months of hearing her characterized as Ryan's state treasurer, the person who had done nothing about the budget mess, many Illinois voters mistakenly thought that the governor appointed the state treasurer. In spite of very high negatives among voters as to the job he was doing and the direction the state was moving in, Blagojevich won by a plurality in a three-way race with a comfortable margin over Topinka and Rich Whitney, the Green Party candidate. Blagojevich's overwhelming advantage in campaign spending even prompted former governor Jim Edgar to reverse a long-held position and publicly call for consideration of contribution limits in Illinois.

Compared to contests for the governor's office, races for the other constitutional offices tend to be low-profile. Under the 1970 constitution, candidates for lieutenant governor run separately under partisan labels in the primary, but the winners are paired with their party's nominee for the general election. For this reason, it is no longer possible to have a governor and a lieutenant governor from different parties. The positions of secretary of state and attorney general are the most strongly contested of the remaining constitutional officers; elections for comptroller and treasurer are very low-visibility contests.

The office of secretary of state has traditionally been seen as the second-largest source of jobs and patronage after the governor's office and as such was prized by state party leaders. Two of the past three governors had previously held the office of secretary of state. Although the duties of the office are limited, one of those duties is to issue driver's licenses and motor vehicle registrations, which ensures a certain level of name recognition for the incumbent. Elections for the office of secretary of state do not generate much attention from interest groups. The amounts spent by the winning candidate have ranged between two and three million dollars for the past three elections, and Democratic incumbent Jesse White won easily each time.

There has been a national trend for the office of attorney general to become more visible as individuals holding this office have taken on consumer, environmental, and public health issues, sometimes with their fellows in other states. The office has also become an attractive stepping stone to higher office. The contrast between the visions of the office presented by the Illinois candidates in 2002 was striking. The eventual winner, Democrat Lisa Madigan, ran to be "the people's lawyer," whereas her opponent, Republican Joe Birkett, focused on a more limited crime-fighting role. Madigan, reelected in 2006, has continued to expand the scope and visibility of the office. Because the office exercises authority in areas such as health care, environment, and financial institutions, major Illinois interest groups have shown increased interest in the office. All this suggests that future elections for state attorney general will become increasingly competitive and expensive.

The saying that no one knows and no one cares who is state treasurer or state comptroller may be a little harsh, but it is not far from public perception of the two offices. But because the state parties are weak and these offices have low visibility, they do present opportunities for ambitious individuals to start political careers by self-recruiting and by self-funding their campaigns. The success of Alexi Giannoulias in the 2006 treasurer's race is only one recent example.

Since 1978 only one Republican candidate for the U.S. Senate has been able to reach beyond the base Republican vote and win election. In 1998 state senator Peter Fitzgerald defeated the party-backed candidate, incumbent State Treasurer Lolita Didrikson, in the primary and then defeated incumbent U.S. senator Carol Mosley Braun in the general election. When Fitzgerald chose not to seek reelection in 2004, the Democrats regained the seat with the election of Barack Obama. The Democrats have held the other Illinois U.S. Senate seat since Paul Simon defeated Charles Percy, the incumbent senator, in 1984. The current incumbent, Richard Durbin, was first elected in 1996 and easily won reelection in 2002 and 2008.

The current dynamic of Democratic dominance in U.S. Senate elections is likely to continue in the foreseeable future. The political demographics of Illinois favor Democratic candidates in statewide elections. In addition, Republicans have not been able to recruit strong candidates in recent campaigns. Getting shut out of statewide elected office in 2006 makes that task even more difficult. A lack of national interest in Illinois U.S. Senate campaigns also plays a role. If a U.S. Senate race is seen as competitive, national senatorial party organizations and national interest groups will engage in recruitment activities and provide support for primary and general election campaigns in addition to efforts within the state. As already noted, the 2008 U.S. Senate election is a strong case in point with the popular, well-funded Democratic incumbent defeating a weak, self-recruited and self-funded candidate who attracted no national attention or support.

The outcome of the 2010 statewide elections will tell us a lot about the future of partisan statewide competition in Illinois. The office of governor and the other constitutional offices as well as a U.S. Senate seat (owing to the appointment of a replacement for Senator Obama) will be open. The Democrats will be carrying the burden of being the party of the impeached Governor Rod Blagojevich. This is an opportunity for the Republicans to field a credible set of candidates and capture some of these offices. If the Republicans are shut out again, and particularly if they are unable to be competitive, then the long-term dominance of Democrats in statewide elections seems assured. If the Democrats control the governor's office and both chambers of the legislature after the 2010 elections, they should be able to draw favorable legislative districts for the 2012 elections without going to a redistricting commission. This would further diminish the prospects for Republican resurgence in the legislative branch.

Legislative Elections: The Illinois General Assembly and the U.S. Congress

In contrast to the U.S. Senate elections, elections to the U.S. House in Illinois present some strategic opportunities for gains and losses that attract the attention of national congressional party organizations and national interest groups. A majority of the current congressional districts in Illinois are considered safe for one party or the other. In these districts, weak candidates for the minority party recruit themselves, receive minimal assistance from local party organizations, and go down to defeat without making an appearance on the radar screens of the national congressional party organizations. For example, following the retirement in 2008 of Ray LaHood, the long-time Republican incumbent, in the Eighteenth Congressional District, a popular Republican state legislator won the primary and easily defeated a Democratic candidate who was appointed to the ballot after the winner in the March Democratic primary withdrew from the race. The selection of Congressman Rahm Emanuel from the Fifth District of Illinois to be chief of staff for President Obama set off a flurry of activity among potential candidates to replace him in office. The only certain thing was that the eventual winner of the 2009 special election in this largely Chicago-based, heavily Democratic district would not be a Republican. Michael Quigley won the Democratic primary, beating five other candidates, and then won the special election for the seat with more than 70 percent of the vote.

Any combination of an open seat in a potentially competitive district and an incumbent with reelection problems will generate interest at the national level as well as within the district. In 2002 Melissa Bean, a Democratic challenger with significant national support, defeated Phil Crane, a long-time Republican incumbent, in the Eighth Congressional District, a largely suburban district in far northeastern Illinois. The incumbent was widely viewed as disengaged and ineffective, and the challenger made that the focus of her campaign. In 2004 the Republicans mounted a strong challenge against Bean, and another suburban district (the Sixth) was strongly contested after the long-time Republican incumbent retired. A strong challenge was also mounted against a Republican incumbent in the Tenth, a northeastern suburban district. Each of these races attracted strong national support. The incumbents were reelected in the Eighth and the Tenth Districts, but the Sixth remained in Republican hands. In 2008 the Tenth District was again contested, and the Eleventh and the Fourteenth Districts, in northern Illinois, were in play owing to the retirement of two long-time Republican Congressmen, one of them the Speaker of the House, Dennis Hastert. These contested seats received attention and support from the respective national congressional campaign committees. The incumbent Republican in the Tenth was reelected, but a Democrat prevailed in a special election in the Eleventh and again in the general election, and a Democrat won the Fourteenth in the general election. Democrats now hold a 12-7 advantage in the Illinois congressional delegation. Nationwide there are a relatively small number of truly competitive congressional seats in each election cycle. Illinois was a key battleground in 2006 and 2008 in the fight for control of Congress. It is ironic that the combination of shifting demographics and retirements by incumbents has overcome the intention of those drawing the 2002 map to create safe districts for the incumbents of both parties.

In elections for the Illinois legislature, the length of the terms of legislators and the structure of the two chambers of the General Assembly set up by the 1970 state constitution create two different rhythms. With house members serving two-year terms, all 118 house seats are up every two years. Each house seat is contested within the state and national political context of that particular election cycle. In the senate, all of the seats are up in a redistricting year (for example, 2012). Each district then fits into one of three patterns of length of terms for the next ten years: 4-4-2, 4-2-4, or 2-4-4. As a result, some senators will be initially elected for four-year terms and some will be elected for two-year terms. In the next election following redistricting (2014), only one-third of the senate seats will be up for reelection. In the third and fourth elections held with the map (2016 and 2018), two-thirds of the senate seats will be up, and in the final election before redistricting (2020), one-third of the senate seats will be up.

Political geography and partisan redistricting combine to produce a striking lack of competition in legislative elections in Illinois. First, achieving competition in districts located primarily in Democratic-dominated Chicago or Republican-dominated DuPage County is not possible. Areas of the state that are dominated by one political party are not going to be competitive in legislative elections. Second, when a party has control of the redistricting process, the goal is not to maximize competition; the goal is to maximize the chances of political control. The strategy is to create as many safe districts as possible where the party in control of the redistricting process can win comfortably and as many as possible where the minority party wins overwhelmingly. In the areas that are naturally competitive or areas where demographic or political trends are favorable, the map-making goal is to configure districts that give the party controlling the process the advantage. The result is a large number of districts with no general election competition and a few districts that become the targets for the legislative leaders as they seek control of the house or the senate.

Under the current legislative map drawn by the Democrats, nearly 58 percent of the winners in house elections and 56 percent of the winners in senate elections had no opponent in the general election. In addition, another 34 percent of the general election winners in house elections and 26 percent in senate elections had weak opponents who spent less than $50,000 and received less than 45 percent of the vote (see table 3.6).

The 2006 and 2008 legislative elections in Illinois continued the dominance of the Democratic Party in both chambers with the redistricting map drawn by the Democrats and adopted prior to the 2002 elections. After picking up one seat in 2006 and three seats in 2008, the Democrats outnumbered the Republicans in the house 70 to 48. In 2006 the Democrats won thirty-seven seats, a gain of six seats, leaving the Republicans with only twenty-two seats. No senate seats changed hands in the 2008 election. It is not all about the map, but a favorable map combined with the Democrats' geographical and political advantages makes winning control of the legislature a very, very difficult task for the Republicans.

When it comes to competition and campaign spending, there are two different worlds of legislative elections in Illinois. In the first world, which constitutes the large majority of the legislative districts, one party has a distinct

Table 3.6. Competition in legislative elections by district

House	2002	2004	2006	2008
Unopposed	71	71	62	59
Weak opponent*	37	38	47	46
Competitive, nontargeted**	4	2	0	3
Targeted by leaders	6	7	9	10
Total number of districts	118	118	118	118

Senate	2002	2004	2006	2008
Unopposed	38	14	15	20
Weak opponent*	14	4	13	15
Competitive, nontargeted**	0	0	0	0
Targeted by leaders	7	4	10	5
Total number of districts	59	22	38	40

Sources: "Show Me the Money," Sunshine Project/Illinois Campaign for Political Reform (www .ilcampaign.org), compiled from primary data from Illinois State Board of Elections (www.elections. state.il.us).
*The losing candidate spent less than $50,000 and received less than 45% of the vote.
**The losing candidate won more than 45% of the vote.

advantage in the district. These are "safe" districts. In the general elections, well-known, well-funded, usually incumbent majority party candidates easily defeat unknown, underfunded candidates representing the party that is in the political minority in the district. Competitive elections do occur occasionally in this world when an incumbent chooses not to run for reelection, but these competitive elections take place in the primary election, not the general. The majority's local party organizations in the counties, townships, and wards exercise great influence in the primary elections in these districts. Success breeds success. The party in the majority tends to control local political offices and hold power on a consistent basis because it is able to raise money and build organizational strength in ways the minority party in the district cannot match. Candidates in primaries in safe districts tend to be recruited by local party organizations or are self-recruited. Legislative leaders rarely get involved with primary elections in safe districts.

In the second world, a small number of contests that will determine control of the legislature are fought between two well-funded candidates backed by professional campaign staffs. These hyperexpensive and usually very competitive races are known as targeted races. The name comes from the fact that they are being targeted by one or both of the legislative leaders in the house or the senate. Initially, the number of potential targets may be 20 of 118 house seats and 5–10 of the one-third or two-thirds of the senate seats that are up for election in a nonredistricting year. Ultimately 8–10 house seats and 4–6 senate seats will be the major targets for the election cycle.[16]

Not all competitive districts become targets, and not all targeted districts become competitive. Regardless of the criteria for designating a district as competitive (for example, 55 percent to 45 percent or 52 percent to 48 percent), it is not possible to know in advance whether a district will be competitive. Legislative leaders and interest groups make reasoned judgments about which districts present the best opportunities or dangers for change and invest in those elections accordingly. After an election is over, a review of the election results and the money and effort spent by leaders on legislative races will show a number of targeted districts with competitive results. But there will also be districts targeted by one or both sides where the race was hugely expensive but not very competitive. Less frequently there will be districts where the outcomes were very close but where little or no money from leaders or organizational resources were directed at the race.

The world of the targeted legislative elections in Illinois is dominated by the legislative leaders, who function as political parties. The leaders recruit candidates, raise money with their personal political committees or leadership political committees, and manage and fund the campaigns. When the legislature comes into session, the legislative leaders provide organization and structure by means of their caucuses. As is discussed in more detail in chapter 5, in the past three decades power in the legislature has become extremely centralized in the legislative leaders. Their power comes from the interrelated dynamic of their ability to raise money and spend it on legislative campaigns, their dominance of the policy process in the legislature, and their monopoly control over the partisan legislative staffs. Although the speaker of the house and the senate president are the most powerful actors in the legislature, each of the leaders in each chamber exercises power in the legislative process through their control of their political caucuses and their partisan legislative staffs. Power in Springfield translates into the ability to raise money and influence legislative elections. It also translates into the ability to build campaign organizations using legislative staff members on leave from the legislature. The resulting strength in legislative elections builds power in Springfield. And the resulting increase in power in Springfield builds power in legislative elections.[17]

As noted above, under Illinois campaign finance law, legislative leaders can raise money from any source in unlimited amounts. Money can also be transferred from one political committee to another without limit or spent on behalf of another candidate without limit. Although the mechanisms vary, over the past three decades legislative leaders of both parties in the house and the senate have become more and more involved with raising money and using it to fund legislative campaigns.

The four legislative leaders operate independently in their election activities. There is usually very little coordination or cooperation between house and senate Democrats or between house and senate Republicans. Elections in house districts in 2008 were contested between the Speaker Madigan "political party" and the Minority Leader Cross "political party"; elections in senate districts were contested between the President Jones operation and the Minority Leader Watson operation. Individual house members sometimes get involved in a senate race, and vice versa, but it is not a regular pattern. For purposes of legislative elections, there is no unified Democratic or Republican party in Illinois. This compartmentalization carries over into the legislative process, further complicating the task of solving public policy problems.

As the legislature comes into session in the spring after the fall general election, the next two-year election cycle has already begun. Each of the legislative leaders will look at the results of the past election and begin planning how to keep a majority or gain a majority. The legislative maps, political geography, and election results will drastically limit the number of districts where there may be a chance of a change in party control. In the senate, the fact that only one-third or two-thirds of the seats may be up will further limit the available options for change. This election calculus is more compressed and complicated following a redistricting because the new districts may not be known until early fall of the first year of the cycle, and new district lines increase uncertainty about the outcome of elections. Each leader will begin with a list of districts where there is opportunity to pick up a seat or the danger of losing a seat. Events such as an unexpected retirement or a personal scandal may alter that list. The leader will also make a judgment as to how favorable the political climate will be at the time of the general election. One leader may pursue an aggressive, offense-oriented strategy that focuses on potential gains; another may pursue a cautious, defense-oriented strategy that focuses on potential losses.

Leaders will become actively involved in candidate recruitment if the targeted district is without an incumbent or if the incumbent is from the other party. If possible, they will work with local parties and interest groups. If the leader has a strong preference for a candidate in the primary, he will provide campaign support that can range from organizational support and candidate training to workers, funds, and expenditures on behalf of the candidate. The financial and organizational support will usually come directly from the leader's political committee rather than from the legislative chamber's political committee in order to avoid the appearance that the legislative party is taking sides in a local primary. If a leader is committed to a candidate, the expenditure of funds on building support for the candidate as a foundation for the fall election can be substantial.

Once the candidates are in place for the general election, the legislative leaders will make another assessment of their election strategy. Since campaigns are relational contests between two candidates, the strength or weakness of the opposition candidate may cause a district to rise or fall as a priority. Any movement beyond an initial level of support may be contingent on the candidate's ability to raise money locally, build an organization, or increase his or her polling numbers. Because the leader's goal is to win seats rather than elect a particular candidate, it is not unusual to see resources shifted from one district to another as the campaigns progress.

Once the candidates are in place, the keys to executing the leaders' election strategies are money and organization. The leaders may transfer money to a candidate directly or spend it on behalf of the candidate in the form of campaign staff, direct mail, or media advertising. The amount of money spent in targeted legislative races is staggering compared to the amount spent in nontargeted races (see tables 3.7 and 3.8). The most expensive house race in Illinois history cost more than $1.9 million, and the most expensive senate race cost almost $2.5 million.

In 2006 there were nine targeted house races with an average total spending per race of $1,123,000 and ten targeted senate races with an average total spending per race of $1,297,000. The leaders were directly responsible for nearly one-half of the money spent by incumbents and nearly two-thirds of the money spent by challengers in these contests. The figures are higher for challengers because incumbents can raise money more easily than challengers. The leadership support figures understate the financial impact of the leaders on targeted races because interest groups who care which party controls the legislature will direct contributions to the candidates whom the leaders support. It is always interesting how a labor union from Chicago or a manufacturing company from Rockford will find candidates in a targeted race in deep southern Illinois. Preliminary figures for the 2008 legislative election clearly show a continuation of the pattern of a small number of hyper-expensive races dominated by the legislative leaders.

As important as the money raised by legislative leaders is in winning targeted races, the organizational support that the leaders provide is just as important. Their control over partisan legislative staff in Springfield has allowed them to build large, professional campaign organizations. A great many people who work on legislative staffs go off the state payroll during election years to run or work on legislative campaigns. These organizations exist from election

Table 3.7. Most expensive legislative races

Total spending	District	Year	Candidates
		House	
$1,924,000	H-107	2006	Granberg (D) vs. Cavaletto (R)
$1,608,000	H-092	2006	Schock (R) vs. Spears (D)
$1,573,000	H-091	2006	M. Smith (D) vs. Dagit (R)
$1,525,000	H-071	2006	Boland (D) vs. Haring (R)
$1,515,000	H-092	2004	Schock (R) vs. Slone (D)
		Senate	
Total spending	District	Year	Candidates
$2,465,000	S-59	2004	Forby (D) vs. Summers (R)
$2,441,000	S-29	2002	Garrett (D) vs. Parker (R)
$2,259,000	S-52	2006	Frerichs (D) vs. Myers (R)
$2,004,000	S-32	2004	Althoff (R) vs. Ouimet (D)
$1,995,000	S-38	2004	Dahl (R) vs. Welch (D)

Data sources: "Show Me the Money," Sunshine Project/Illinois Campaign for Political Reform (www .ilcampaign.org), compiled from primary data from Illinois State Board of Elections (www.elections .state.il.us).

Table 3.8. Average spending in Illinois legislative races, 2006

		Average spending	Number of races
House	Targeted	$1,123,000	9
	Nontargeted (excluding legislative leader)	$195,000	107*
Senate	Targeted	$1,297,000	10
	Nontargeted (excluding legislative leader)	$327,000	27**

Data sources: "Show Me the Money," Sunshine Project/Illinois Campaign for Political Reform (www. ilcampaign.org), compiled from primary data from Illinois State Board of Elections (www.elections. state.il.us).

*Only 47 nontargeted districts had two candidates, and only 22 of those 47 losing candidates reported any spending; the average amount spent was $45,000.

**Only 13 nontargeted districts had two candidates, and only 5 of those 13 losing candidates reported any spending; the average amount spent was $44,000.

to election. They work for the leader, not for individual candidates. Many staff are experienced organizers or specialists in campaign media and communications. Their loyalty is to the leader, and their ultimate success is measured by his or her political success. If the leader decides to pull staff from one race and move them to another, they will shift campaigns and candidates. This stands in sharp contrast to the loyalty of the personal campaign organization of a long-time incumbent in a safe district; that organization exists solely for the incumbent. The impact of legislative staff and leadership control is addressed in more detail in chapter 5.

Unless there are significant changes in the political culture, the redistricting process, the style of legislative leaders, and Illinois campaign finance laws, the two worlds of legislative elections will continue. One will be characterized by safe, one-party districts with noncompetitive elections, the other by targeted districts with extremely expensive, leadership-controlled elections. Whoever has the greatest success in that second world will control the General Assembly.

Illinois Elections: Power and Policy

Elections in Illinois are best seen in two different lights. First, they reflect the political demographics and geography of the state. Illinois is strongly Democratic when it comes to statewide elections, both federal and state-level. It is also a state of political regions that shape strategies for statewide elections. Illinois leans Democratic in legislative elections, but legislative maps and regional political geography make legislative elections more complex and their overall outcome less certain than is the case with statewide elections. Under the right circumstances Republicans can win statewide, but they must overcome the substantial advantage that any Democratic candidate begins with. Given control of the redistricting process, Republicans could shape a legislative map that would give them a chance to win control of the legislature, although the trends in the political demographics of the state make that more difficult than was the case in the 1990s. And at that time, the Republicans, operating with a map that they drew, were able to win control of both chambers of the legislature for but a single session.

Second, Illinois elections both reflect and reinforce the dominant individualistic, power-oriented, nonideological political culture in the state. The election and campaign finance laws work against those without money or power and reward those who have power, especially those who are the most effective at acquiring more power and exercising it, either as individuals or as political organizations. Rather than promoting participation and policy innovation, the election process reinforces a politics that is status quo–oriented and risk-averse when it comes to dealing with policy problems. The pragmatic orientation of the legislative leaders and the weak position of rank-and-file legislators do not encourage risk taking and innovation.

Statewide elections could be vehicles for promoting fundamental changes in process and policy. But the record of the last three to four decades is a record of very little progress in addressing the serious fiscal and policy problems facing Illinois. Two governors, Walker and Blagojevich, were elected on the basis of promises to fundamentally change the nature of Illinois politics. Walker foundered on his own ineptitude and the intransigence of the state's political culture. The same fate, accelerated by his personal corruption, overtook Blagojevich. The 1994 election gave the Republicans in Illinois control of both chambers of the legislature and all of the constitutional offices. The 2006 election provided the same opportunity for the Democrats. In 1995–96 nothing occurred in Illinois while it was under Republican control to fundamentally change the role of government or the foundations of public policy to match what was happening at the national level after the Republicans took control of Congress. Nothing took place in 2007–8 to suggest that the Democrats, with complete control over state government, will be any more successful. The political culture prevails. Winning and control, in and of themselves, are the major goals of Illinois elections. Policy positions and outcomes are means to those ends rather than the ultimate goals of Illinois politics.[18]

4.

Constitutions

• • • • • • • • • • • • •

State constitutions provide the dimensions of the ballpark in which the game of politics is played. The charters provide the structure of government and enumerate elective offices to be filled. Equally important, constitutions grant powers and impose limitations on government in general and on the legislative, executive, and judicial branches in particular. Unlike the federal government, which has had only one Constitution since the Articles of Confederation, Illinois has had four constitutions since its admission to the Union in 1818.

The number may be misleading, though, because the first "frontier" constitution was written hurriedly. Drafted, debated, and passed in three weeks, it was a rough document in a state with little knowledge of its future. Twice in the following fifty-two years, as the state evolved and Chicago emerged, the constitution was rewritten, but the versions of 1848 and 1870, like the first constitution, often created new problems while trying to resolve earlier ones.

For one hundred years between the 1870 vote and the approval in 1970 of the current constitution, the state moved forward in spite of the 1870 constitution's restraints; leaders tried again and again to rewrite or amend the state framework but failed each time. They were victims not only of the restrictions written into the constitution they hoped to improve but also of poor preparation, a leaning toward partisanship, and opposition from special interests. Then, in a triumph of nonpartisan effort, 116 delegates gathered in 1969 in Springfield, deliberating a new charter in the historic Old State Capitol. This was no ordinary group—many of the state's future leaders were delegates—and they took on the task with vigor. During a nine-month period, under the skilled and energetic leadership of longtime constitutional advocate Samuel W. Witwer, they overhauled the law of the land and engineered a political alliance to gain voter support for ratification. It was a major achievement in Illinois history and one of the best examples of the state's occasional ability to overcome its individualism to address a common problem.

Nature of Constitutions

Constitutions are designed to serve as the bedrock on which a government's structure is built. This is a risky engineering feat in almost any case, and it certainly was in early Illinois, where the framers were unsure of the kind of building that was to be erected on their foundation. Still, they made use of a major concept that appears in all state constitutions except that of Delaware: it must be harder to change than a simple state statute; the constitution can only be amended with the voters' approval in addition to the legislature's.

As evidenced by the United States Constitution, this primary set of rules need not be long, and many argue that it should not be. Rather than being filled with provisions detailing exactly how government should be structured and what offices should be filled at what salary, a short-form constitution is little more than a framework of rights and responsibilities. Idealists say that a constitution should contain fundamentals (although there is disagreement about what is fundamental) and that nonfundamentals should be placed in legislation or statutes. For instance, idealists would say the basic organization of state government into three branches is fundamental but that creation of a specific state agency (for example, the state board of elections created by the 1970 Constitution in Illinois) is not fundamental. Another point of contention is how restrictive a state constitution should be. A "negative" constitution is one that contains many restrictions on state and local governments. Illinois's second constitution had a number of such negatives, many intended to rein in the power of the legislature. One of them limited legislators' pay to a penurious two dollars per day; this backfired in that it spurred creation of a system of "fees" paid by private interests for introduction of bills.[1]

When Illinois's constitution is compared to California's, for example, the former looks quite basic. The current Illinois document does not include many negatives and nonfundamentals, whereas the California Constitution is very lengthy and full of details. The other major difference is that the latter provides for the "general initiative," by which voters can propose constitutional amendments by citizen petition (rather than through the legislature). It is common for the voter to face twenty constitutional and other initiatives and referenda at a primary or general election. Although this system provides far more avenues for debate about constitutional issues, it also turns constitution writing into a highly politicized undertaking in which advertising and financial backing play major roles. A general initiative for Illinois was discussed by the 1970 Constitutional Convention but was not given serious consideration because of the negative reaction of delegates to the California experience.[2]

Although important in establishing general rules for a state's government, state constitutions and their construction do not often attract the public's attention. The exception is when a controversial amendment is proposed or, as happened in the 1960s in Illinois, a complete rewrite is contemplated. This is the case even though, in accordance with Illinois law, high school students and some college students have to pass a test concerning the contents of the state's constitution.

Constitutional Compromise in 1818

The first Illinois Constitution was adopted in 1818 as a condition of statehood. One issue that received much attention—and had national implications—was the question of slavery. The original draft language, borrowed from Ohio, prohibited both slavery and involuntary servitude, and although indentured servants were to be allowed, the indenture had to be voluntary and for no longer than one year. Proslavery delegates argued, however, that use of slaves would bring economic benefits to Illinois and would continue generating revenue from the salt springs in Gallatin County. They were smart enough to avoid advocating full slavery, knowing that such a provision could doom the constitution's review by the U.S. Congress and president. But they inserted language that protected existing property rights, including the holding of indentured servants, and that allowed continued "renting" of slaves from Tennessee and Kentucky to perform the backbreaking work in the salt mines.

The final constitution also omitted a provision that had been included in the Ohio and Indiana constitutions expressly prohibiting amendment to allow the introduction of slavery. The phrase's absence sparked debate when the U.S. Congress reviewed the document, but opposition from northern states was insufficient to prevent passage. On December 3, 1818, Illinois became a state.

That this omission was intentional was later confirmed when proslavery forces pushed for a constitutional convention in 1824. They succeeded in both houses of the legislature but were defeated at the polls after a vigorous antislavery campaign by many of the state's leaders.[3]

The first constitution gave the legislature so much power and the governor so little power that the system was ripe for abuse. The constitution enacted in 1848 contained some improvements. It reduced the legislature's ability to control the judiciary through appointments, provided legislative authority to create corporations or associations with banking powers, and eliminated the option of using a "viva voce" system of voting in elections (in which the voter calls out his vote and thus must publicly show his preference) in favor of the written ballot.

The product of the 1870 convention was longer and more detailed than earlier documents, signifying the growth in complexity of the state's needs and problems. The convention delegates, according to the historian Robert Howard, "cured most of the faults of the 1848 constitution. They drafted a new basic law that was voluminous in detail and in time would be criticized as being a straitjacket on progress. Nevertheless, the new constitution endured for a century as Illinois kept abreast of its sister states while advancing from a predominantly rural civilization into the atomic age."[4]

One of the most controversial side issues put to the voters in 1870 provided a new method of electing members to the House of Representatives. The cumulative voting method was devised to reduce regional tensions by means of a controversial system of "minority representation." The system allowed each voter to cast three votes for representatives, splitting them or giving them all to one candidate. Because many voters took advantage of the three-in-one "bullet" vote, a Republican could often be elected in a predominantly Democratic district and vice versa. Cumulative voting was eliminated by constitutional amendment in 1980.

The 1870 constitution proved to be very difficult to amend "because the leaders of the state's important interests were afraid to upset the balance of forces established by the compromises," according to Elazar.[5] It presented many problems for state officials, especially in regard to financial matters. For example, because of the strict limitations on local government debt, a large number of special districts were established that would later be blamed for Illinois's and especially metropolitan Chicago's parochialism and lack of coordinated planning. In addition to the limitations and the level of detail, narrow court interpretations of the constitution made it difficult for elective officials to govern. For example, in 1932 the state supreme court ruled that the constitution did not permit the state to levy an income tax, something that would remain a badly needed revenue source in decades to come.[6]

Witwer's Long Road to Reform

After World War II, a coalition that included the League of Women Voters and the Chicago Bar Association decided to push for a convention. They appointed a Committee on Constitutional Revision and asked a respected

Chicago attorney, Samuel W. Witwer, to be chair. "As Witwer recalls it," write Elmer Gertz and Joseph P. Pisciotte, "'in a weak moment,' he agreed to do so, being assured by them that the committee would have its work done in a matter of only a few years."[7] In fact, it would take the next twenty-five years of his life.

Witwer recruited a blue-ribbon committee to help him plan the campaign but found to his dismay that there was almost no written documentation about the weaknesses of the 1870 constitution. So he set out to become an expert on the subject and was well prepared in 1947 when he appeared before a senate committee to lay out the need for change. The senators, it turned out, "had no real desire to hear from the Witwer committee,"[8] and some hardly listened to the presentation. Witwer was infuriated and became more determined than ever.

Constitutional reform gained momentum when Adlai E. Stevenson became governor in 1949. Stevenson presented a constitutional convention package to the legislature that year. Handling the matter for Stevenson was Richard J. Daley, who at the time was Stevenson's director of revenue. The proposition lost on a close vote in the House of Representatives.

The Republicans in the legislature offered an alternative to Stevenson's "con-con" package—the gateway amendment. It eased the ratification requirement for constitutional amendments by providing that an amendment could be adopted by a favorable vote of two-thirds of those voting on the amendment itself, loosening the prior requirement of a majority of all those voting in the election. It also provided that three amendments instead of one could be submitted in each general election. The legislature, with Stevenson's support, approved the gateway amendment and submitted the question to the voters on a separate blue ballot that bore the notice: "The failure to vote this ballot is the equivalent of a negative vote."[9] The blue ballot has been identified with constitutional revision questions to this day. Thanks to the special ballot and a strong campaign, the gateway amendment received an overwhelmingly favorable vote.

Many felt at the time that constitutional revision by amendment was more desirable than a constitutional convention. The gateway provisions were used by the General Assembly in 1950 and in subsequent years. But enthusiasm for this approach diminished because the track record of constitutional revision was not impressive. From 1950 to 1966, fifteen amendments were submitted to the voters and six were approved. Only two of those adopted were far-reaching—a 1954 reapportionment amendment and a 1962 judicial reform amendment. Three defeats of amendments to revise the revenue article, which was badly out of date in its restrictions on government's powers of taxation, discouraged reformers.

The major development that gave renewed attention to constitutional re-vision was the 1964 at-large election for the house. This unusual election resulted from the failure of the legislature and the governor to redraw house district lines. Among those elected were many successful men and women new to politics, including Earl Eisenhower, brother of the former president, and Adlai Stevenson, son of the former governor and ambassador. When the legislature convened in 1965, they were ready for change. Among the reform they enacted was the creation of a legislative Constitution Study Commis-sion. The commission, composed of legislators appointed by the legislative leaders and public members appointed by the governor, was given an open-ended charge to "study any and all provisions" of the constitution, to deter-mine whether "any part or all" should be revised, and to determine whether any revision should be accomplished by a constitutional convention or by piecemeal enactment. After two years of study, the commission concluded that "a Constitutional Convention is the best and most timely way to achieve a revised Constitution."[10]

As recommended by the commission and approved by the legislature, the call for a convention was on the November 1968 ballot. After a strong campaign by a citizens' organization, the Illinois Committee for Constitutional Revision, the call was approved by 71.4 percent of those voting in the election.

Convention Success at Last

The delegates were elected in the fall of 1969 on a nonpartisan basis, and the Sixth Illinois Constitutional Convention convened December 8, 1969—one hundred years to the day after the start of the 1869 convention. Witwer, who had been quietly building trust and alliances during the previous two decades, was elected convention president. He knew many of the 115 other delegates and many knew each other because the room was filled with rising stars in the state's political hierarchies. Richard M. Daley, son of the Chicago mayor, was there. So were Michael Madigan, future speaker of the house, black civil rights leader Al Raby, future state senator and gubernatorial hopeful Dawn Clark Netsch, and a broad spectrum of representatives from labor, women's groups, and other walks of life.

Witwer negotiated hard to create twelve balanced committees that would not break down along partisan lines or be overwhelmed by a single controversial issue. For the most part he succeeded. The committees set to work in a collegial atmosphere with a strong staff behind them. Executive director Joseph P. Pisciotte oversaw a small army of clerks, lawyers, writers, researchers, committee aides, messengers, and doorkeepers as well as a parliamentarian. This staff and structure were based on those of other states' conventions and help explain the volume and quality of work that was turned out by the delegates.

One important decision had been made before the convention: the approval of the flat-rate income tax in 1969. The tax was upheld by the state supreme court in August 1969;[11] if this decision had been reversed, the tone of the convention might have been quite different because the give-and-take concerning the revenue article might have overshadowed debate about other controversial issues.

Many of the changes made in the 1970 constitution were important; others were relatively minor. The convention delegates were concerned with cleaning up the ancient document; they revised, deleted, and reorganized the old material, cut four thousand obsolete words, and excised many outdated provisions such as references to the 1893 Columbian World's Fair and the Illinois Central Railroad.

Of more importance was the constitution's clarification of the separation of powers, especially those of the legislative and executive branches. Thus the lieutenant governor was removed as the presiding officer of the senate, and the legislature was given the power to call itself into special sessions. The office of auditor general, created in the new constitution, was clearly spelled out as a legislative officer. The provision with the biggest impact in this area was the new veto power given to the governor. Before 1970 the governor had the regular veto and the line-item veto and used them frequently. Added in 1970 were the reduction veto, used for appropriations bills, and the amendatory veto. These changed the gubernatorial-legislative relationship because the governor no longer has to be a major actor during the legislative process; he can modify legislation using his veto powers. (See chapter 6 for a discussion of gubernatorial use of these expansive veto powers.)

Another significant change was the grant of home rule to cities and counties. Before 1970, Illinois had been a Dillon's rule state, which meant that local governments had only the powers granted to them by the legislature. Home rule reversed this relationship by providing that, with certain limitations, local governments had all the powers not denied them by the legislature. The home-rule provision proved instrumental in the later political alliance that helped pass the final document; it was one of four items on Mayor Richard J. Daley's "must" list. The others were classification of property taxes in Cook County, an elective judiciary, and continuation of cumulative voting. Home rule and property tax classification were put in the main package;

the other two were advanced as side issues. With all four of the key issues under control, Daley endorsed the main body of the proposed constitution (though not until two weeks before the public vote) and swung his machine behind it. The endorsement made support clearly bipartisan and resulted in a noticeable jump in favorable ratings in public opinion polls, paving the way for victory.

The 1970 constitution made changes in state offices elected statewide. The governor and the lieutenant governor now run as a team in the general election and must be of the same political party. The attorney general, treasurer, and secretary of state continue to be elected officials, but the secretary no longer serves as the chief election official. A new State Board of Elections was created to handle these duties. The superintendent of public instruction was replaced by the State Board of Education, which could be elected or appointed. The General Assembly decided to make the board an appointed body. The elected office of auditor of public accounts was replaced by the elected state comptroller and by the legislative office of auditor general, a position appointed by the legislature.

The voters took less notice of numerous smaller changes that most observers felt strengthened the state's foundation. A Judicial Inquiry Board was created to provide a method of investigating courtroom misconduct, and new rights were added to the Bill of Rights, the most important being the prohibition of discrimination based on sex and provisions protecting the rights of handicapped persons. The former (the state Equal Rights Amendment) was surprising in that in 1980 the Illinois legislature played a part in defeating a similar amendment to the U.S. Constitution.

The treatment of the State Board of Elections shows conflict between the moralistic and the individualistic impulses of the writers. Instead of specifying a nonpartisan, independently appointed board, the new constitution allowed the legislature to determine the makeup of the board and the method of selection of its members. Ultimately it settled on appointment by the governor with required balance between the political parties. This method ensures a status quo–oriented board that has at times been unable to act (as seen in 4-4 votes) and generally protects the interests of Republicans and Democrats against major change or the influence of third parties. In a 2009 case, however, the Illinois Supreme Court ruled unanimously in *Cook County Republican Party v. Illinois State Board of Elections* that dismissals of complaints by a tie vote "are subject to judicial review of all questions of law and fact presented by the record, including whether the complaints were filed on justifiable grounds."[12] As a result of this decision, tie votes by the Illinois State Board of Elections might be taken directly to the appellate court for adjudication.

The 1970 convention, like most of its predecessors, submitted a "package" and four side issues. These provided for lowering the voting age to eighteen, abolishing the death penalty, choosing between appointive and elective selection of judges, and continuing cumulative voting for state representatives.

On finishing their business in an atmosphere of tired jubilation, the convention delegates decided to submit the proposed constitution to the voters at a special election on December 15, 1970. A new citizens' campaign, Illinois Citizens for the New Constitution, was established at the urging of Governor Richard B. Ogilvie. Many interest groups supported the new constitution; others opposed it. Special campaign groups were organized to support or oppose certain issues such as an appointive judiciary.

The new constitution passed statewide with bipartisan support by a 56 percent favorable vote. As for the side issues, the death penalty was retained, cumulative voting was chosen instead of single-member, single-vote districts, the elective judiciary was retained, and the option of reducing the voting age to eighteen was rejected.

The vote was more favorable in Cook County than in downstate Illinois. Only 30 of the state's 102 counties supported the document, but they represented three-fourths of Illinois's population. Sixty-five percent of Cook County's voters supported the main document, as opposed to 45 percent of downstate voters. Voting followed historic geographical patterns set by constitutional amendments (1950–66) and the call for the 1969–70 Constitutional Convention: northern counties generally voted favorably on constitutional questions and southern areas consistently voted negatively.

Thus Illinois had a new constitution. It was a remarkable achievement in a large, divided industrial and partisan state and in turbulent times. It also was remarkable because Illinois is not considered a reform state. Daniel Elazar said the new constitution was "one of the most advanced in the country."[13] It was a compromise between the political and managerial approaches to governance.[14]

Standing Up over Time

The test of time has shown that the package approved in 1970 seems to be working for the people and the special interests of Illinois; no major efforts have been initiated to discard it. Unlike the constitution that preceded it, the 1970 document allows two ways to create improvements without undue hardship: through amendments, which have been used fairly frequently, and by calling a convention, which must be put to a public vote every twenty years.

Legislators have made some attempts to reverse the decisions of the constitutional convention, but few have reached the ballot. Since 1970, only seventeen amendments have been placed on the ballot, and of these, ten have been approved. One amendment with a major statewide impact was the so-called cutback amendment of 1980, approved by a two-to-one margin, which reduced the size of the House of Representatives and eliminated the controversial minority representation (cumulative voting) system. Another amendment was approved in 1988, when the voting age was reduced from twenty-one to eighteen years to conform to the U.S. Constitution.

An amendment passed in 1992 falls in the "motherhood and apple pie" category. It amends the Bill of Rights to add a crime victims' rights section. Crime victims shall have "the right to be treated with fairness and respect for their dignity and privacy throughout the criminal justice process" and nine other rather innocuous "rights."[15] It was adopted during a push to get tough on crime, and some academics say that it illustrates the inclusion of nonfundamentals. Two more changes were added in 1994. Voters ratified a proposal to encourage earlier passage of bills by the General Assembly; the new deadline of May 30 means that bills passed after that date are not effective until June 1 of the following year unless passed by a three-fifths majority. Voters also approved limiting the right of an accused criminal to meet the witnesses face to face during trial proceedings. Children who have been sexually abused may now testify from a separate room, via closed-circuit television, to prevent intimidation and additional psychological harm from facing the alleged abuser.

The strongest measure of the value of the staying power of the 1970 convention is that voters rejected an opportunity to call for a new convention. The 1970 constitution provided for a vote every twenty years on whether to call a convention; the attorney general ruled that the first call would be on the ballot in November 1988. In preparation for the debate about the question, the legislature created the "Committee of 50" to provide material to help the voters. The Committee of 50, which included political and civic leaders, held hearings and reconvened the living delegates from the 1969–70 convention. There was no strong sentiment for another convention on the part of the committee or the former delegates.

In the media and among the public, there was considerable opposition. Interest groups such as the Illinois Chamber of Commerce, the AFL-CIO, and the League of Women Voters opposed the call for different reasons. Some felt that the 1970 constitution had served the state well; others questioned the cost of another convention (the 1970 affair cost about $14 million). Still others felt that new controversial issues, such as abortion rights, would be brought up in a convention. And the business community wanted to maintain the flat-rate, 8:5 ratio between corporate and individual income taxes.

There was some vocal support for another convention. Some wanted merit-based selection of judges, others wanted the initiative and referendum system used in California. Supporters mentioned other changes, such as a revised tax system with more progressive taxes. The *Chicago Tribune* spoke for most voters when it declared in an editorial:

> The Tribune strongly recommends a "No" vote on the proposal for a state constitutional convention. Illinois already has a modern, workable Constitution, a model for other states. Delegates to the 1969–70 Convention that wrote it thought voters should have an opportunity at 20-year intervals to decide whether it needed an overhaul. They underestimated the excellence of their work. The Constitution they drafted is still a fine fit for Illinois, dealing only with the basics: the scope and authority of state government, the powers of local government, the mechanics of amendment and the guarantee of individual rights. It keeps its nose out of other matters, and that is one of its great strengths.[16]

Seventy-five percent of the 3.6 million voters agreed with the editorial and in 1988 soundly defeated the call.

The question of calling a constitutional convention was on the ballot again in 2008. And once again, a coalition of business, labor, and civic groups, including the state League of Women Voters, came out in opposition to the call. Operating as the Alliance to Protect the Illinois Constitution, the coalition raised $1.6 million and ran radio and internet ads featuring popular former governor Jim Edgar. Proponents of a new constitution included Lieutenant Governor Pat Quinn and a couple of small conservative groups organized specifically to push for a new constitution, which raised only $121,000.

Some opponents privately feared that a new convention might affect provisions dear to them. For example, labor interests worried about elimination of the pension guarantee for public employees, and business interests opposed changing the flat-rate income tax into a graduated rate. Progressives among the opponents feared that a new convention called in a time of large state budget deficits and general economic distress might saddle the state with unworkable constraints on budgeting, such as a limit on appropriations increases and a requirement of a super-majority to adopt annual state budgets. In other words, the present we know is better than a future we don't.

Proponents welcomed the idea of opening the constitution to change. Quinn and others favored the adoption of the initiative, referendum, and recall available in California. Conservatives wanted to change the constitution to rein in state spending. But proponents lacked adequate funding to get their message out. This time they did have the support of the *Chicago Tribune,* which stated in an editorial that a con-con might be able to address what they considered as the dysfunctional and corrupt state political and governmental system.

Following a campaign that was mostly invisible to the electorate, the opponents of a con-con carried the election 58 percent to 42 percent. Only 60 percent of those voting in this presidential election year bothered to vote on the question of a constitutional convention.

By most measures, then, the 1970 constitution has been a distinct improvement over the 1870 version. It is a political document and thus not perfect from the reformers' perspective; for example, it continues the election of officials to a number of state offices that are filled by appointment in other states. Neither does it do away with election of judges, which has been blamed for corruption and favoritism in the courts. One national observer, Neal Peirce, wrote in his book *The Megastates* that the 1970 constitution was "not a terribly distinguished piece of work."[17]

From a national perspective this may be so, but from the vantage point of Illinois, whose history of constitution making has been less than brilliant, the document was a major step forward. At least as important as the content of the constitution was the process it created. Illinois leaders from both sides of the aisle and all walks of life, respectful of each other and mindful of the state's needs, convened and hammered out solutions to long-standing problems. In the individualistic culture of Illinois, such a process is rare enough that the 1970 Constitutional Convention can fairly be called a triumph for the common people.

Prior to the 1970 convention, academic and reform debates generally focused on the need for strong governors in state government. The result was that in Illinois the governor has very strong formal powers, especially with the reduction and amendatory vetoes and with the ability to call special sessions of the General Assembly.

The Illinois Constitution is a living document. For example, during the Blagojevich administration (2000–2009), the governor and House Speaker Michael Madigan battled over the constitutionality of the governor's expansive use of the amendatory veto and of the legislature's Joint Committee on Administrative Rules (JCAR).

The amendatory veto was generally thought to be an instrument for correcting technical flaws in legislation so as to avoid the necessity of starting a bill anew to make the corrections. As of 2008, the Illinois Supreme Court had not resolved the issue definitively. On one hand, the court has ruled that it may not be used for the substitution of complete new bills (*Klinger v. Howlett,* 1972). On the other hand, it has ruled that it is to be more than "a proofreading device" (*Continental Illinois National Bank & Trust v. Zagel,* 1979) and that the amendatory veto "was intended to improve the bill in material ways, yet not alter its essential purpose and intent" (*City of Canton v. Crouch,* 1980).[18]

Blagojevich used the prerogative extensively. In a series of amendatory vetoes in 2008 that were characterized by the former governor's office as "Rewrite to Do Right," the governor took, for example, a tax increment finance bill for a small community and changed it by amendatory veto to a bill that eliminated property taxes for disabled veterans.

Expect one or more of the governor's amendatory vetoes to be contested in the courts in the future, in hopes of further clarification as to the limits of use of the amendatory veto.

The JCAR reviews rules promulgated pursuant to legislation by state agencies to determine whether the rules conform to legislative intent. Blagojevich simply ignored the committee's rejection of rules that sought to prevent him from expanding his health care coverage programs. He claimed that the committee was an unconstitutional intrusion of the legislative branch into the executive branch's authority. A lower court ruled in 2008 that Blagojevich exceeded his authority in ignoring JCAR. Expect further court actions relating to this issue.

With the state constitution and court interpretations thereof providing the framework in which the other branches of government may operate, we now turn to those branches, first the "people's branch," the legislature.

5.

The Legislature

• • • • • • • • • • • • • •

The Illinois legislature is a fiercely partisan body where horse-trading and sophisticated political stratagems often appear more important to lawmakers than the particular issues to be decided. High-pressure lobbying and generous contributions to legislators' election campaigns tie them closely to labor, business, and other influential interests. Whereas short hours and low pay marked the early legislatures,[1] today lawmaking is a full-time endeavor for many, and good pay and generous pension benefits have lured many to make a career as a legislator.[2]

Legislators of Every Stripe

Legislators tend to reflect the habits and mores of the districts they represent. In the Capitol rotunda, you might see people in brightly colored sports jackets and casual shoes standing toe-to-toe with those in black wing tips and somber pinstripes. Southern Illinois lawmakers are likely to be deeply concerned about jobs and capital improvements for their comparatively poor region. Chicago legislators pay special attention to funding for the city and protection of its home-rule authority. Suburban lawmakers are most concerned about improving the transportation network to unclog crowded roadways and slowing the growth of property tax rates.

Today's Illinois General Assembly is a full-time, professional branch of state government. Voters elect two house members from within each of fifty-nine state senate districts. Ninety-four of the 177 lawmakers in both chambers described themselves in 2006 as "full-time legislators."[3] Many of the others generate all or a significant part of their income from legislative salaries that range from $63,141 to $88,719, with the higher amounts going to the four-fifths of the lawmakers who serve as chairs or minority spokespersons for the scores of legislative committees.

The Illinois legislature spends about $90 million per year and employs about seven hundred persons as partisan staff for leaders, members, and committees and as nonpartisan staff for support agencies such as the bill drafting and research units.[4]

The legislature is, like the state, highly diverse. Among the 177 members of the house and senate in 2006 were 48 women, 28 African Americans, and 11 Latinos.[5] The 37 lawyers represent one-fifth of total membership; 7 members are farmers, and 3 are schoolteachers. The roll call also includes a minister, a paralegal, a writer, a police officer, a professor, and an entrepreneur.

These legislators are real people with needs, ambitions, doubts, and anxieties. It takes great motivation to raise $500,000 or more for a targeted reelection campaign and devote endless evenings to running for a position that may grind down one's nonpolitical career. People are spurred to candidacy for various reasons, including a sense of civic responsibility, a need to prove oneself, the challenge of the competition, professional advancement, especially for Chicago Democrats for whom politics is often a lifelong career, the salary and attractive pension benefits, and opportunities to get involved with well-known figures and to work on important issues. Many legislators, especially those from downstate, see the General Assembly as the culmination of their public service. Others see it as a stepping-stone to higher office.

Legislators want to feel good about what they are doing. They want to feel that their work is important and to take pride in having contributed to a better hometown and state. For all these reasons, legislators enter the General Assembly with high hopes. Often these hopes go unfulfilled. Each lawmaker is but one in an unwieldy group of 177. Moreover, a legislator's direct participation in most issues often is limited to a final passage vote on policies largely shaped without his or her actual involvement.

Alas, legislative leaders, the governor, and their unelected staffs often seem to be the ones in overall control of the legislative process. Nowadays that perception is more real than rank-and-file legislators care to admit.

Life in the Political Trenches

This does not mean that there is little to do for ordinary legislators. Usually there is more to do than time permits. Legislators must shepherd bills of their sponsorship along the winding legislative path; help process legislation in committees and on the floor; respond to hundreds of phone calls, letters, and emails weekly; and host visiting constituents. They also must read until the pages blur—bills, staff analyses, interest group position papers, letters, newspapers, and research reports. They must return endless phone calls from lobbyists, constituents, and reporters.

Back home, legislators serve as advocates for their constituents, dealing, for example, with the secretary of state for driver licensing matters, the Department of Transportation for road improvements, the Department of Revenue concerning tax matters, the Department of Professional Regulation for occupational licenses, the Department of Natural Resources for park improvements, the Department of Public Aid for social services, and the Department of Public Health regarding nursing home care. This is the bread-and-butter work of a career politician. Constituents appreciate a legislator who takes care of a problem by guiding them through the bureaucracy of state or local government agencies, and they often show their appreciation on Election Day and, perhaps, at fundraising events.

In order to build visibility with voters, lawmakers maintain from one to three offices in their districts. Some downstate legislators do regular "circuit-riding" to meet constituents at courthouses throughout the district, and their constituents and the weekly newspapers and local radio and television stations often treat them as celebrities. Meanwhile, legislators in Chicago and the surrounding suburbs rarely enjoy media coverage. Instead, they struggle to achieve name recognition by mass-mailing glossy, picture-laden "after-session reports" to their constituents and greeting riders on CTA elevated platforms and Metra train stations near Election Day. Several host cable television shows or write columns for local newspapers, and many attend countless community events. If any time and energy remain, lawmakers look after what might remain of their law practices or businesses.

As a result, lawmakers must establish priorities. The most important goal for nearly all is reelection. They often regard all other activity as a means to this end. Many legislators specialize. For the sake of simplicity, they usually fit in one of four categories: the issues advocate, the district advocate, the committee specialist, and the broker. The issues-oriented lawmaker might be a committed conservative, populist, anti-tax, or gay rights advocate who sponsors legislation that supports his or her ideological commitment. The district advocate focuses more on issues of specific benefit to his or her constituents such as highway and park projects, the location and staffing of a new prison, or funding for university campuses. All legislators sit on committees, but some sit on the same one for many years and become experts in the specific policy issues covered by that committee. Finally, there is the broker, a pragmatic legislator who enjoys getting things done by means of the bruising work of stitching together bipartisan, regional, and other majority coalitions for or against controversial bills.

Despite cultural and regional differences among lawmakers, the legislature is a close-knit political club in which a degree of camaraderie develops. Liberals and conservatives may disagree about issues just as downstate farmers and Chicago corporate lawyers enjoy different cuisine, but they also have a great deal in common. All have run for office; raised campaign funds; and endured potshots from opponents, disgruntled groups, and the media. The voters elected all of them; those who want to stay will have to go through the process again. All must respond to constituent inquiries, meet visiting school groups, listen to lobbyists, and typically spend more than eighty nights a year in Springfield, eating and drinking in the same few places.

For this reason, patterns of mutually useful behavior have developed. Legislators generally treat their colleagues with trust and respect and engage in good-faith negotiations. Thus they avoid becoming personal in the heat of debate, keep their word and commitments, reciprocate favors done, and help one another whenever possible. These patterns help explain what would otherwise be paradoxical behavior. For example, legislators will often help a colleague from the other party to get his or her bill out of committee. If the committee vote looks close, a committee member might change his vote with language such as the following: "so that my respected colleague can get his bill reported to the floor for the full debate it deserves, even though I may have to vote against it at that time." This helps the colleague get a little favorable publicity in the home district; regrettably, it also clogs the legislative process with bills that legislators must consider later on the chamber floor even if they are unlikely to enact them.

Conflict and Resolution

Once they have indebted themselves to others so that they might be reelected, legislators typically find themselves in a pressure tank where conflict, accommodation, and interdependence characterize relations among themselves, the governor, and interest groups. Conflict between lawmakers and governors is natural, for there is an inherent clash of perspectives. Lawmakers mainly focus on the people in their districts, whereas the governor must think about the whole state. Legislators go about their business in a piecemeal fashion, each developing bills based on individual interests and special knowledge, whereas the governor has to be comprehensive in his or her annual state of the state and budget messages. The legislator's job has a short-term focus because about seven of ten Illinois lawmakers are up for election every two years.[6] The voters elect a governor every four years, and they expect him or her to take a long-term view, to present a vision for the future.

As a result, each branch frustrates and exasperates the other. They contend on fairly even terms. The governor has greater formal powers, information resources, stature, and visibility; as a single actor, the chief executive can be decisive. Nevertheless, the legislature has its own strengths: strong leadership in the four caucuses, sophisticated staffs, nearly full-time commitments by most legislators, and the political will to live up to its billing as a co-equal branch.

The legislative cycle lasts two years in Illinois, with each year known as a biennial session; the biennium in 2007–8 was the 95th General Assembly. The legislature convenes each year on the second Wednesday in January and continues to meet, with periodic recesses, during the two-year period. Typically, the legislative leaders divide each year into three phases: the regular spring session, the interim summer period, and the fall veto session.

The spring session generally begins slowly in January and traditionally ends with a roar in late May or early June. Legislators enact laws by means of bills only, and bills may originate in either house with the sponsorship of one or more members. The Illinois Constitution confines bills, except bills for appropriations and for the codification, revision, or rearrangement of laws, to one subject and limits appropriation bills to the subject of appropriations. Typically, all legislators combined introduce about nine thousand bills in the course of the biennium, most during the spring of the first year, hundreds of these during the first week. The president of the senate and the speaker of the house assign bills to the Senate Assignment and House Rules committees, which assign the bills to standing committees. The speaker and the president, who are the leaders of the majority party in each body, control the rules committees and therefore control which bills advance or languish in the rules committees.

In contrast to the U.S. Congress, where committees control bills, legislative sponsors steer their bills through the Illinois legislative process. Tradition dictates that the committee chairperson schedule a hearing date for a bill in order to accommodate the sponsor, if possible. Timing is important because a sponsor must gather support and count votes in committee as well as at the passage stage. Each bill receives three formal readings by title on the floor of each house on three separate days. The first reading occurs at introduction, the second takes place after committee action, when the bill returns to the chamber floor,[7] and the final reading occurs when the members of the chamber vote to either approve or reject the bill. The Illinois legislature records all votes electronically at the stage of final bill passage.

Even with the imposition of successive deadlines, a logjam of unfinished

Fig. 5.1. Cartoon by Bill Campbell (Courtesy of Carl Sandburg College)

bills typically develops as the spring session approaches its scheduled adjournment date. This is understandable because the pressure of a deadline is a critical component that keeps the legislative process running and induces brokering and compromise among lawmakers. The parties are often evenly balanced, and no region—Chicago, the collar counties, or downstate—has a majority in either chamber. Coalition-building is often imperative. Bills must receive a majority of the votes of all those elected, sixty in the house and thirty in the senate, rather than simply a majority of those voting.

Drafters of the 1870 and 1970 Illinois constitutions sought to encourage negotiation and final legislative action by June 30 (now May 31) of each year and to avoid having sessions go into overtime. As a result, all bills passed after that date could not take effect until the following July unless they were passed by three-fifths of those elected. Attaining an extraordinary majority generally requires cooperation from the minority party in each house, so the constitution's framers assumed that the presiding officers in the General Assembly would do their best to get the job done before or very close to the deadline.

On the other hand, whenever the two parties divided control between the governorship and at least one house of the legislature, the three-fifths proviso occasionally discouraged on-time adjournment. In overtime session, votes from both parties would be required in order to adopt the annual budget and controversial or unpopular legislation. Thus, the governor and legislative leaders tended to delay serious negotiations until the three-fifths proviso imposed the political necessity for compromise and shared responsibility. For example, the governor and the legislature could then enact budget cuts and increase cigarette taxes only with bipartisan support. In 1991, with a new governor, legislators could not reach an agreement before the spring session ended on June 30. That forced the legislature into overtime session, and they finally reached an agreement on July 18. In 1993 the overtime spring session lasted until July 13.

As a result, in 1994, the legislature considered a constitutional amendment to move the deadline from June 30 to May 31, the date after which an overtime session starts and a three-fifths majority is required in order to pass bills with an immediate effective date. Both houses enacted the amendment unanimously; in November 1994 the voters ratified it.[8] The deadline change reflected the reality of the political dynamic at the time of divided state government.

The second phase of the legislative process occurs after the spring session adjourns and the legislators depart Springfield for the summer. During this interim period, the governor's staff, the Governor's Office of Management and Budget (GOMB, formerly the Bureau of the Budget), and agency managers face the task of reviewing the thousand or so bills passed by the legislature in a typical spring session. The constitution requires that the governor receive a bill from the legislature within thirty days of passage. Then the governor has sixty days to sign the bill or impose one of several types of vetoes. Legislators commonly refer to this as the bill's "drop" date. In the rare event that a bill is neither signed nor vetoed within sixty calendar days after it is presented to the governor, it becomes law.

Legislative staff members are busy during this interim period compiling summaries of the spring session and analyzing gubernatorial actions on bills.

Other legislative staff prepare for and attend public hearings of legislative subcommittees, special committees, or task forces to gather testimony and other evidence and make recommendations about how to resolve certain public policy issues.

In the third and final phase of the legislative process, the lawmakers reconvene in the fall for a veto session that allows further debate and action on bills vetoed by the governor. In odd-numbered years, the fall veto session generally opens in October; in even-numbered years, lawmakers reconvene in mid-November following the general elections. The fall session typically lasts six to twelve days. A vetoed bill returns to the house where it originated, and the members have fifteen calendar days in which to act. If the legislature overrides a veto in one house, then the bill moves to the second house, where the same fifteen-day deadline applies.[9]

The expanded veto power given the governor in the 1970 constitution has an unintended consequence. The delegates institutionalized the fall veto session as a countervailing legislative power that ensured that the legislature had an opportunity to override vetoes. Delegates intended to prevent a pocket veto, which the U.S. Constitution permits;[10] however, the legislature often takes up not only vetoes but also postponed or new legislative initiatives during the fall session. It gives legislators another bite at the apple and affects their strategy with regard to matters that might be too hot to handle during the spring session, especially in even-numbered election years—items such as tax increases and pay raises.

Because of retirements and defeats in even-year elections, numerous lame-duck lawmakers may feel less responsive to caucus leaders' demands and constituency pressures during a fall veto session. Some will even reverse themselves and become proponents of certain parts of the governor's program because the governor can provide a job with good pension benefits in addition to salary. In other words, all bets are off during even-year fall sessions.

Role of Committees

Much of the work of committee is routine and has little effect on the policies embedded in a bill because even if a bill dies, legislators may resurrect the main idea later. Committees are almost meaningless because bad bills often get out so easily.

Regular committee members feel the influence of caucus leadership strongly. House Democratic leaders regularly circulate bill lists with arrows that point up or down to indicate the position of the leadership. Because of the strong party discipline that has routinely been imposed in recent years on committee members, lobbyists often considered a bill dead if it had "down arrows" from the speaker's office. Thus they lobbied hard with the speaker, his staff, and assistant leaders to get the arrows reversed or at least removed to indicate a neutral position. When Lee Daniels was briefly speaker (89th General Assembly, 1995–96), he attempted to impose a similar rigid type of arrow system on the house Republican caucus. Owing to stiff resistance among the caucus members, the arrows soon became merely leadership "recommendations." In the senate, where marching orders regarding legislation are typically more informal and less routine, leaders tend to limit their coercive influence over committee members to major or controversial bills.

In the house, leaders also have authority to replace committee members with others from their party's legislative caucus. The house rules state, "A member may be temporarily replaced on a committee due to illness or if the member is otherwise unavailable."[11] House leaders routinely interpret the phrase "otherwise unavailable" broadly. When considering an important bill, a house caucus leader can replace for that day a committee member who refuses to follow leadership's position on the bill with another member who will. Senate leaders interpret a similar rule narrowly, and they seldom invoke its authority to replace a member.

The number of standing committees in both chambers has significantly increased since the 90th General Assembly (1997–98), when the house had twenty-eight standing committees and the senate had sixteen. In the 95th General Assembly (2007–8), the standing committees in the house numbered forty-eight and those in the senate twenty-five. As the number of standing committees increases, so does the number of legislators who serve as committee chairs and minority spokespersons and receive a stipend of about $9,000 in addition to their base salary. The leaders make all committee appointments, and so this arrangement gives the leaders an opportunity to reward or punish that they can use to enforce caucus discipline.

Moreover, with more bills in the legislative process, more committees will meet and hold hearings that consume more of members' scarce time. Leaders can exploit this opportunity to exercise further control over members by manipulating the committee meeting schedules and the assignment of bills to the committees. Busy members have less free time to act on their own or in combination against the leaders' wishes. In order to cope with the demands of ever-increasing committee workloads, regular members must heavily rely on the professional staffs, who work for the leaders. A member who acts in opposition to the leadership's agenda in committee might have to do so unassisted by staff.

Staff Professionals Working the System

Forty-five years ago, there would have been very little to write about legislative staff because there were so few, but today staff members outnumber legislators and have a significant effect on the dynamics of the legislative process.

There are four staffing categories: those who report directly to the leaders or their assistants; those who provide analysis and staff the committees; those who provide clerical or administrative assistance for individual legislators in their Springfield offices; and those who work for the legislature's various support agencies, including the bill-drafting reference bureau, research unit, committee on administrative rules, and information service. Legislative leaders hire and assign those in the first three groups on a strictly partisan basis, and their work assignments continue at the sole discretion of the leaders. Those who work for the support agencies do so for the most part on a bipartisan basis. It is common for a legislative agency director to be affiliated with one party and the assistant to be affiliated with the other.

Regular legislators hire their own district office staff using their district office allowance, which is about $80,000 annually for every member. Normally, the allowance is enough for basic clerical staff, office space rental, and the cost of supplies, though adequacy varies depending on the location of the district office and the regional cost differences. In addition, the leaders might provide extra district office staff for selected members, generally those who the leaders predict might be targeted for defeat in the next election cycle. This incumbency protection stratagem bolsters the selected members' constituent services and presumably their reelectability. This is yet another example of calculated member dependence on leaders and their resources.

Legislative staffers are typically in their twenties and are working on or already have master's or law degrees. Like the legislators for whom they work, staff members have ambitions, priorities, and frustrations. Some see staff work as a stepping-stone. United States senator Richard Durbin and former governor Jim Edgar are among scores of former staffers who have subsequently served as elected officials, agency heads, gubernatorial aides, and lobbyists.

In the shorter term, however, what most staff members want is to see their ideas, bill drafts, amendments, and budget recommendations become law and implemented as public policy. Those who work and negotiate with staff, including lobbyists, appreciate the objective of having one's idea adopted by a respected legislative staffer, which is often an important initial step in the legislative process. Staff members also want recognition for the work they have done, in spite of the hard and fast institutional requirement that all credit go to the boss. They appreciate people who thank them for their contributions to the process. Finally, staff members are usually open to bipartisan cooperation, even within the context of partisan assignments. Committee staffs from both parties often share information while their bosses publicly engage in partisan debate about the same issues.

Each committee has at least two staff analysts, one for each party. Before each committee hearing, staff members prepare analyses of each bill. Typically, an analysis includes a synopsis that outlines the proposed change in the law; current law and descriptions of possible problems to be resolved; discussion of the positions of the caucus, affected agencies, interest groups, and the governor's office or affected state or local government agencies; and suggestions for member's questions at the hearing. In most cases, the analysts will have contacted the pertinent government agencies and other interested parties to generate information for their detailed analysis of the proposed change in statutory law. This detailed groundwork provides the foundation on which lawmakers build legislation and public policy.

A Sometimes Long and Winding Road

Some bills will work their way, step by procedural step, toward passage without major incident, but a likely fate for major appropriations bills and controversial pieces of substantive legislation is a long and winding road. Thus a bill might seem irretrievably lost before its essence suddenly reappears in another bill, making a frantic dash for final passage before a scheduled deadline or adjournment.

Persuasion of fellow legislators is stock-in-trade in the legislative arena, but subtler techniques such as timing and personal knowledge of other legislators are often just as effective. A legislator shepherding his or her bill through a committee hearing tries to match the timing to the moods of the committee. For example, the lawmaker may have arranged for testimony on a bill by interest group representatives and other experts. Some of these people may have come hundreds of miles for the hearing and will want to have their full say in the matter. But if other bills have consumed a great deal of time, and if tired committee members are fidgeting in their chairs, the bill's sponsor may well size up the chances of a favorable vote and, if the count looks promising, curtail or eliminate his team's testimony to request a well-timed vote.

Most committee work is more hard-headed, especially when money is involved. The governor must make his budget recommendations to the legislature by the first Wednesday in March. The GOMB prepares individual appropriations bills for about sixty agencies; together these bills represent the governor's budget, which in fiscal 2008 totaled about $59.5 billion. Although the executive branch develops its budget over an eight-month period, the legislature must react, evaluate, and authorize the budget in the three-month period from March through the conventional late May adjournment. Each house conducts this work in appropriations committees.

Since the mid-1990s, the legislative leaders have designated the "budgeteer" for the caucus, usually one of the appropriations committee chairpersons. The budgeteer and appropriations committee staffs have then altered the governor's proposed budgets outside the hearings without the active participation of committee members. Strong, experienced, and knowledgeable budgeteers and staff budget directors have also shifted spending authority from a governor's objectives to those that reflect the preferences of the legislative caucus leaders.

The appropriations bills provide a good example of how the professionalized legislature with its full-time, partisan staff fully counterbalances the executive branch. In the case of appropriations, however, they do this at the expense of the active participation of regular committee members in the process. The appropriations bill for each agency proposes dollar amounts for line items such as personnel, contractual services, equipment, travel, and telecommunications. Appropriations committee staffers require agency responses to detailed questions to justify what the amount allocated for each line item would buy. Because staff analysts specialize in different areas, their questions cannot be derailed easily. Analysts from one or both parties will meet with the agency's fiscal officer and sometimes the agency head to discuss the proposed budget, laying groundwork for future legislative floor debate or actually brokering a deal outside of the committee hearing. During the public committee hearing, members play the role of receiving hours of agency testimony about the governor's budget proposals and may even make the news by grilling hapless agency officials, but the committee members rarely join in the actual process of negotiations and drafting of the budget bills.

Other technical and little-known tools used by leaders to various degrees for crafting compromises on controversial issues include conference committees, "shell bills," and "agreed bills." A conference committee reconciles differences between the house and senate versions of a bill. Five members are appointed from each chamber, three by the presiding officer and two by the minority leader. Generally, they appoint the bill's sponsor and committee members who are specialists on the bill's subject matter.

These short-lived committees were traditionally not required to meet publicly or to meet at all. Often a legislator or staffer would simply circulate a conference committee report based on agreement between two or more key conferees, with approval of the leadership, seeking the six signatures needed to file the revised bill with the two chambers. For important bills, staffers for the governor and legislative leaders and key lobbyists routinely hold quick meetings in a corridor off the senate or house floor or in the privacy of a leader's office.

Such a system allowed bills to be changed significantly or completely re-written by conference committees. During the sometimes chaotic windup of the spring session, a score of conference committees were in existence simultaneously.

Skilled legislators and staff often manipulate this esoteric process. In 1989, for example, senate Republicans under the leadership of minority leader James "Pate" Philip forced a change in senate rules on the pretext of curbing the abuse of conference committee reports. The new rules required that a conference committee report lie on senators' desks for one day before a vote can be taken, that sponsors of bills be appointed to conference committees that will deal with their bill, and that all amendments adopted in conference committees be germane, that is, pertinent to the subject matter of the original bill.

After a decade of having the Democratic majority outmaneuver them, Philip and the senate Republicans in 1993 took advantage of their new ma-jority status and adopted rules that require the Senate Rules Committee to approve a conference committee report before the senate can consider it. These rules, which remain in effect,[12] considerably reduce the ability of a few people to make changes in legislation without the knowledge of other members and out of public view.

While ostensibly preventing abuse of process, the leaders had designed such rule changes as part of the overall tightening of leadership control in the legis-lative process, which over time has resulted in a dramatic shift of power away from the regular membership to the leaders. Since the mid-1990s, the leaders of the majority caucuses of both parties consolidated their power through ever-tightened rules designed to enable them to manipulate the legislative process at the expense of regular members, and they did so under the disingenuous guise of reform and with the acquiescence of the regular membership. In recent years, Speaker Madigan has refused to allow the use of conference committee reports, and shell bills have been used instead.

The shell bill is another tightly controlled vehicle used by legislative lead-ers to revive dashed hopes. It allows leaders to introduce, late in a session, new proposals as well as compromises hammered out among leaders and the governor in closed meetings. Because new bills cannot be introduced after a certain date set by rule each session, the party leaders introduce early in the process a number of innocuous shell bills, empty of substantive content, that later can contain new or revived legislation or amendments. Leaders cannot use just any bill because amendments must deal with the same chapter of the state statutes as the bill they would amend. Thus dozens of shell bills are moving along at any given time, available at strategic moments to carry forward late-developing compromises or to resurrect ideas seemingly killed earlier.

Legislative leaders in years past used the agreed bill process when their caucus members felt caught uncomfortably in the middle of intense conflicts between major interest groups on subjects about which the lawmakers have less expertise than the groups. For example, proposed changes in workers' compensation for injuries divide labor unions and management. Legislative committees sometimes direct the interest groups to try to iron out their differences outside the legislative chambers and then come back with an agreed bill, which the legislators would probably ratify. The agreed bill process sometimes works, especially if the interest groups think the legislative solution might be worse than their agreement.

Four Tops—and the Governor

Legislation is a complex business in which byzantine procedures and layers of committees and staffs are among the many barriers to turning a bill into a law. Its complexity ensures that a core of leaders will develop to guide the regular membership. The structure and political makeup of the General Assembly has led to the institution of a four-leader system that includes the majority and minority leaders of both chambers, known since the 1980s as the "Four Tops." They have generally shared control of the legislative process with the governor, who by the stroke of his veto pen has the discretionary power to undo years of legislative labor.[13]

The Four Tops bring significant legislative experience to their roles. Although experience and longevity explain their success in part, the rest of the story consists of their "near monopolies" on campaign fundraising and professional legislative staff and of the acquiescence to their caucus leaders' agenda by increasingly dependent regular members.[14]

An exception to this collaborative approach among the Four Tops sometimes occurs when one party has complete control of both chambers and the governorship. The majority leaders occasionally exclude the minority leaders from the negotiating table, leaving Two Tops and the governor. For example, this happened at times during the 89th General Assembly (1995–96), when the majority Republicans had one-party control. The tables were turned during the 93d, 94th, and 95th General Assemblies (2003–8), when the Democratic governor and the majority Democratic Tops occasionally excluded the minority Republican Tops from the negotiating table. Finally, a majority Top might boycott the other Tops because of intraparty fighting, for example, when the speaker refused to attend negotiations with the governor of his party during the 95th General Assembly and sent the majority leader instead. Nevertheless, except in the case of one-party rule or intraparty political power struggles, the governor and the Four Tops generally collaborate and control the legislative process and the creation of public policy in Illinois.

The power of legislative leaders had begun to grow in the early 1980s, when leaders centralized selection and management of the partisan staffing for committees. Staffers are now loyal to the leadership and not to the committee chairpersons, who once had a say in the selection. Many of these staff assistants have also become skilled at campaign management and take leaves of absence during campaigns to help direct reelection efforts of members with difficult races, further tying them into the political apparatus of the legislative leaders.

Because of their powers, the leaders have become aggressive and successful at raising campaign funds that, along with campaign management services, they allocate to their members. Each of the four leaders directs a caucus political action committee and his or her own leader's fund, and in the case of house Democrats, the Illinois Democratic Party funds. During the 2006 campaign cycle, spending among the leaders ranged from $5.1 million to $7.6 million.[15] Most contributions from big interest groups flow not to individual members' campaign accounts but to the leader-controlled funds.

The leadership of each party targets a small number of legislative districts for special effort based on the potential for gaining a seat by defeating the other party's candidates in the next election. The leadership also protects members whom the other caucus has targeted by assigning committee staff to assist them in drafting and sponsoring popular bills and getting the bills through the legislature. The press staff publicizes the targeted members' legislative achievements in Springfield and in hometown news media. Members targeted in tough reelection contests sometimes vote the way the opposition might vote, with the tacit approval of their leadership, to avoid becoming vulnerable to attack by the other caucus's candidate. Veteran members know by hard experience that in a heated reelection campaign, a political attack launched by an opponent in a press release might cost a candidate tens of thousands of dollars in campaign funds because it forces him or her to buy expensive media advertising or mailers to explain or defend a controversial vote. Indeed, legislators who are in somewhat safer districts often vote with the targeted members. As a result, leaders designate a member to be the caucus whip, whose job it is to keep caucus discipline and see to it that caucus members in nontargeted districts vote as the party leadership demands.

Leadership powers are not without limits. Each caucus's membership is diverse, with varying ideologies, personalities, ambitions, and rivalries. Perfect discipline is impossible, and a lawmaker may be more loyal to his or her district interests than to a leader. Moreover, leaders depend on their members for support to win and retain their positions. As a result, leaders who run roughshod over members risk losing their position. Instead, they generally try to apply their powers in ways designed to generate credits among members, and leaders can draw on that political capital as needed.

Conversely, in order to have influence in the legislature, a regular legislator must get the big picture and be well informed about the legislative process and policy issues and well connected with the powers-that-be. The ability to influence the legislative process usually comes together in the few lawmakers who possess a robust combination of intuition and sound reasoning and enjoy a district where reelection is a safe and therefore an inexpensive proposition.

Balance of Power

The 1970 Illinois Constitution altered the balance of the power between legislative leaders and the governor by providing the governor with powers of veto in addition to the total veto of bills and the line-item veto. The new powers included the reduction veto for appropriations bills, which allows for the reduction in appropriated amounts, and the amendatory veto, which permits gubernatorial changes to substantive bills enacted by the legislature. This combination of veto powers explains why "Illinois is considered a strong executive state."[16]

If the legislature disagrees with a governor's total, amendatory, or line-item vetoes, they can override them by a vote of three-fifths of the members elected to each chamber. Restoration of an appropriation reduced by the governor requires only a majority of the members elected to each chamber. Thus after 1970 it became easier for the legislature to override a governor's vetoes by reducing the required majority to three-fifths from the previously almost insurmountable two-thirds.[17] Both sides soon tested these new constitutional powers, ultimately forcing a showdown.

Governor James Thompson set the stage with his prolific use of the amendatory veto in the 1980s. Both chambers of the legislature at this point had firm Democratic majorities, and they fired back by overriding Thompson's vetoes.[18] Thompson kept the veto pen busy until, in 1987, Madigan refused to call up a number of bills that Thompson had sent back with amendatory vetoes. Thompson wanted these bills; nonetheless, Madigan's inaction had the effect of killing them by placing them in parliamentary limbo.[19] Thompson eventually "got the Speaker's message" and began to temper his use of the amendatory veto.[20]

The interest groups also play a balancing role in decision making. Indeed, the "Third House" is an informal association of lobbyists. Whereas Republican and Democratic camps bisect the legislature, economic philosophy and specialization fragment interest groups. One of the few positions on which most agree is that campaign contributions are a worthwhile approach to gaining influence with governors, the Four Tops, and their assistants.

Taking note of the power structure in the legislature, interest groups have recently directed more of their contributions to the campaign committees of the four leaders and several assistant leaders. This represents mutually advantageous accommodation as well as interdependence. These contributions increase the power of the leaders as they dole the money out to their appreciative rank-and-file members. Not surprisingly, in election cycles from 2003 through 2006, the speaker controlled $17.7 million, the senate president $14 million, the senate minority leader $12.1 million, and the house minority leader $10.6 million. Interest groups have an easier life because their lobbyists can focus more time, effort, and campaign contributions on four leaders and less on the full complement of 177 legislators.

How Legislators Make Decisions

A legislator makes thousands of decisions each year, from the insignificant to the momentous, in committee, on second reading, at passage stage, and in response to lobbyists, constituents, and reporters. The lawmaker must apply a split-second calculus to many of these decisions. Should he or she help a colleague get a dubious bill out of committee (an easy affirmative decision for most)? How should he or she vote on possibly career-threatening tax increases or abortion legislation? A legislator cannot blithely abstain from voting, allowing those who know more about an issue to make the decision. The Illinois Constitution requires that bills receive a majority vote of all those elected, so failure to vote or a formal present vote operates in the same way as a no vote. There is no easy way out.

Barack Obama, a former Illinois state senator, discovered this when he ran for president in 2008. During the contentious Democratic primary elections, Hillary Clinton attacked Obama for voting "present on 129 bills and 11 personnel appointments out of roughly 4,000 votes cast during his nearly eight years in Springfield."[21] Few states allow a present vote, and Obama discovered that it is difficult to explain this quaint Illinois practice to a national audience. One explanation given was that it is an appropriate vote for legislators who have a conflict of interest that prevents them from voting yes or no on a bill. Regarding some of the votes, Obama, a law school instructor, explained he was for some parts of a bill and voted present because he believed other parts unconstitutional. Yet some critics charged that the present vote was a cagy way of avoiding a difficult no vote, while having achieved the same result.

An Illinois lawmaker's political party affiliation and the position of his or her caucus leaders' positions provide the most apparent guides to decision making. For routine and noncontroversial matters, the party line is a good guide to the way a legislator will vote, but with difficult or unpopular issues, leaders impose positions on their members only to the extent necessary to achieve their objectives. Leaders take into account that the attitudes of voters in a legislator's district may be at odds with a caucus's partisan position, particularly for members facing a targeted race. In those cases, the leaders try to structure majority roll calls without demanding support from those who would have to vote against their constituents' wishes.

Voters' attitudes as reflected in mail and personal contacts also provide indispensable cues for lawmakers, especially for those in competitive or targeted districts. Most voters, especially those in large urban or suburban districts, have little or no idea how their legislators are voting, let alone who they are. Legislators understand this, so one might conclude that lawmakers could act without concern for constituents' attitudes. This is generally not the case, because careerist lawmakers view their political world in terms of actions that might increase or decrease their electoral base. Endorsement by large membership organizations of realtors, farmers, and labor unions can add scores or hundreds of votes to one's base of support, as can support from advocates of gun ownership or the pro-life and pro-choice causes. This is why small but intense groups often wield more influence than their numbers would seem to represent.

The institution has developed approaches to reducing conflict in decision making, especially concerning the many issues that lack strong partisan, constituent, or regional considerations. One of these is "going along," that is, voting for legislation unless there is visible opposition. In committee, as members try to wrap up a long hearing, one often hears a legislator ask, "Is there any opposition to this bill? If not, I move the attendance [or partisan] roll call." Legislators generally give their colleagues' bills the benefit of the doubt.

Reciprocity is another consideration. It makes more sense to help a colleague than to stand in the way, for his or her assistance may be useful another day. Reciprocity often takes place in committees; it is one reason so many bad bills get out of committee to clog floor action later. Passing a problem along seems to simplify decision making: "Let the other chamber clean up the problems" or "Let's send it to the governor, and let him resolve the conflict."

Making commitments early reduces conflict as well. Keeping one's commitment has been a hallowed norm, though it seems to have been breached more frequently in recent years. An early commitment to a colleague or lobbyist regarding a controversial bill that is going to plague the legislature all session effectively takes the committed lawmaker out of the lobbyists' crosshairs.

Not all conflict, of course, can be resolved, pushed along, or reduced. For the scores of decisions that involve conflict, the lawmaker complements his or her own values and knowledge with cues provided by the leadership, staff, colleagues, lobbyists, the governor's office, the press, and constituents.

Information is an important factor. Legislators have more information available than they can digest, and the amount they do absorb is impressive. Nevertheless, with regard to any one decision, the information is likely to be incomplete. Thus, the credibility of the information or of the person who delivered it becomes critical. The best cues tend to come from expert colleagues, veteran lobbyists, senior legislative staff, and longtime state agency experts.

A former legislator recalls one use he made of informational cues on the house floor: "I respected my seatmates to my left, right and in front of me. One was on the judiciary committee, another on local government and agriculture, the third on revenue. I was on appropriations and education. We had most of the committees covered among us. So on third reading as each bill came up we would ask who had it in committee, what he remembered, and how he was going to vote. While we didn't always agree, it was an invaluable set of cues."[22]

Power: Sometimes the Luck of the Draw

Of great importance in the balance between the two political parties is the drawing of new electoral districts every ten years. Reapportionment represents the essential trench warfare of politics, for after a mighty struggle, new battle lines are set for a full decade.[23] The process begins following the decennial census and is intended to be a bipartisan effort of the legislature. Nevertheless, since candidates win or lose elections depending on where the lines are drawn, the redistricting processes of 1990 and 2000 became deadlocked in the legislature. The constitution requires that the new map be drawn by a commission of legislators and nonlegislators that comprises four Democrats and four Republicans selected by the legislative leaders. Because these commissions could not reach agreement by August of the redistricting year, a ninth member was chosen to break the tie, as provided by the state constitution. The state Supreme Court submits the names of one Democrat and one Republican, and the secretary of state randomly selects one of them.[24] After the 1990 census, the Republicans won the draw; the following decade the Democrats did. Not coincidentally, the Republicans controlled the senate from 1992 to 2002, but after the 2000 census and remapping, the Democrats took over.

Districts should be equal in population, compact, contiguous, and nondiscriminatory. Within those rules, the players draw boundaries that favor the party in control of redistricting. Computers are at the heart of the procedure, processing census information on a precinct-level basis so that legislators can tell instantaneously how moving a district line by one city block will change the population, political, racial, economic, age, and other dimensions of the proposed district.

The basic techniques for achieving partisan advantage are to pack your opponents and their voting strength into as few districts as possible or dilute your opponents' strength. Districts that are equal in population and acceptably compact and contiguous can be drawn to benefit either party.

To illustrate, consider Champaign and Urbana, which are contiguous central Illinois cities located in the heart of Champaign County. Put simplistically, the twin cities form a doughnut hole in which the two major parties are competitive, while the rest of the county is predominantly Republican. Over the years, depending on which party is in control after each new census, so goes the legislative map. In 1981 the Democrats were in control, and using the urban doughnut hole they drew a map with a solid Democratic house seat and divided the rest of the county among several Republican districts. After the next census, Republicans drew the map, and they split up the twin cities to produce house districts that Republicans won every year except 1992. In 2001 Democrats drew the next map, which reunited Champaign-Urbana into a single safe house district easily won by a Democrat and divided the rest of the county into three Republican house districts.

Conflict is inherent. Although party leaders want to increase their respective total membership numbers, individual lawmakers are more interested in "safer" districts from which they can easily win reelection. Leaders of African American, Latino, downstate, collar county, and Chicago interests want safer districts and more of them.

The rise of the Latino Caucus is an interesting example. In 1987 a strong independent leader who got his start in Chicago politics as a community advocate became the first Latino senator in Illinois history. Senator Miguel del Valle swiftly moved up through the ranks to become an assistant majority leader. By 1994, as the number of Latinos in Illinois surpassed nine hundred thousand, their political and economic power began to be felt.[25] Because of more favorably drawn district maps, four Latino legislators served in the General Assembly and often worked together with the Black Caucus.

By 2003, as Democrats came back to power as the majority in both houses, the number of Latinos serving as legislators nearly doubled, and they formed the Latino Caucus and began to push for political change.[26] By the convening of the 95th General Assembly (2007–8), because of rapid Latino population growth in the Chicagoland area and favorably drawn district maps, the Latino Caucus included four senators and nine representatives, all of whom were Democrats. But when Senator del Valle retired in December 2006 to become the clerk of the City of Chicago, a bitter fight broke out over who would replace him in senate Democratic leadership. The repercussions strained the ability of the senate president to hold his caucus together during the tumultuous 95th General Assembly, especially the internecine power struggle among house and senate Democrats and the governor.

The Latino population in Illinois will presumably continue to grow, and the drawing of future legislative district maps will affect the extent of the political influence of the Latino Caucus. The question in the meantime, however, is whether the Latino Caucus will become a significant voting bloc in the Democratic caucuses during future General Assemblies. They have sufficient numbers to be influential, but that would require them to put aside their differences and consistently work together.

An Epic Power Struggle

For most of his turbulent tenure, Governor Rod Blagojevich (2003–9) clashed with House Speaker Michael Madigan over control of the budget and over the governor's efforts to expand health care coverage in the face of legislative opposition. The two powerful officials often fought to a draw, with the governor winning budget battles and Madigan prevailing with respect to the legislature's supremacy as policy maker. The battles are worth recounting, for they illustrate the uses of the formal powers of all three branches of government.

The epic power struggle that followed burst into public view in the 2007 spring session as a bitterly fought battle over the fiscal 2008 budget. On one side were Madigan and his erstwhile allies, the house and senate Republican leaders. On the other side was Blagojevich, who lined up with his chief

THE END OF ANOTHER LONG, HOT, DUSTY DAY IN THE SADDLE.

Fig. 5.2. Cartoon by Bill Campbell (Courtesy of Carl Sandburg College)

ally, senate president Emil Jones. Madigan wanted a utility rate freeze and a budget to meet the state's basic obligations. Blagojevich wanted a new $3 billion health care program paid for by a new gross receipts tax (GRT) on business. Jones wanted new funding for education paid for by a Chicago casino. Republican leaders wanted new building projects paid for by gaming. The house unanimously rejected the GRT by a vote of 107-0. The spring session lurched into a record-breaking overtime session that would drag on for ten weeks until the legislature finally passed the fiscal 2008 budget.

During the overtime period, Blagojevich issued special session proclamations sixteen times. The governor even filed a lawsuit against Madigan for not convening special sessions on the exact date and at the exact time he specified.[27] In a memorandum in support of his motion to dismiss the complaint,

Madigan argued that in the five years since the governor had taken office he had called for thirty-three special sessions—an astounding number given that throughout state history all governors combined have called eighty-nine.

After the budget passed both houses, the governor vetoed parts of it. Specifically, he cut member initiatives (spending projects for individual legislators) for house Democrats and senate Republicans, while he spared the senate Democrats and house Republicans, as if to attempt to drive a wedge between the minority caucuses. He proclaimed that he had cut the "pork" from the budget, but critics charged that the vetoes blatantly rewarded political friends and punished opponents in the legislature.[28] Moreover, the governor said he would use the "savings" generated, which totaled about $463 million, to pay for his unilateral expansion of state-sponsored health care, notwithstanding the lack of legislative approval or funding.[29]

The house voted overwhelmingly to override most of the vetoes and reductions. Nevertheless, Emil Jones, whose Democratic caucus had escaped vetoes or reductions of their pet projects, refused to call the governor's veto message for a vote in the senate. It was impossible, therefore, to override the vetoes and reductions, because to do so the constitution required a three-fifths vote in both chambers.

So, after the dust settled from the fiscal 2008 budget battle, who were the winners and losers? The speaker and the governor were essentially stuck in a politically balanced standoff. Madigan got the limited-growth budget he wanted, but without the vetoed member projects; the governor did sign a utility rate relief bill backed by the speaker. On the other hand, the ambitious health care plan announced by the governor had shrunk drastically to a much smaller scheme.

Another conflict soon flared up when a legislative commission rejected emergency rules proposed by the state Department of Health and Family Services (DHFS). The governor sought approval from the Joint Committee on Administrative Rules for emergency rules to expand FamilyCare. The committee is a legislative commission that reviews rules to ensure compliance with the legislative intent of their authorizing statutes. The DHFS sought to add about 147,000 adults from middle-income families to the program. This was a part of Blagojevich's attempt to circumvent the legislature and unilaterally expand FamilyCare, a state-sponsored health insurance program. Contrary to state law, he then deemed the JCAR decision to be merely advisory and attempted to expand the program anyway.

Illinois businessmen subsequently filed a complaint against the governor in which they alleged that he unlawfully expanded FamilyCare by acting without legislative approval and without specific appropriations to spend state funds to pay for it. A Cook Judicial Circuit judge issued a preliminary injunction against expanding the program pending trial. The governor appealed. In *Caro v. Blagojevich,* the appellate court affirmed the preliminary injunction on the basis that DHFS had exceeded its authority.[30]

While the parties were arguing *Caro* in the appellate court, the legislature, in the 2008 spring session, surprised many seasoned observers by sending the governor a budget that was out of balance by $2 billion, which means expenditures exceeded anticipated revenues by that amount.

The governor responded by cutting the budget by about $1.4 billion using reductions and line-item vetoes. The legislature acquiesced with most of his spending cuts.

Throughout the 95th General Assembly (2007–8), state leaders filed lawsuits, traded personal insults, and made outlandish charges against each other as overtime and special sessions dragged on. The epic power struggle, which was paralyzing state government, showed no sign of letting up.

The Legislature and the Power to Impeach

In the November 2008 general election, voters nationwide elected Barack Obama the next president of the United States. Before taking office he resigned as U.S. senator, leaving a vacancy that the federal constitution and Illinois state statutes give sole discretion to the governor to fill.[31]

On December 9, 2008, the agents of the Federal Bureau of Investigation arrested Blagojevich. The sworn complaint was based in large part on intercepted statements by the governor. The complaint alleged that he and his chief of staff, John Harris, conspired to sell the vacant U.S. Senate seat to the highest bidder and that they conspired to force the firing of a *Chicago Tribune* editor and shake down a children's hospital for a campaign contribution in return for state funding.[32] All this happened in the face of the widespread press coverage of several ongoing federal investigations of the Blagojevich administration, including allegations of "endemic hiring fraud" going back to January 2003.[33]

Within a week of the arrest, the house initiated unprecedented impeachment proceedings against the governor. The speaker and the minority leader appointed a bipartisan special committee to conduct an investigation to determine whether cause existed to impeach the governor.[34] Blagojevich refused to attend or testify during the house impeachment proceedings; instead, criminal defense attorney Edward Genson appeared for him.[35]

Article 4, section 14 of the Illinois Constitution gives house members the sole power to conduct legislative investigations to determine whether cause exists to impeach a governor. Impeachment proceeding was deemed in the 1970 constitution to be remedial rather than criminal in nature because it was designed by the framers as a proceeding "to protect the public from an officer who has abused his position of trust."[36]

On January 8, 2009, the investigative committee found that "the total-ity of the evidence warrants the impeachment of the Governor for cause."[37] The committee noted that the sworn criminal complaint, which was based primarily on the governor's "own words," was "sufficiently credible to dem-onstrate an abuse of office of the highest magnitude and conduct that is en-tirely inconsistent with the Governor's constitutional oath." Moreover, the committee was convinced by the evidence adduced at the hearing that there was in fact a link between campaign contributions and official actions. In addition, the evidence was persuasive that the governor "defied JCAR and expanded a health care plan without legal authority or a funding source." Finally, the testimony of the auditor general showed, to the committee's sat-isfaction, that the governor's abuse of power related to other programs.[38] On January 9, 2009, the house members voted 114-1-1 to approve the article of impeachment, thereby impeaching the governor for abuse of power. Five days later, the newly sworn house members of the 96th General Assembly (2009–10) voted 117-1 to impeach a second time.

The impeachment trial in the state senate, pursuant to rules adopted by the senate and presided over by the chief justice of the Illinois Supreme Court, began on January 26, 2009. After four days of proceedings, on January 29, the senators convicted Blagojevich on a vote of 59-0. The senate ordered his immediate removal from office and banned him from ever holding public office again. Lieutenant Governor Patrick Quinn was elevated to the gover-norship to hold office until the end of the term in 2010.

Since the 1960s the Illinois General Assembly has successfully developed strong professional staffing. The legislative leaders have consolidated their control over the staff as a part of the steady concentration of power in their offices. Moreover, since the 1980s leaders have achieved almost complete control of the legislative process in their respective chambers by tightening the procedural rules and by the acquiescent dependency of regular members on leaders' largesse to finance expensive campaigns. Finally, given the im-peachment of the governor and his removal from office in 2009, it is evident that the legislature has the capacity to operate as a branch of government co-equal to the executive.

6.

The Executive

• • • • • • • • • • • • •

A Golden Gloves pugilist as a teen, Governor Rod Blagojevich (2003–9) struck a combative tone with the legislature at the beginning of his second term in 2007, when he surprised lawmakers with massive proposals to provide health coverage for nearly everyone in the state and a $7 billion gross receipts tax on business to pay for the new program. Both were summarily rejected by the legislature, but the governor proceeded to expand his health program, called Illinois Covered, prompting lawsuits from Republicans that charged him with an unconstitutional usurpation of the legislature's authority to appropriate funds.

Blagojevich might well be characterized as an unpopular populist who early in his governorship adopted populist themes of taking on the political system, helping the disadvantaged through expanded health care, and protecting the little guy from an increase in income or sales taxes. Because of never-ending wrangling with the legislature and the indictment or conviction of several close associates on corruption charges, the governor's approval ratings had sunk by late 2007 to roughly 20 percent, with 51.9 percent of those polled saying they would vote to recall the governor from office if they had the opportunity.[1]

In the summer of 2007 Blagojevich called sixteen special sessions of the legislature, generally without providing lawmakers with proposed legislation to react to, the special sessions coming on successive days. In addition, the governor filed two suits against the legislature in 2007. The first asked Speaker of the House Michael Madigan to hold special sessions on the days and at the times the governor wished to force representatives to show up for sessions. The second asked a judge to order the house clerk to record the governor's budget veto message on a specific date, rather than some later date, as part of political maneuvering over possible veto overrides. As long-time capital reporter and analyst Charles Wheeler put it: "In the surreal world of here-and-now Illinois politics, the suits are among the latest signs of the toxic environment infusing government under the control of the state's dysfunctional Democratic leaders (governor, Speaker of the House and President of the Senate)."[2]

According to Taylor Pensoneau, Blagojevich had been quite successful in his first-term legislative initiatives—hiking the minimum wage, passing ethics legislation, and, after decades of failed attempts, passing gay rights legislation.[3] Expanded health care and improved children's services were, however, the hallmarks of the Blagojevich administration. In his first term he created the All Kids plan, which sought to offer health coverage to all Illinois children, and a program of universal preschool for three- and four-year-olds.[4]

In the governor's second term (2007–9), things began to fall apart. The challenge in all of the Blagojevich health care initiatives had been to find the money to pay for the expensive programs. Indeed, the governor went deeper into deficit spending in each year of his first term simply to pay for regular programs (see chapter 10, "Taxing and Spending"). Adhering to his campaign promise of not increasing general sales or income taxes, he turned to other revenue initiatives: the $7 billion business tax, mentioned above, lease of the state lottery to generate a reported $12 billion up-front, massive increases in gambling, and long-term borrowing of $12 billion on the premise that the cost of borrowing money would be less than the interest income earned.

All of these proposals were repeatedly rejected by the legislature. So the governor and Speaker Madigan checkmated one another. The governor declared he would veto any general tax increase, which dampened any interest among lawmakers in casting tough tax increase votes that would come to naught. At the same time, Madigan blocked all the revenue initiatives proposed by the governor. In addition, personal acrimony developed among the state's three top policy makers: Madigan and Blagojevich disliked one another, and then–senate president Emil Jones was aligned with the governor; Jones and Madigan lost trust, so critical in politics, in one another.

As noted elsewhere, federal agents arrested Blagojevich in December 2008 for having been heard on a wiretap allegedly trying to sell the appointment of a successor to the U.S. Senate seat previously held by President Barack Obama. This became an international news story. Exasperation with the governor's confrontational tactics had been building among legislators since at least the beginning of his second term. Failure to consult with the legislature on major new initiatives in health care and then proceeding to implement the health care expansion without legislative appropriation or approval were fundamental factors in lawmakers' anger toward the governor. The authors doubt, however, that Blagojevich would have been removed from office absent his arrest for allegedly trying to sell the U.S. Senate seat. "Gov. Blagojevich shattered the ethos, the set of values by which we have operated," observed veteran lobbyist Jim Fletcher. "We believed in getting out on time, protecting old programs, budgeting incrementally, and not proposing big new programs until the base spending was assured."[5] All the while, as of the spring of 2009, the state had gone nine years without a major capital investment program of building and maintenance for highways, mass transit, universities, colleges, schools, and state agencies.

All this has apparently taken a toll on the management of state government. In the March 2008 report "Grading the States," *Governing* magazine and the Pew Center on the States awarded an overall grade of C to Illinois, whereas the states overall received a B– grade.[6] In twenty categories concerning the state's handling of money, people, infrastructure, and information, Illinois was graded weak in nine, to wit: long-term outlook, budget process, structural balance (are revenues keeping up with spending?), workforce planning, training and development, managing employee performance, capital planning, maintenance, and budgeting for performance. Only in the category of online services and information did Illinois rate better than mid-level.

Governing did have a few good words to say for Illinois. The magazine pointed to increased use of performance measures. "And some of the yardsticks now used, such as the percentage of ex-offenders who avoid going back to prison, are measuring solid outcomes." The evaluators concluded, however, that such measures are vital "in a state where long-term financial prospects are frightening."[7]

The lessons learned from the governor's confrontational politics are that (1) success in major public policy initiatives requires the active support of both the executive and legislative branches, and (2) significant preconditioning of lawmakers and legislative leaders is needed before they are willing to consider taking on expensive, major new programs and revenue initiatives.

Approaches to Leading Illinois

Since Shadrach Bond first took on the job in 1818, twenty Republicans and twenty Democrats have served in the state's top post. Each brought his own approach to the job of governing. As the late Robert P. Howard explained in *Mostly Good and Competent Men,* several of the chief executives left lasting imprints as managers, builders, or social reformers.[8]

Thomas Ford (1842–46) was one of the managers. He inherited a huge debt from an overly ambitious internal improvements scheme to build railroads, canals, and plank roads throughout Illinois. Ford determined that, painful as it would be, the state must pay the principal and interest so as to restore the state's integrity as a place to invest. He sold government land and passed a permanent tax to pay off the debt, and he arranged new mortgage terms for completion of a canal between Lake Michigan and the Illinois River that would link the Great Lakes to the Gulf of Mexico. In so doing, Ford "made possible the future solvency and prosperity of Illinois."[9]

Another manager was Republican Frank O. Lowden (1917–21), who reorganized 125 boards and commissions, many of which operated as political fiefdoms, into nine executive departments. He also centralized the state's budgeting and accounting systems and became a leading candidate for president at the 1920 GOP convention. But after nine ballots in which Lowden was deadlocked with General Leonard Wood and Senator Hiram Johnson of California, the convention turned to Warren G. Harding.

The most recent manager, some would say visionary, was Richard B. Ogilvie (1969–73), who created the executive Bureau of the Budget (now the Governor's Office of Management and Budget) and staffed it with bright young professionals. Ogilvie established a strong Environmental Protection Agency before the federal government took similar action. He also imposed the state's first income tax and shared part of the revenues with local governments.

Governors who were builders measured the success of their tenure by the amount of concrete poured and steel erected. Helped by a bond issue and planning initiated by his predecessor, Governor Len Small (1921–29) took Illinois out of the mud and onto seven thousand miles of concrete pavement. Year after year he set new national records as a road builder. He rejected road bids of $40,000 per mile, threatened to have the state rather than contractors do the work, and ultimately reduced the costs to $27,000 per mile. Small also put state aid to schools on an equalization basis designed to help fiscally weaker districts.

William G. Stratton (1953–61) widened U.S. Route 66 to four lanes and by the end of his eight years in office took credit for 7,057 miles of new roadways and 638 bridges. Stratton imposed tolls to finance a network of superhighways for the burgeoning metropolitan Chicago region. He sponsored major bond issues that won approval in referenda and financed creation of new university campuses and a network of mental health centers. In addition, Stratton reformed the state court system and revised the state's malapportioned legislative districts for the first time in half a century.

The social reformers were perhaps the least easy to fit in the mold of individualistic Illinois politics. Edward Coles (1822–26) was an idealistic aristocrat from Virginia who freed the slaves he inherited. Robert Howard credited Coles with preventing Illinois from becoming a slave state: "Coles reacted quickly when the legislature's pro-slavery majority ordered an 1824 referendum on the calling of a constitutional convention that would have legalized the de facto human bondage that existed in early Illinois. Lacking power to veto the resolution, he assumed leadership in defining the issue, raised money for publicizing his views, and mobilized public sentiment against the pro-slavery movement. In what seemed to be a hopeless campaign, the cause of freedom triumphed—6,640 to 4,972."[10]

John Peter Altgeld (1893–97) became one of the heroes of American liberalism. Altgeld spent surpluses built up by his predecessor to open teachers' colleges at DeKalb and Charleston and insane asylums at East Moline and Bartonville; he increased appropriations for the University of Illinois and encouraged its expansion in graduate programs and medicine. Altgeld made his mark, however, in social reform. He appointed Florence Kelley, a protégé of Jane Addams, to enforce a new factory inspection law; the law also limited employment of women to eight hours per day and strengthened an earlier child labor statute.

According to Howard, the turning point in Altgeld's career was his eighteen-thousand-word justification for pardoning three anarchists who had been convicted on flimsy evidence of a bombing at the famous Haymarket Square labor rally in 1886 in Chicago. "This courageous but belligerent action made him the most hated man in Illinois and wiped out any prospect of his being elected to another office. Thereafter he devoted his multiple talents to the protection of the poor and downtrodden and to the enactment of progressive legislation."[11]

It is easier to leave a lasting imprint when financial resources are available to build lasting infrastructure, as was true of several of the governors whose careers are sketched above. Henry Horner (1933–40), the state's first Jewish governor, presided during the depths of the Great Depression. He financed unemployment relief by shifting the state's major tax burden from property to sales and worked effectively with fellow Democrats from the New Deal administration of President Franklin D. Roosevelt. "By background and performance, he was ideally suited to serve as Depression governor," according to Howard, who considered Horner among the state's best governors.[12]

Thompson the Super-Salesman

In a state that has no term limits, James R. Thompson was elected governor four times and served from 1977 to 1990, longer than any Illinois governor. He decided not to run for a fifth term that many observers thought he could win. Most remarkable about his string of victories was that Illinois went through a tough economic transformation on Thompson's watch. Hundreds of thousands of well-paid manufacturing jobs were wrung out of the state's economy and replaced by comparable increases in jobs in a rapidly developing service sector that ranged from fast-food restaurants to financial services and information technologies. Illinois suffered a deep recession in the early 1980s and uneven economic growth thereafter, with strength in the collar counties but weaknesses in rural areas and Chicago. Yet Thompson kept on winning.

He responded to the economic woes as did governors in other struggling states. He expanded the state's economic development agency, infused it with money for job retraining, and created incentives for industry. He established more state offices overseas than any other state (eleven by 1990) and became the state's chief salesman abroad.

Governors, Thompson declared, ought not devote much time to direct management once they have learned the job. Indeed, many agency directors did not see him personally on state business in a year's time. Yet Thompson will probably be given his highest marks for having administered the state effectively. Overall, he hired and retained high-quality staff and agency directors, and he gave them the latitude to do their jobs. Remarkable for Illinois, with its well-known history of political corruption, no scandals were reported during his fourteen years in office.

Thompson came into office without a clear picture of where he wanted to lead the state. He addressed problems as they arose, with intelligence and an attitude that government could make some difference, albeit not fundamental. Though he tried and had good people to help him, he became resigned to the limits of government in solving fundamental social problems. He did not, however, see it as his role to exhort the larger society to transform itself. Maybe he, like other policy makers, did not know what to prescribe for society's shortcomings.

This governor thought of himself as a builder.[13] In Chicago he constructed the State of Illinois Center, later to be named for him. It resembles a huge, glimmering, ungainly spaceship, plopped awkwardly in the heart of the city's Loop. He embarked on what appeared to be a major infrastructure renovation program called Build Illinois, which evolved instead into a potpourri of projects awarded in large measure to the districts of favored lawmakers or to those whose support was needed.

Thompson was elected as a crime-busting U.S. attorney who promised reform (he successfully prosecuted a former governor, Otto Kerner). At his first inaugural in 1977, Thompson declared: "No job will be bought, no favors will be sold. No citizen seeking help will be asked his or her party allegiance or political loyalty."[14] But by his final year, most state job vacancies were filled on the basis of party allegiance or sponsorship by lawmakers, and in 1990 the U.S. Supreme Court struck down elements of his extensive patronage system.[15] In 1986 he raised an unprecedented $7.11 million for his final campaign,[16] much of it in contributions of $10,000 to $100,000 from businesses, interest groups, law firms, and individuals who did business with the state or who were interested in legislation that would come to his desk.

There was nothing illegal in these patronage and fundraising practices, but there was no reform. Illinois politics appeared to change the onetime reformer more than he changed the state, repeating a pattern that has marked political life throughout the state's history. Big Jim Thompson probably reflected the values, aspirations, and individualistic political culture of Illinoisans better than most governors before him.

Edgar the Low-Key Manager

Thompson's protégé and successor was Jim Edgar, a study in contrasts with Thompson and many of his predecessors. Edgar was the first governor in sixty-two years to succeed a governor of the same party, a reflection of the state's historic competitive partisan balance. Thompson is a native Chicagoan who in his latter terms in office operated state government primarily from that city, where he resided during his governorship. Edgar, who grew up and went to college in Charleston (population twenty thousand), was both the first downstate governor and the first nonlawyer in thirty years. Thompson had had no previous state government experience; Edgar has spent his entire career in state government and state politics.

Thompson is open and gregarious; Edgar is reserved and private. Thompson relishes the black-tie social life and spends expansively on fine art and antiques. Edgar is a family man and church-oriented person; alcohol was not allowed in his executive mansion.[17] Edgar was even known to mow his own lawn at a cabin-style home north of Springfield, where he and his wife spent as much time as possible. His image was so squeaky-clean that reporters filed stories when they observed a state trooper assigned to him atop the riding mower at his retreat home.

Because of his restrained personality and lifestyle, Edgar appeared to have more limited objectives and less power than his predecessor. There were no major initiatives during his first term, in part because of a campaign pledge that there would be no tax increases, a promise he fulfilled. When the *Chicago Tribune* in 1994 endorsed Edgar for a second term rather than challenger Dawn Clark Netsch, it had to acknowledge that "if Edgar thinks he can glide along for another four years, then the state is headed for trouble."[18] The editorial noted that in his first term Edgar had backed down on legislative initiatives for a ban on assault weapons, riverboat casinos in Chicago, and experimental charter schools. It pointed out that the opposition had come not only from Democratic nemesis Michael Madigan in the house but also from Republican senate president James "Pate" Philip. Big Jim and Pate Philip got along famously, and Philip would often sponsor Thompson initiatives that he opposed personally.

Edgar and Thompson were alike in one respect—neither was a reformer. Like Thompson, Edgar courted big campaign donors and rewarded his political friends with contracts and patronage whenever possible. But he trimmed the state bureaucracy and scaled back on Thompson's propensity to award big incentives to lure jobs to the state or help existing companies expand. If he had to be assigned to a category, Edgar would be a manager.

Ryan the Tragic Dealmaker

After serving as chair of the Kankakee County Board, speaker of the Illinois house, lieutenant governor (two terms), and secretary of state (two terms), George Ryan entered the governor's mansion in 1999. Ryan had all the political skills to be a builder in the fashion of Jim Thompson as well as an effective, favor-vending dealmaker. Because of some of his deal-making, a federal jury found Ryan guilty in 2006 on twenty-two counts of trading governmental favors for personal gain. He was sentenced to a term in federal prison.

The Republican Ryan accomplished much in his single four-year term.[19] He raised license plate fees and liquor taxes to finance $12 billion in a program of bricks-and-mortar highway and school construction known as Illinois First. He ended decades of political deadlock over rebuilding the lakefront home of the Chicago Bears by doing a deal involving the team, the City of Chicago, and the legislature. Ryan broke with Republican suburban mayors and agreed with Democratic Chicago mayor Richard M. Daley to expand O'Hare Airport.

Ryan loved to play a part in making big deals happen, and he disdained the details. He once told James D. Nowlan, with a note of pride, that in his decade as a state legislator (1973–83) he "never read a bill." He left the details to aides, some of whom took advantage of his trust.

Definitely a hands-off manager, Ryan generated an immense stock of credits with legislators and others over the years, based on favors that ranged from special license plates to pension-boosting jobs in his offices for legislators to myriad favors as speaker of the house in moving legislation along or blocking it.

In 2003 Ryan gained international notice, most of it favorable, when he commuted to life terms the death sentences of all 167 convicts on Illinois's Death Row.[20] He may be the only convicted felon ever nominated for the Nobel Peace Prize.

A Sprawling Executive Branch

Like the Chicago suburbs, the executive branch of government in Illinois is a huge and sprawling operation, with 125,000 employees in 2007.[21] Of these, about three-fifths work directly for the governor and another 40,000 are employed by state universities. If the estimated state revenues for 2007 of about $44 billion were equated with corporate revenue, Illinois would rank in the top 50 on the Fortune 500 list of leading American corporations.

The executive branch is complex and highly diversified. It delivers health care each year to 2.5 million of Illinois's 12.8 million residents, most of them low-income workers, children, and the elderly. A different function is provided by the small Department of Financial and Professional Regulation, which examines, licenses, investigates, and sometimes disciplines about eight hundred thousand persons across forty-one occupations, from physicians and architects to boxers and wrestlers. The sprawling Department of Human Services spends $6 billion per year on community services, residential facilities, and hospitals for the mentally ill, the developmentally disabled, the addicted, the blind, and youth and children, among others. The Department of Corrections houses 45,000 inmates in twenty-eight correctional facilities.

The organization of Illinois state government is about as complex as the state is diverse. By the second decade of the twentieth century, the bureaucracy had grown into a sprawling, unmanageable collection of entities that Governor Frank O. Lowden cut down to nine executive departments in 1917. Since then, the number of departments expanded to twenty. In addition, twenty-seven major boards and commissions were created, each linked to the governor on the organization chart and through members that he appoints. The executive branch had become so layered, in fact, that cabinet meetings in the Thompson administration had to be held in the ballroom of the executive mansion.

Governor Rod Blagojevich used his executive reorganization powers to consolidate several agencies into a huge Department of Human Services and a consolidated Department of Financial and Professional Regulation.

The first problem a chief executive faces in Illinois is that the executive branch is not his or hers alone. The executive powers are divided by the Illinois Constitution among five independently elected officials: the governor, the secretary of state, the attorney general, the treasurer, and the comptroller (see figure 6.1). This system contrasts with the executive branch of the U.S. government, in which the president appoints all other constitutional officers.

Independently elected officers often use their offices as springboards to the governorship, as in the cases of Republican secretaries of state Jim Edgar and George Ryan. In 1990 Edgar faced Democratic attorney general Neil Hartigan in the race for governor. Seeking to move up the ladder, the other three executive officers that year ran for the posts being vacated by the gubernatorial candidates.

The statewide officials also often make life difficult for their fellow executives. In 1994 the comptroller, Dawn Clark Netsch, frequently criticized Governor Edgar's management of his budget and ran against him in the 1994 election. By 2007 all executive officers were Democrats. That did not, however, stop Attorney General Lisa Madigan from investigating allegations of wrongdoing in the office of Governor Blagojevich. In 2006 Republican treasurer Judy Baar Topinka ran unsuccessfully for governor against Blagojevich

The attorney general is the chief legal officer for the state. Among other responsibilities, the attorney general and his or her staff provide advisory opinions for state and local officials and represent in court more than three hundred boards, departments, and commissions of state government (though the governor retains legal counsel for his office and that of most of his agencies). The attorney general also collects monies owed the state and works with county-level state's attorneys to prosecute certain criminal cases.[22] Attorney General Lisa Madigan (elected in 2002) has used the office aggressively in her self-perceived role as "the people's lawyer." In the summer of 2008, for example, during the depths of the sub-prime housing crisis, her office brought suit against Countrywide Insurance, a mortgage lender that many see as a culprit in the housing crisis for its lax lending procedures.

The secretary of state is best known for administering motor vehicle registration and drivers' licensing; in addition, the office oversees the state library and archives and administers laws relating to incorporation in Illinois. The secretary of state has far more employees (about four thousand) than does any other state-level elected official except the governor.

The comptroller keeps the state's "checkbook" and pays all the state's bills. Comptrollers have used the information at their disposal to evaluate and

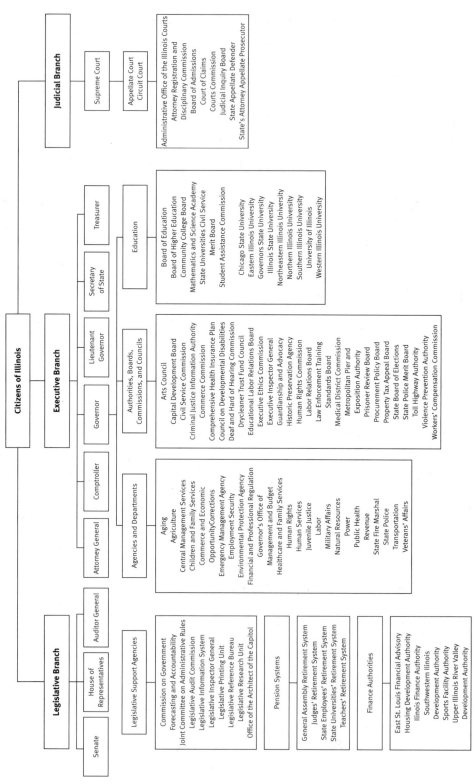

Fig. 6.1. State of Illinois organizational chart. Source: Illinois Office of the Comptroller, 2007.

comment on the financial condition of the state. The treasurer is responsible for receiving, investing, safeguarding, and disbursing (on the order of the comptroller) all monies paid to the state.

Although these thumbnail sketches fail to describe all that the governor's fellow elected executives do, their offices remain, when compared with the office of the governor, narrow and generally ministerial. For this reason, these officials have worked over the years to broaden the scope and visibility of their offices by enactment of statutes that assign them responsibilities beyond the few set forth in the constitution and added by personal initiative.

For example, the lieutenant governor has no constitutional duties other than to fill the office of governor when it is vacated. Yet the report on that office in the *Illinois Blue Book* (2005–6) has sections about the lieutenant governor's activities as chair of various groups such as the governor's Rural Affairs, Broadband Deployment, and Main Street Councils, among others, and about his work as an advocate for taxpayers and consumers. Recent attorneys general have been active in environmental protection and in concerns for senior citizens and consumer affairs. When he was secretary of state, Governor Edgar expanded his motor vehicle responsibilities to crack down on drunk driving and used his role as state librarian to champion adult literacy programs.

These activities make political sense because these offices are often used as launching pads to higher office.

Powers of the Governor

The governor has strong formal and informal powers, thanks in part to the enhanced veto and management powers provided by the 1970 constitution. An Illinois governor needs all these powers, which are described below, because he is expected to fill several roles beyond those of administering the state's business and managing his own bureaucracy.

By virtue of the governor's constitutional responsibilities to give formal state of the state and budget messages to the legislature each year, the chief executive is expected by legislators to propose comprehensive policies and a detailed budget, to which the legislature will react. In addition, his political party expects him to wear the mantle of state party leader. He or she is also expected to be the state's chief negotiator, the one who brings legislative, business, union, and civic leaders to the executive mansion or to the Thompson Center to resolve prickly conflicts such as school strikes in Chicago and legislative impasses that pit labor against management. In other words, there are great expectations for an Illinois governor.

Because the state economy struggled during the 1980s, Governor Jim

Thompson—with great relish—took on the role of chief salesman, or economic developer. He set up economic development offices in eleven overseas cities, from Moscow to Sao Paolo, Kyoto, Tokyo, Warsaw, and Budapest, and he took two or more trips overseas each year to trumpet Illinois products and business opportunities. Governors since have continued with at least a few international outposts; Blagojevich had nine.

In order to carry out these tasks effectively, the governor needs powers to do things *for* people, especially for lawmakers, and powers to do or threaten to do things *to* people. He has a significant stock of such powers, though not always enough to accomplish his objectives. Among his fundamental powers are those to veto bills passed by the legislature; initiate comprehensive legislative programs and annual budgets; dispense patronage jobs, appointments, and contracts; and administer his sprawling executive agencies.

The governor has the advantage of being a single decision maker who confronts a two-house legislature characterized by sometimes divided party majorities, scores of committees, and as many points of view as there are members. The governor can also benefit from the stature, authority, and perquisites of the office.

The president of the United States, who can sign or veto a bill in its entirety, would undoubtedly be envious of the additional veto powers granted the governor of Illinois, powers among the most extensive in the fifty states. In addition to the whole bill veto, he has the authority to make substantive changes in enacted legislation (the amendatory veto), to reduce the amount of money in appropriations bills (the reduction veto), and to eliminate specific line items from these spending bills (the line-item veto).

Since 1970 governors have used these powers frequently. Governor Dan Walker (1973–76) had difficult relations with the legislature. He vetoed 468 bills in their entirety during his single four-year term, more than 14 percent of all bills passed. The legislature was able to override only one in fourteen of his vetoes with the required three-fifths majority in each house.[23]

Thompson used the amendatory veto more extensively than have other Illinois chief executives. In 1989–90, he applied amendatory language to 140 enacted bills. The legislature was able to override, or strip away, his changes on only 8 bills.[24] In the 1991–92 biennium, the legislature enacted 1,528 bills. Governor Edgar applied one of his four veto powers to almost one-fifth (290) of them. His vetoes were overridden just sixteen times.

In his first year in office in 2003, Rod Blagojevich applied 115 vetoes of various kinds and was overridden twenty-one times by the legislature.

As the political scientist Alan Rosenthal points out, however, the legislature often expects the governor to bring coherence to legislation: "An example is the crisis over Acquired Immune Deficiency Syndrome (AIDS), in which many bills have been introduced by legislators seeking to demonstrate concern and gain credit for action. The Illinois Legislature in 1987 passed 17 different AIDS bills, a number of which contradicted one another. Governor Thompson vetoed four, applied the amendatory veto to three, and signed 10 others, trying to fashion a coherent program out of a potpourri of legislation."[25]

The governor's ability to award jobs and contracts and make appointments represents another kind of negotiating power. In the 1980s just about every vacancy that occurred under Thompson's jurisdiction was scrutinized to see whether a lawmaker or political party leader had a qualified candidate. If so, that patron had a good chance of seeing his candidate selected. If the patron had a candidate who was not yet qualified by examination, the position was often held open for months while the candidate tried to become qualified.

Legislators sometimes sponsor themselves for job appointments in anticipation of voluntary or involuntary retirement from their elected posts. In addition to continuing their careers in government, these persons can add handsomely to their legislative pension benefits by holding such jobs. This interest in a post-legislative career can persuade a lawmaker to cast difficult votes on behalf of the governor's program.

The governor also fills by appointment nearly 2,100 positions on more than 282 boards and commissions plus nineteen interstate compacts. Most are unpaid, yet many of these appointments are prestigious, such as those to the University of Illinois Board of Trustees and the Illinois Arts Council. Others are highly prized for the recognition they bring within a profession, such as the forty-one boards that oversee licensure for engineers, architects, physicians, real estate agents, and other regulated occupations.

Finally, there is the award of so-called pork barrel projects and the construction contracts that go with them. Thompson's Build Illinois program melded the concept of economic development with projects that benefited lawmakers. According to Alan Rosenthal, Thompson adopted projects selected by legislators, and he agreed that about one-fifth of the funding would be allocated among the Republican and Democratic caucuses of the house and senate.[26]

Each project provided for contracts that benefited contractors, financiers, and law firms. These beneficiaries were expected, some would say, to show their appreciation with large campaign contributions, and they helped Thompson raise several million dollars per year for his campaigns. In addition to financing reelection campaigns, campaign funds are used to help legislative candidates and to provide birthday, anniversary, and holiday gifts for friends and politicos.

Because of these powers, a legislator will frequently seek a governor's support and assistance. Years ago, during a closed conference of Republican members of the house, several GOP lawmakers were loudly criticizing the governor (Ogilvie, also of their party). Finally, a sage veteran silenced the bickering with this remark: "Okay, so the governor is an SOB. But just remember and appreciate this—he's *our* SOB!"[27]

The governor of Illinois has more latitude than do many governors in administering the executive branch. Although the executive is divided, the lion's share of state government functions and personnel are within the governor's domain. He appoints all his department heads and has statutory authority to terminate without cause several hundred senior civil service executives at the end of their four-year appointments.

The 1970 constitution grants governors the power to reorganize state agencies by executive order, subject to rejection by the legislature. In 1995 Edgar used this power to merge the Departments of Conservation, Mines and Minerals, and Energy and Natural Resources and units of other agencies into a single Department of Natural Resources. As noted above, Blagojevich used the powers to consolidate several social service agencies into the Department of Human Services and consolidate a number of agencies into the Department of Financial and Professional Regulation.

A Peer of Corporate Executives

The most important informal power of the governor lies in the stature of the office itself and the perquisites that come with the job. With rare exceptions, the governor alone among state officials and lawmakers can become, by virtue of his office, a peer of top corporate chief executives. The governor has the assurance that they will return his phone calls when he needs their counsel or assistance. His comments are often on the front page and on evening television, whereas those of most legislators are relegated to the back pages, if covered at all. His personal presence often generates interest and increased participation in fundraising events for legislators.

In Springfield the governor has at his disposal a handsome executive mansion for entertaining. Just down the street from the mansion is an even more impressive building, an expansive, restored manse designed by Frank Lloyd Wright and owned by the state. He also has a small fleet of aircraft and, in Chicago, impressive offices atop the James R. Thompson Center in the heart of the central business district.

Although this stature and the resources of the office are real, the personal style of the governor determines how effectively they will be put to use. Richard

Ogilvie (1969–72), Dan Walker (1973–76), and Jim Edgar (1991–98) lacked the expansive, outgoing personalities of Thompson, Ryan, and Blagojevich. The first three used the stature and resources of office less, and less effectively, than did Thompson and Ryan, who genuinely enjoyed entertaining and rubbing elbows with legislators, lobbyists, the media, and business leaders. Thompson used the mansion and funds from his campaign chest for annual as well as spur-of-the-moment parties and dinners. A Protestant, Thompson regularly celebrated certain Jewish holy days with Jewish lawmakers and friends. At the adjournment of each legislative session—often beginning at 2 A.M. or later—Thompson and later Ryan hosted legislators, staffers, lobbyists, and journalists for a lively pre-dawn party on the lawn of the executive mansion.

Alan Rosenthal observes that to be effective with legislators, a governor generally needs several traits. One is to "stand tall," that is, to have a strong personality and presence and be willing to use that personality to "get tough" from time to time. The chief executive also needs to be willing to rub elbows with the lawmakers, consult with them, massage their egos, and "talk turkey," that is, be willing to use the powers of his office in making deals on legislation.[28]

If a governor is selective in his proposals, makes use of blue-ribbon commissions to generate consensus, takes his case to the people (which Thompson and Blagojevich did with enthusiasm in whirlwind fly-around press conferences throughout the state), and works the legislature from the inside, he can achieve considerable success in getting his programs enacted.[29] Thompson did all of these things with gusto. As a result, he had generally good, though not always successful, relations with the legislature. Blagojevich had a more confrontational style with the legislature, once referring to them as a "bunch of drunken sailors" in their spending habits.

A governor needs all the powers and skills he can muster, for powerful constraints are imposed on him. In addition to sharing his authority with other executive officers, a governor confronts a legislature that is often controlled by the opposition party. The legislature tries to live up to its textbook billing as an independent, co-equal branch of government. During the fourteen years Thompson was governor, the Democratic opposition controlled both chambers of the General Assembly, with the exception of 1981–82, when Republicans had a majority in the house.

The role of the federal government in state government also limits and frustrates a governor. Many of the laws enacted in Washington are designed to be administered by the states and paid for with a combination of state and federal funds. Prime examples include air and water pollution programs, the Medicaid program for the poor, the No Child Left Behind education program, vocational rehabilitation, and transportation. Federal funds account for about one-quarter of the Illinois budget; the U.S. Congress and federal bureaucrats leverage that funding to direct the manner in which major state programs are run.

During the 1980s, for example, there was a major difference of opinion between the federal and Illinois environmental protection agencies about how to meet federal clean air standards. The U.S. Environmental Protection Agency (EPA) insisted on an automobile inspection program; Illinois countered that it could achieve the objectives more effectively and less expensively in other ways. The EPA rejected the Illinois proposal and threatened to withhold $350 million in federal highway funds. Governor Thompson appealed personally to President Ronald Reagan, to no avail. With no other recourse, Illinois set up automobile inspection programs.

The state and federal courts also tell a governor how to do his job. During the early 1980s, for example, the state often reduced prisoners' sentences by more than ninety days to alleviate prison overcrowding. In 1983 the Illinois Supreme Court ruled that the executive branch lacked legislative authority to cut sentences by more than sixty days. Prison populations began rising immediately.[30] Dealing another setback for gubernatorial authority, in a major 1990 decision the U.S. Supreme Court, by a 5-4 vote in *Rutan v. Republican Party of Illinois*,[31] declared unconstitutional Thompson's awarding of thousands of jobs based on merit examination combined with political party sponsorship.

Inside the Governor's Office

Of the governor's several roles, management of state government occupies less time and attention than might be imagined. As Thompson put it: "Governors really, especially in the latter part of their service, don't manage the state. If they're still managing the state after their first term, they ought not to be governor."[32] Most governors derive greater personal satisfaction and political rewards from the pursuit of other functions such as formulating policy, steering programs through the legislature, building popularity and support among the public, and helping develop the state's economy.

Ogilvie enjoyed the management role. Yet a study of his schedule for one month, done by one of his assistants, found that he spent less than one-fifth of his time on management of state government.[33] As state government's responsibilities have grown, so has the complexity and size of the governor's office. In 1993 there were 190 employees in the office itself, ranging from schedulers to Washington lobbyists and "ethnic group assistants."

Rod Blagojevich operated with a governor's office staff of 99 persons in 2007.[34] He clearly did not relish the hands-on management role. He rarely worked from either his Springfield or his Chicago office, instead preferring to deal with staff through conference calls from his home office.[35]

This staff helps the governor make decisions—for instance, what legislation to propose, how to resolve a policy dispute between two agencies, whom to appoint as an agency director, how to satisfy the demands of an interest group, and which speaking invitations to accept.[36] In performing this role, the staff provides two important and related services: it manages the flow of information to the governor and serves as a surrogate with the groups that want the governor's attention.

Information flows in a variety of ways: memos, email, audio-video hookups between Chicago and Springfield, discussions with staff or agency personnel, staff debates within the office, contact with outside advisors, newspaper articles, and meetings with interest groups or legislators. Because it is impossible for the governor to attend to all who seek his favor, a staff member acting in the governor's stead can have a strong impact on the boss's image.

The use of staff as a go-between has some obvious tactical advantages. It tends to preserve flexibility on issues because the governor can always disavow the position taken by a subordinate. The surrogate also can sometimes say no for the governor, insulating him from that unpleasant duty.

A governor typically delegates the coordination of his staff to a deputy who has been called chief of staff, deputy governor, or chief of governmental operations. The deputy governor's job is a bit like being a secretary-general of the United Nations because the governor's office is at times not so much an organization as an alliance among nations. The reason is twofold. First, the organization of the office reflects the conflicts that are a fundamental part of state politics. Differences among staff members mirror the conflicting interests of the state's various political viewpoints. Second, it is difficult for any governor to delegate power. A governor draws legitimacy from being the person elected to do the job. The authority of anyone acting in the governor's place can be easily undercut or become suspect unless continually supported by the governor directly. Because power is personal and not hierarchical, the notion of organization can become something of an exotic concept in the governor's office.

Ideally, the deputy governor runs the office to accommodate the decision-making style of the governor. That style may involve open debate among staff, preparation of detailed decision memos by staff, acted on without much discussion, advice from people outside government, or a combination of approaches. Thompson's style encouraged staff at various levels to have direct communication with him in policy deliberations. Edgar operated a more traditional hierarchical office, with policy recommendations flowing up to the chief of staff through a "super cabinet" of seven executive assistants, each with functional areas of responsibility. A hands-off manager, Blagojevich delegated extensive responsibility to deputy governors, a chief financial officer, and the director of the Governor's Office of Management and Budget (GOMB).

This office is part of the executive office of the governor yet generally operates somewhat apart from the rest of the governor's staff. The budget process gives the work of the GOMB a much more structured focus than other staff activities. Budget analysts are hired by senior GOMB staff, and there is less major staff turnover with a change in governors. For these and other reasons, the office tends to have an institutional life of its own,

During the budget process, conflict sometimes arises between the GOMB, which sees its role as to constrain agency spending, and the agencies, which typically want increased spending authority. Some disagreements can only be resolved by the governor. Influential interest groups also have a stake in the process. Most groups tend to want more spent on behalf of their constituents. All must be dealt with, and often the governor must take the lead.

The GOMB plays a significant role in the governor's office because mistakes in budgeting can cost the governor dearly. There are tremendous political pressures to spend more tax dollars or to give tax relief and virtually no pressure to control that spending. Yet the constitution requires a balanced operating budget, at least in cash terms, and a governor who allows spending to get out of control runs the risk of severe embarrassment. Thus the GOMB must carefully monitor both revenues and agency spending. For example, spending for the $13 billion Medicaid program doubled during Jim Edgar's first term, growing each year far beyond GOMB estimates. This created turmoil for the rest of the budget and forced the governor to cut spending in other areas and pare back growth in education appropriations.

Links to Agencies and the Legislature

Executive assistants based in Chicago and Springfield provide the governor with primary day-to-day linkages with more than sixty state agencies, including many not under his direct control, such as the state boards of education and higher education. The executive assistants are also the chief executive's eyes, ears, and voices in relations with interest groups, the legislature, and citizens. Each has an area of policy and management responsibility such as education, human services, or economic development.

Executive assistants try to increase cooperation among agencies and often have to mediate disputes among them. Agencies often have narrow responsibilities that overlap with those of others. Children's services, for instance, are delivered by several agencies, including the Departments of Children and Family Services, Healthcare and Family Services, and Human Services and the State Board of Education. Regulation of drinking water is shared by EPA and the Department of Public Health. Public Health shares responsibility for inspecting and certifying nursing homes with the Departments of Labor, Financial and Professional Regulation, Healthcare and Family Services, and Human Services, along with the State Fire Marshal.

The governor and his staff face even stiffer challenges in maintaining effective relationships with the General Assembly. The legislature must enact substantive legislation—much of it proposed by the governor and his agencies—and pass the annual budget. The legislature also oversees the executive branch through committee hearings, biennial audits by the auditor general, and review of agency rule-making by the Joint Committee on Administrative Rules. The legislature thus maintains a presence in virtually every area of executive branch activity, which makes good relations with lawmakers crucial to the success of a governor's tenure.

It is not surprising that a governor will often select a former lawmaker or legislative staff member to supervise his legislative office. For example, former legislator Jim Edgar, before serving as secretary of state and as governor, was director of Governor Thompson's legislative office. Familiarity with the members of each house, their personalities, and the politics of their districts is essential if the head of legislative affairs is to be an effective strategist for the governor.

Generally, the legislative office lobbies for passage of the governor's budget and other initiatives and works against bills that would be politically embarrassing for the governor to sign or veto. The legislative office channels information about legislative developments back to the governor and other members of the governor's staff, serves as a contact point for legislators who wish to deal with the governor or an agency, and provides legislative advice to other gubernatorial staff and agencies.

In order to be effective, the office must develop a close working relationship with the leaders of the governor's party in each house of the legislature. The staff must work through the leadership in selecting sponsors for administration bills, communicating the governor's position with regard to major legislation, scheduling legislative activity, and developing overall legislative strategies. Because much legislative work is done in committee, the staff must also work closely with the committee chairs and the minority spokespersons.

The governor maintains a traditional lawyer-client relationship with the lawyers on his staff. They advise him about the extent of his statutory and constitutional authority and explore with him the legal implications of individual decisions. Usually the governor appoints a chief counsel who supervises several lawyers. In addition to providing assistance with specific issues, the legal staff spends a considerable amount of time working with agency lawyers on litigation—particularly cases that are politically sensitive, involve large judgments against the state, or could commit the state to new and recurring program expenditures. The attorney general is designated by the constitution as "the legal officer of the state," but with the exception of environmental issues, the bulk of the governor's legal work is conducted by agency lawyers with the attorney general's concurrence.

The legal staff also engages in more routine activities. The constitution allows the governor to "grant reprieves, commutations and pardons" to convicted criminals. Four times each year the Prisoner Review Board refers fifty or so requests for commutation from prisoners to the governor's office. The legal staff reviews each one and makes a recommendation to the governor.

The lawyers also draft executive orders, which must be limited in scope to operations within the executive branch, and review all legislation passed by the General Assembly for adherence to the constitution and for legal consistency. The latter activity keeps the lawyers well occupied from July to September.

Shifting Role for Patronage

With the largest bloc of jobs in the state under their control, governors often depend on personal contacts and political recommendations when hiring employees. Patrons have been political party leaders, legislators, influential lobbyists and interest group leaders, elected officials, their staffs, and friends.

The political culture that dominates Illinois has long tolerated the practice of sponsored jobs; it was understood that elected officials would use their influence to gain employment for supporters, friends, and relatives. In return, the people assisted would provide support to the governor and his party.[37]

Federal courts, however, have placed significant constraints on patronage. In 1972 a federal court in Chicago declared that it was unconstitutional to fire an employee for political reasons. As a result, patronage activity in Illinois shifted its focus to job openings, inasmuch as it was still acceptable to hire qualified employees on the basis of patronage considerations. During the Thompson years, nearly every one of about five thousand job vacancies that occurred annually came under intense scrutiny by the governor's patronage office to see if an important patron had a candidate he or she wanted to sponsor for the opening.

As noted above, in 1990 the U.S. Supreme Court declared it unconstitutional to use political party affiliation or support as a consideration in hiring, promoting, transferring, or recalling non-policymaking employees.[38] The decision appears to be narrowly focused on patronage related to political party affiliation. In other words, it is now unconstitutional to favor one job candidate over another solely because one has a record of voting for the party of the governor and the other does not. The decision does not appear to address the practice that expanded in the 1980s wherein legislators of both parties would personally recommend job candidates.

Despite these legal limitations, a strong expectation continues among participants in the web of Illinois government and politics that job openings should be filled after consideration of the desires of patrons. Meeting these expectations legally is the job of the governor's patronage office.

The head of the patronage office has often been a key political advisor to the governor and a major link to influential people. Virtually every employee hired by the state must meet some qualification in the form of educational credentials, experience, or test results. When two candidates meet the job requirements, the role of the patronage office is to ask, "Why not hire the person friendly to our administration, or earn a credit with a legislator who can be helpful to us later?" It is a difficult role to perform, as recalled by Donald Udstuen, patronage director for Governor Richard B. Ogilvie:

> It's an impossible job in a lot of ways. On the one hand, you've got county chairmen crawling all over you thinking that all you've got to do is snap your fingers and their guy's got a job. Then you've got the agencies and the personnel system to deal with.
>
> Let's say you get an agency's okay, then you still have to make sure all the civil service requirements are met. That can take a lot of time and a lot of party people get impatient. They can't understand the delays. That's one of our biggest problems. That, and the fact that there are just not enough jobs.[39]

Political patronage in hiring and promotions in non-policymaking positions exacts a price from the professional civil service system. Paul Craig, himself a veteran former senior civil servant in Illinois, notes, "When politicians use their office and power to advantage someone, they seldom ask who is being disadvantaged."[40] Craig cites illustrations of career civil servants having been denied deserved promotions because of political placements. This,

Craig avers, diminishes overall professionalism in state offices and reduces the important "discretionary effort" from civil servants who have been demotivated and demoralized by unfair or inequitable personnel treatment.

Many appointments are to nonpaying positions on boards that advise agencies on such subjects as endangered species, group insurance for state employees, migrant labor camps, swine brucellosis, and beekeeping. But there are also boards with significant regulatory powers and paid commissionerships such as the Illinois Commerce Commission, the Pollution Control Board, and the Liquor Control Commission. Other appointed boards such as the Dangerous Drugs Commission and the Delinquency Prevention Commission actually administer programs. In most cases, there is a requirement that no more than a majority of members appointed to a board or commission may be of the same political party.

The existence of so many boards and commissions stems from several factors. There is the desire to provide a formal mechanism for public participation in agency programs, including that of technical specialists. They have also been created to separate sensitive quasi-legislative and quasi-judicial functions from direct executive control in order to promote the perception of fairness or to keep these functions out of politics, which they generally do not. Governor Blagojevich and his office apparently kept a tight rein on his appointees to boards and commissions, who reportedly were expected to behave as directed by the governor's office.

Most governors since Ogilvie (1969–72) have maintained special units to receive and process citizens' complaints and to serve as outreach offices for certain programs or constituencies. Under Governor Edgar there were special assistants for Asians, Latinos, ethnic minorities, African Americans, and women.

Other sections of the governor's office provide basic support services. For example, the scheduling office receives scores of invitations each month for the governor to speak or appear at various functions. The staff processes and organizes these invitations and works with the governor, his personal aides, and senior staff to arrange the governor's schedule.

Agencies Try for a Low Profile

Although the governor and his staff are not involved in day-to-day management of the twenty departments under the chief executive's jurisdiction, the governor's performance is often judged on how well these agencies function. This can be problematic, because even here the governor does not have unfettered discretion. The major interest groups expect to have some influence over who is selected to run the programs that affect their members or constituents. The unions, for example, expect to have a say in who heads the Department of Labor; at the Department of Agriculture, it is the Illinois Farm Bureau; and so it goes throughout the organization chart. Groups that object strongly to a gubernatorial appointment can attempt to stall or prevent required confirmation by the senate.

Once appointed and confirmed, directors gradually become part of a bureaucracy, with concerns and interests that often differ from those of a governor. Agencies and their subdivisions have long-standing relationships with local and federal bureaucracies, old ties to legislators and legislative committees, and strong commitments to existing procedures. The directors may owe their appointments to the governor, but they are quickly exposed to new claims on their loyalties.

For these reasons, subtle tensions often develop between the governor's office and an agency director and her staff. A former social services director observes:

> The biggest burden in running an agency is that created by many people who have their fingers in our pie. For example, you have: the governor's liaison with this agency; the governor's liaison to the rate review board [which sets purchase of service rates paid by the state]; the patronage director; the legislative liaison office.
>
> And the Governor's Office of Management and Budget, which is "knee deep in what we can and can't do"; the appropriations staffs in both houses, as well as between parties . . . ; several key legislators who have an interest in the agency; Art Quern and Paula Wolff in the governor's office [former chief of staff and program office director], and the interest groups. All of which makes for a great number of people telling you how to do your job. However, the buck stops with the director. These other people are not accountable and indeed often back away very quickly when something goes wrong.[41]

Government agencies are not run like a business, nor can they be. There are no profit-and-loss measures of accountability, and, indeed, state agencies feel a strong need to spend all their money by the end of the fiscal year or their budgets might be cut the following year. On-the-job performance is also difficult to assess. The quality of foster care provided to thousands of children is more difficult to evaluate than is the production rate of zero-defect earthmovers or cellular phones.

The lack of a clear bottom line allows a governor and agency directors to slip into fuzzy measures of success. Thus "no news is good news" is a byword for how well a director is doing. If the director keeps bad news about an agency from popping up on the evening news, then presumably everything is going well. Other techniques are to prevent problems from reaching the governor's desk, stay within the budget, and keep the lid on situations that could become volatile.

That sounds simple enough, but it has been a Herculean task for the directors of complex, demanding agencies such as the Department of Corrections, the Department of Human Services, and the Department of Children and Family Services. Each of these agencies has been given responsibilities and public expectations that cannot be met with the funding provided, if at all.

Skilled agency directors and senior staff are crucial teammates of effective governors. Without them, the chief executives become reactive, defensive administrators and have little opportunity to become mentioned in the history books among the strong managers, great builders, or social reformers who have now and then made their mark in Illinois.

7.

The Courts

● ● ● ● ● ● ● ● ● ● ● ● ● ●

The entangling of the courts with politics should come as no surprise to anyone in a state that elects its judges. Illinois voters nominate judges in partisan primaries and elect them to the bench in general elections. It is easy to see that in cases tried or appealed in the courts there will always be winners or losers. In any case, court decisions resolve conflicts, enforce community norms, stigmatize people, apply statutes or determine their constitutionality, and legitimize or reject decisions made elsewhere in state or local government. Clearly, litigants have the opportunity to wield power through the courts for political purposes.

The judicial branch of Illinois state government handled more than 4.5 million cases in 2007.[1] On a day-to-day basis, the courts hand down decisions rooted in constitutional, statutory, and common law in civil and criminal cases. At trial, the trier of fact—either a jury or a judge without a jury (in a bench trial)—will weigh the evidence adduced at trial, and based on the findings of fact the judge will then render a decision and enter a final judgment on the merits of the case. Subject to the rules of the supreme court, the parties in the case may have a judgment or order reviewed on appeal.

Litigation falls into two general categories: civil and criminal. In civil cases a complaint typically involves disputes about divorce, child custody, contracts, mortgage foreclosure, personal injury, or property damage. Civil cases usually pit individuals or businesses against each other, and both sides usually pay private attorneys to represent them while they litigate the cases in court. The court may enter judgments for money damages or orders that declare the rights of the parties to a case or controversy, or it may issue injunctions.

In contrast, a criminal case directly implicates the government's fundamental responsibility to preserve public safety and order. A state's attorney, on behalf of the people of the state of Illinois, prosecutes a defendant individual or business for violations of the criminal code. On a finding of guilt, the court may enter judgment that sentences a criminal defendant to penalties that range from monetary restitution to victims to imprisonment in a county jail or state prison to, in capital cases, death.

Given the tremendous power vested in the courts, the question often arises whether the people should elect judges. Should we replace elections with an appointment process that selects judges based on their legal qualifications? Should the people depend on the judges to keep watch over themselves and protect the public from judicial corruption or abuse? What should the process be to remove corrupt judges from the bench? What is the appropriate balance of power among the co-equal branches of state government? How far can the legislative and executive branches of government go in telling the courts how to sentence criminal defendants? How far should the courts go in interpreting statutes, rules, or procedures, in determining their constitutionality, or in resolving conflicts between the executive and legislative branches of government?

This chapter examines these questions after explaining the framework of the court system and examining the major issues that confront the Illinois courts.

Unified System with Three Levels

In contrast to many states, Illinois has a court system that is neat and orderly in structure. Under the current unified system, there are only three layers of courts statewide with no overlapping jurisdictions: the circuit courts, the appellate courts, and the supreme court, which oversees the administration of the entire system.

The supreme court has seven members elected from five judicial districts; the larger first district (Cook County) elects three judges. The voters elect justices on a partisan ballot for a ten-year term. If a judge decides to serve a second (or additional) term, he or she is placed on a retention ballot. The judges are nominated in party primaries. In 2009 the Democrats had a four-to-three majority on the Illinois Supreme Court.

The justices have historically been white males, but following developments elsewhere in the electoral process, the first African American was elected to the court in 1990 and the first woman in 1992. In 2009 two women and one black male sat on the court.

The intermediate courts are the appellate courts. The judges sitting in these courts also serve ten-year terms and are subject to a retention vote. An appellate court is located in each of the five judicial districts. In 2009 there were twenty-four appellate judges in the first district (Cook County), nine judges in the second district, seven in the third district, seven in the fourth, and seven in the fifth, for a total of fifty-four appellate judges.[2]

The trial courts of general jurisdiction are the circuit courts. The state is divided into twenty-three judicial circuits. Cook, DuPage, Lake, McHenry, and Will Counties each consist of a single circuit. The legislature determines the number of judges in the other circuits, which depends on the circuit's size and amount of business; the minimum number is three judges. In 2007 there were 525 circuit judges in Illinois, 186 of whom were in Cook County.[3] The term of the circuit judges is six years, and the retention ballot is used.

Legislators in the General Assembly often try to increase the number of judges in their districts. Each circuit has at least five judges. Each county also has at least one resident circuit judge, who is elected from that county alone, bringing the total number of downstate circuit judges to more than two hundred.

The constitution provides for the appointment of associate judges who have limited jurisdiction. The elected circuit court judges appoint the associate judges to four-year terms and, like elected judges, they must be licensed attorneys. In 2007 there were about four hundred associate judges in Illinois.[4]

The Circuit Court of Cook County is much larger than downstate circuit courts; indeed, it is the largest court in the world. As a result, its structure is more complex.[5] It has much more specialization than do the twenty-two downstate circuits. Cook County has a separate section for mechanics' liens and a whole division for domestic relations, for example, and it uses "holiday" (weekend) and evening narcotics courts to keep the wheels of justice moving seven days per week.

The Illinois Constitution places administrative authority for the entire system in the supreme court; it is exercised by the Chief Justice.[6] The supreme court submits the annual judicial budget to the General Assembly. It also appoints certain support staff headed by an administrative director, makes temporary assignments of judges, appoints judges to vacancies, and creates rules to provide for the orderly flow of judicial business.

State government pays for the salaries and benefits of the judges on all three levels. County governments provide office and courtroom space and support staff to assist the circuit judges, primarily through the county-level office of clerk of the circuit court.[7]

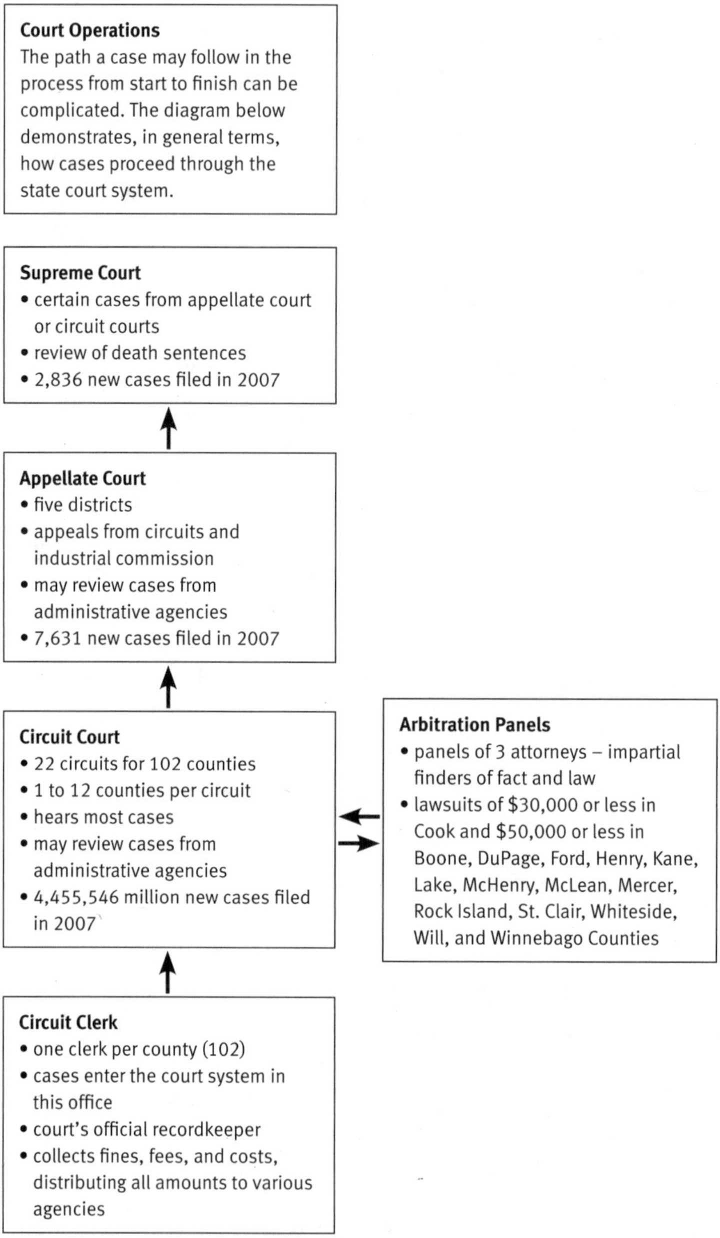

Court Operations
The path a case may follow in the process from start to finish can be complicated. The diagram below demonstrates, in general terms, how cases proceed through the state court system.

Supreme Court
- certain cases from appellate court or circuit courts
- review of death sentences
- 2,836 new cases filed in 2007

Appellate Court
- five districts
- appeals from circuits and industrial commission
- may review cases from administrative agencies
- 7,631 new cases filed in 2007

Circuit Court
- 22 circuits for 102 counties
- 1 to 12 counties per circuit
- hears most cases
- may review cases from administrative agencies
- 4,455,546 million new cases filed in 2007

Arbitration Panels
- panels of 3 attorneys – impartial finders of fact and law
- lawsuits of $30,000 or less in Cook and $50,000 or less in Boone, DuPage, Ford, Henry, Kane, Lake, McHenry, McLean, Mercer, Rock Island, St. Clair, Whiteside, Will, and Winnebago Counties

Circuit Clerk
- one clerk per county (102)
- cases enter the court system in this office
- court's official recordkeeper
- collects fines, fees, and costs, distributing all amounts to various agencies

Fig. 7.1. Illinois court system. Source: Illinois Supreme Court, 2006.

Judges for Sale in Cook County

Although many want to take politics out of the courts, this issue motivates only a fraction of those who push for merit-based selection. Most proponents want a merit or appointive system because they believe that it is essential to reduce the unethical or criminal behavior that has steadily cropped up throughout the history of Illinois's judicial system.

Although the judicial disciplinary system has generally been successful elsewhere in Illinois, it has not been in Cook County. In the 1980s and early 1990s, for example, federal (not state or county) prosecutions resulted in the sentencing of sixteen judges for crimes including racketeering, bribery, mail fraud, and perjury. The judges were part of a deep-seated case-fixing network that involved crooked lawyers, bagmen, Chicago alderman Fred Roti, and Illinois state senator John A. D'Arco. In the two separate investigations known as Operation Greylord and Operation Gambat, fifty-seven attorneys were also convicted along with twenty-six criminal justice employees, including court clerks, deputy sheriffs, and police officers.[8]

Attorney Terrence Hake, who posed as a crooked lawyer, and a downstate judge, Brocton Lockwood, who wore a tape recorder inside his boot and played the role of a good old boy who needed extra cash to support his womanizing and drinking, gathered much of the evidence for the Greylord convictions.[9] It took Hake three months to gain entry into the clandestine network that could fix cases with certain judges,[10] while Lockwood worked his way into the fraternity of opportunistic judges. Over a three-year period, the moles, with the support of FBI agents and U.S. Attorney Dan Webb, developed cases against dozens of individuals, whose court testimony in turn implicated dozens of others.

Judge Richard LeFevour's corrupt system provided acquittals of drunk-driving and other traffic cases in return for $100 bribes. "The miracle workers [crooked lawyers] would leave a list of the cases they wanted fixed and in what courtrooms. Judge LeFevour would then assign bribe-taking judges to those courtrooms. Later the attorneys would drop off their payments with the judge's cousin and bagman, Jimmy LeFevour.[11]

Judge Reginald J. Holzer corrupted the chancery court, which heard civil cases involving injunctions, class actions, mortgage foreclosures, declaratory judgments, and contract matters. Judge Holzer had a different scheme: he "borrowed" money from parties whose cases were before him. He awarded receiverships to Ernest Worsek, a businessman who in turn loaned the judge $15,000, then $10,000 more and then another $10,000, which the judge never paid back. Holzer squeezed $10,000 from attorney Russell Topper, who stood to earn $200,000 in fees in a damage suit before Holzer. Bernard S. Neistein, a former state senator, arranged a $10,000 bank loan for Holzer. When the judge made no payments, Neistein paid it back himself.[12]

Eleven other judges were convicted in the Greylord scandal, each with his own corrupt system and circle of accomplices. While those cases went to trial and made the Chicago headlines, Operation Gambat was using a corrupt lawyer who had turned informant, Robert Cooley, to infiltrate Chicago's infamous First Ward organization.[13] Long rumored to have ties to organized crime, the organization was run by Alderman Fred Roti and his party secretary, Pat Marcy, who used politically connected judges to fix cases involving everything from civil matters to murder. Cooley passed $72,500 to Marcy and Roti after Judge Thomas J. Maloney acquitted four men of the murder of Lenny Chow. In another case, Marcy handed Cooley an envelope containing $7,500 to reward Judge Frank Wilson for finding accused hitman Harry Aleman not guilty. Wilson later committed suicide. In a third case, this one in the chancery court, Marcy encountered difficulties. Judges were apprehensive because of Operation Greylord, and a new system of random computerized case assignments made it difficult (but not impossible) to place a case before a cooperative judge. When the computer picked Judge David Shields, Marcy thought the case was lost. Then he learned from attorney Pat DeLeo that Shields would "do whatever we want. . . . This thing is no problem."[14] The fix cost $5,000 and led to convictions of both DeLeo and Shields.

The operations had the approval of the chief judge for the U.S. District Court for the Northern District of Illinois (Chicago) and the U.S. Department of Justice and were groundbreaking for their use of hidden microphones in the private chambers of two judges. Some observers questioned whether federal prosecutors had been too aggressive in using a sting operation to increase the number of convictions.[15] However, Judge Lockwood concluded his book with a defense of the approach: "I believe the Jimmy Hoffa case, Watergate, Abscam and Operation Greylord were all necessary and appropriate steps in re-establishing the very basic principle that, in this country, no person or group regardless of power and prestige, is above the law."[16]

Leaving aside the issue of sting operations as an investigative tool, the point for this book is that the Illinois judicial disciplinary system did not bring about the many convictions. This is not to say that the local powers had not investigated the courts in Cook County; they had, and the Judicial Inquiry Board filed complaints against several Cook County judges over the years. Nevertheless, the disciplinary process had clearly been inadequate to address the biggest breakdown in the history of the Illinois judicial system.

Selection of Better Judges

The corruption issue drives the question of whether there is a better way to select judges. Voters in Illinois have elected trial, appellate, and supreme court judges since 1848. A 1962 amendment to the constitution reaffirmed the election of judges and provided a new method for voters to evaluate judges in office. Judges who seek another term notify the secretary of state of their desire. A question is placed on the ballot that asks whether the judge should be retained in office for another term. There is no party designation on the ballot. The 1970 constitution requires a three-fifths majority vote for retention.[17]

Supporters of election of judges tend to be populists of the Andrew Jackson school of thought. They believe that the people should pick their own judges just as they elect officials to the executive and legislative branches. Election, they argue, provides accountability by allowing voters to remove judges who have failed to maintain standards of judicial conduct or who have become incapacitated. In the 1970 vote on a new state constitution, voters decided to retain the election of judges in a side issue to the main document.

The argument for appointment of judges, often termed a "merit" system, is that it will bring better qualified attorneys to the bench and provide a more independent judiciary. Elections, some argue, involve judges in political matters that might later affect their independence on the bench, leading to the type of corrupt practices uncovered by Operation Greylord.

Proponents of the appointive system and their allies in the legislature have tried since 1970 to get the issue on the ballot as a constitutional amendment. No proposal has passed both legislative chambers yet. One reason is that subsidiary issues have divided the proponents. Some want local option, with each circuit or county deciding whether to have an appointive system. Others say appointments should be limited to the supreme and appellate courts. Most proponents, including the bar associations, have argued that the governor should make the appointments after receiving nominations from a screening committee.[18]

In what may be a boost to proponents of judicial merit selection systems in the future, the U.S. Supreme Court has ruled that federal due process required disqualification of a state court judge from participating in the decision of a case in which a litigant had contributed three million dollars to the judge's campaign for election. The court reasoned that the appearance of impropriety required the recusal of the judge.[19] The decision seems to add weight to the argument that the way to avoid undue influence in the courts is to replace judicial elections with merit selection systems.

Choosing from a Field of Unknowns

One enduring criticism of the elective system is that voters usually have little or no knowledge of the candidates on the ballot. The bar associations over the years have issued evaluations of candidates for the judiciary,[20] as have the state's major newspapers, but these endorsements attract little attention among voters. In the 1986 Cook County spring primary, three judicial candidates endorsed by Chicago mayor Harold Washington won despite being rated "unqualified" by the Chicago Bar Association. The *Chicago Sun-Times* in 1994 acknowledged the ineffectiveness of the primary system when it editorialized: "Once again, unqualified candidates in abundance are guaranteed subcircuit judgeships by merely surviving a crowded and confusing primary election."[21]

This is not so surprising when one considers that the various lawyers' groups cannot agree among themselves as to which judicial candidates are qualified.[22] In 1986, for instance, the bar associations did not disapprove of the performance of Judge Joseph E. McDermott, who had been publicly accused of taking bribes in traffic court and who was willing to go to jail rather than testify before a federal grand jury. McDermott received the largest vote in the primary and the second-highest in the general election of any judicial candidate. He did not serve, however, owing to his eventual conviction in federal court.

Another factor in the election of judges, particularly in Cook County, is the large number of candidates on the ballot. In 2008 in Cook County, seventy judges were up for retention in the general election. The Chicago Bar Association found that all but four were qualified. On Election Day, the voters looked over the excruciatingly long list of judges and retained them all.

Even the conscientious voter who consults newspaper editorials and advertisements of the bar association ratings is likely to be overwhelmed by such a list. In practice, many voters work down the list with no real knowledge of the candidates or skip the judicial part of the ballot entirely.

Campaigns for the Bench

Traditionally, Illinois judicial candidates have campaigned for office in a less obtrusive manner than those running for the legislature or statewide constitutional offices. Although the amount of money spent on judicial campaigns has increased, it had been far less than the increases in funds spent for other elective offices. Nonetheless, the mold of understated judicial campaigns was broken in 2004 in the contest for the supreme court in southern Illinois.

The 2004 race pitted an incumbent Democratic appellate court justice, Gordon Maag, against a challenger, Lloyd Karmeier, a Republican circuit court judge. A former clerk for an Illinois Supreme Court justice and a federal judge, Karmeier had spent eighteen years on the bench. He eventually won what many at the time considered the nation's costliest judicial race.[23]

Rather than candidates' qualifications, the public policy issue of tort reform dominated the elections. The race turned into a full-blown battle between trial lawyers and labor unions, on one hand, and business and the medical profession, on the other, led by the U.S. and Illinois Chambers of Commerce and the Illinois State Medical Society. The dominant issue involved the size of jury awards for individuals or classes of individuals allegedly injured by smoking or acts of medical malpractice. The campaign cost a total of $9.3 million, more than eighteen of the thirty-four United States Senate races decided on Election Day, and at the time more than any American judicial race.[24] *Business Week* magazine ran a story on the extraordinarily expensive race with the headline "The Threat to Justice."[25]

The unprecedented spending in the race was not an accident. According to a judicial watchdog group, Illinois's Fifth Appellate Judicial District, anchored by Madison County, had earned a national reputation for large tort jury awards, including a $10.1 billion award against tobacco giant Philip Morris.[26] Moreover, supreme court justices make appointments to fill lower trial court vacancies within their respective districts, so this particular race became a "must-win" contest of wills and treasuries between the rival interest groups.

A subsequent race for the Illinois Appellate Court in the same judicial district in 2006 cost $3.3 million, a replay of the fight over tort reform with a similar configuration of combative interest groups. Clearly, those spending large sums of money in judicial campaigns believe that the judiciary affects their interests. In addition, while polls show that the public appears to favor either public funding of judicial campaigns or appointment of judges, there is little movement by the legislature toward either policy.[27]

The Judiciary and State Government

As a co-equal branch of state government, the judiciary has many interactions with the executive and legislative branches as it vigilantly struggles to uphold its independence. In 1992, after the Greylord and Gambat scandals, the supreme court formed the Illinois Supreme Court Special Commission on the Administration of Justice. In their final report, known as the *Solovy Report* after chairperson and attorney Jerold S. Solovy, the commission declared, "Judicial independence is an essential feature of democracy. Yet the

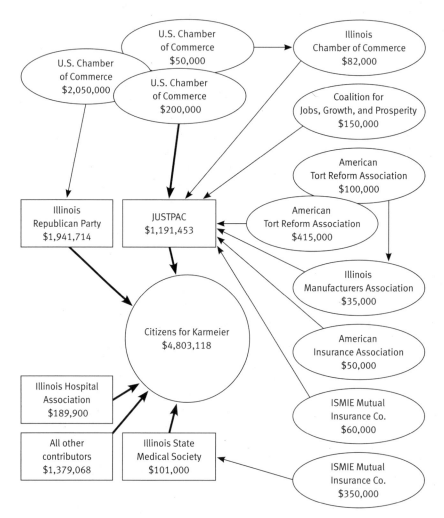

Fig. 7.2. Illinois campaign finance reporting: Business and medical interests. The figure illustrates campaign finance reporting by significant business and medical donors. Entities other than Citizens for Karmeier, including political parties and PACs, may have received contributions in addition to those illustrated here. In addition, amounts contributed to those entities could be spent for purposes other than Karmeier's campaign. Consequently, amounts received by those entities will not necessarily equal amounts contributed to the campaign. Source: Illinois Campaign for Political Reform, 2005.

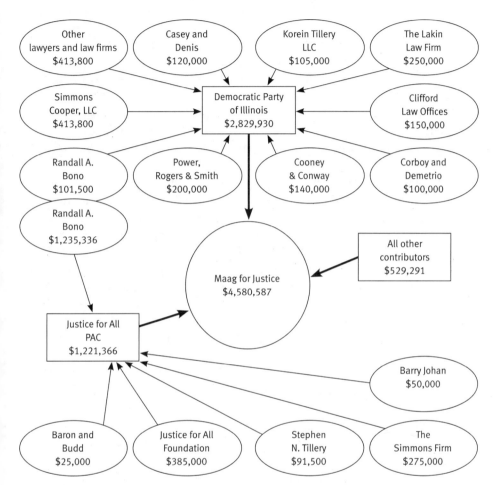

Fig. 7.3. Illinois campaign finance reporting: Lawyers and law firms. The figure illustrates campaign finance reporting by significant lawyer and law firm donors. Entities other than Maag for Justice, including political parties and PACs, may have received contributions in addition to those illustrated here. In addition, amounts contributed to those entities could be spent for purposes other than Maag's campaign. Consequently, amounts received by those entities will not necessarily equal amounts contributed to the campaign. Source: Illinois Campaign for Political Reform, 2005.

principle of judicial independence is seriously eroded when elected officials or other political figures are able to manipulate judicial cases and the selection of associate judges. Enhancing judicial independence by insulating the judiciary from the political system remains an urgent need."[28]

It would be very difficult if not impossible to completely extricate the courts from the entanglement of politics. With regard to some issues the judiciary has the final word, but with others, it simply does not. An obvious example is that, though the supreme court prepares and submits its own budget, it depends on review by the legislature, passage by both houses, and the approval of the governor for the enactment of appropriations bills that include the court's budget.

Illinois has a strong separation of powers clause that states: "The legislative, executive and judicial branches are separate. No branch shall exercise powers properly belonging to another."[29] Separation of the courts from the legislative branch was tested in a ten-year running controversy between the supreme court and the auditor general, a constitutional officer appointed by the legislature.[30] The main issue was whether the auditor general could audit the funds of two judicial agencies administered by the court: the Attorney Registration and Disciplinary Commission and the Board of Law Examiners. These two funds are not appropriated by the legislature; rather, the court collects fees from lawyers and candidates for the bar for the respective funds.

The auditor general nonetheless ruled that these were public funds, but the supreme court claimed that the commission and the board are not state agencies under article 8 of the constitution. The media generally were on the side of the auditor general, as were the delegates to the 1970 Constitutional Convention when they reconvened unofficially in 1987. They passed a nonbinding resolution saying it had been their intent to give the auditor general the power and duty to audit these two agencies. Even so, the supreme court considered its refusal to permit the audit a matter of constitutional principle: "The independence of the Judicial Branch of State Government is a fundamental precept of government which is grounded on the constitution's separation of powers clause and the inherent power of courts to safeguard their authority. The branches of government must cooperate with each other but such cooperation is subordinate to the doctrine of separation of power."[31]

As it turned out, personalities may have had as much to do with the battle as constitutional rights. In 1990, after the legislature appointed a new auditor general, the court made overtures to heal the division and requested that the new official audit the very same judicial agencies.

In 1997 yet another clash between the legislature and the courts took place. The Illinois house launched impeachment proceedings against the Chief

Justice of the Illinois Supreme Court, James D. Heiple, to remove him from the bench. The controversy erupted from his alleged misconduct during a series of traffic stops in which the judge was accused of disobeying police and abusing his position to avoid speeding tickets. A special house investigative committee, on a vote of 8-2, issued a report that concluded that Heiple "was 'imperious,' 'arrogant' and discourteous to his colleagues, but that those shortcomings still did not amount to an impeachable offense."[32] The two dissenters were also the only two who were not attorneys. Heiple, who was the first Illinois judge threatened with impeachment by the legislature since 1833,[33] retired when his term on the court ended on December 3, 2000.

Another lesson concerning separation of powers unfolded in the process involving the fiscal 2003 budget. Thirteen years earlier, the Compensation Review Board had determined that judges' salaries should include cost of living adjustments (COLAs), adjusted annually. The legislature suspended the COLAs, however, including those for judges. The legislature later acknowledged that this violated the constitution, which read in part, "Judges shall receive salaries provided by law which shall not be diminished to take effect during their terms of office."[34] Accordingly, to remedy the situation, legislature included payment of the fiscal 2003 COLAs in the budget for fiscal 2004.

When the fiscal 2004 budget bill reached Governor Blagojevich's desk, he vetoed the judicial COLAs. The supreme court issued an order—without any pending complaint or petition before it—to State Comptroller Dan Hynes and ordered him to pay the COLAs, but he refused to obey. Circuit court judges then filed a class action suit demanding payment of the COLAs for judges, and the trial court found that their elimination was unconstitutional and ordered payment. On appeal, the supreme court found that the COLAs had fully vested in 1990 and that efforts to block their payment violated the constitution. Moreover, the court ruled that a defense of legislative immunity was inapplicable and that the judiciary had authority to compel payment without a specific appropriation.[35] Thus the skirmish ended, and the state paid the judges' COLAs.

Blanket Clemency and Justice

Under the state constitution, the legislature has the power to enact statutes that specify the sentences the courts may impose on criminals convicted of serious crimes. The legislature enacted the statutes codified in the Illinois Criminal Code that defined classes of crime from first-degree murder down to Class C misdemeanors and provided parameters for sentencing for each crime. This sentencing approach has raised some controversy in Illinois, especially because the state's "get tough" policy resulted in longer sentences and a skyrocketing state prison population. For offenses designated Class X crimes, including such offenses as armed robbery, home invasion, and trafficking in controlled substances, the sentencing statutes eliminated probation and mandated the courts impose lengthy prison terms up to sixty years.

Governor James Thompson, a former federal prosecutor, pushed these statutory changes to sentencing through the legislature in fulfillment of a campaign promise. In a special message to the legislature on October 25, 1977, Thompson said, "To the criminal, Class X says that if found guilty, you will go to jail for a substantial period; you will not beat the system through probation or a slap on the wrist. To the prosecutor, Class X says no more lenient sentences for violent offences. Class X is a message that everyone can understand. It says the people of Illinois will no longer tolerate violent crime. That is the message we need to make a dent in the unacceptable rate of violent crime."[36]

Earlier in 1977 Thompson had signed legislation reinstating the death penalty. The first execution was held on September 12, 1990. The second, in May 1994, was that of serial killer John Wayne Gacy. By that time, there were 154 others awaiting execution on Illinois's Death Row.

The last execution in Illinois occurred in 1999. That was George Ryan's first year in office, and it was evident that there were serious doubts about the death penalty—the courts had overturned several murder convictions because of insufficient evidence. Because of this, Ryan appointed a commission to study the death penalty. In the meantime, the governor, with the cooperation of Attorney General Jim Ryan, declared a moratorium on executions. At the time, no death row inmates had completed all of the necessary appeals, which meant that there was no case ready that would require the attorney general to petition the supreme court for a final execution order, which was necessary before an execution could occur. As a matter of law, a governor has no authority unilaterally to suspend a final execution order; rather, the constitution gave a governor the power to grant reprieves, commutations, and pardons. In reality, the governor's moratorium was based upon the tacit agreement by the attorney general not to seek any final execution orders from the supreme court in the event that any death row inmate completed all appeals.

Meanwhile, the governor's commission reviewed all cases of death row inmates and heard testimony from prosecutors, private defense attorneys and public defenders, and other interested groups and individuals. The commission recommended extensive changes in the law and procedures involved in the investigation and trial of capital cases. Legislation was introduced that incorporated the commission's recommendations, but the legislature did not enact it before Governor Ryan left office in January 2003.

In the final months of his administration, Governor Ryan had concluded that he could not trust the justice system in all death penalty cases. During his last year in office, all inmates on death row either had filed a clemency petition or had one filed without their consent by a third-party advocate. In January 2003 the governor announced a "blanket clemency" for all inmates whom the courts had sentenced to death. Thus he chose to give full pardons to four inmates and commuted the death sentence of the remaining 167 death row inmates to life without parole.

Death penalty opponents praised this action, but Attorney General Lisa Madigan filed a writ of mandamus in the Illinois Supreme Court that challenged the action on several grounds. *Mandamus* is a Latin word that means "we command." A writ of mandamus is a court order that requires another court, government official, public body, corporation, or individual to perform a certain act. The attorney general asked the court to command the director of Department of Corrections and the wardens of Pontiac and Menard state prisons to refuse to record commutation orders by Governor Ryan or expunge the orders if they had already recorded them. The court denied the petition.

Madigan alleged that a governor lacked authority to commute sentences for inmates who failed or refused to consent to their clemency petitions. The court acknowledged that the Illinois constitution grants authority to the legislature to regulate the clemency application process, and in fact statutes enacted required an inmate's consent.[37] Nonetheless, this did not restrict the governor's constitutional authority to act on such terms as he thought proper. Rather, the Illinois Constitution granted a governor unlimited power to issue as many pardons or commutations as he wished to whomever he wanted, even if an inmate had not requested it.[38] Nor did the governor's action create a separation of powers issue, because he had not exercised any power of the judiciary when he granted the blanket clemency. However, the court's opinion concluded with this admonition to future governors: "As a final matter, we note that clemency is the historic remedy employed to prevent a miscarriage of justice where the judicial process has been exhausted. . . . We believe that this is the purpose for which the framers gave the Governor this power in the Illinois Constitution. The grant of this essentially unreviewable power carries with it the responsibility to exercise it in the manner intended. Our hope is that Governors will use the clemency power in its intended manner—to prevent miscarriages of justice in individual cases."[39]

When Governor Rod Blagojevich took office in January 2003, he ostensibly continued the moratorium, though Ryan had obviously rendered the issue moot when he emptied death row. On the other hand, in Blagojevich's first term, the legislature did pass most of the reforms recommended by Governor Ryan's commission on the death penalty, which Blagojevich signed into law. From 2003 until early 2009, homicide convictions have resulted in about thirteen death sentences; those inmates await execution on death row. Nevertheless, because the appeal process in a death penalty case takes several years to complete, as of early 2009, no inmate sentenced to death by an Illinois court had completed the appeal process. Until that has occurred or a death row inmate has waived all remaining appeals, there would be no pressure on an attorney general to seek a final execution order, nor a genuine test of a governor's moratorium on the death penalty.

Judicial Review and the Age of Statutes

Today most law is of the statutory kind, and the statutes enacted by the legislature are the primary source of the state's public policy. Before the mid-nineteenth century, however, the judiciary in Illinois typically made public policy using the common law. This differed from statutes enacted by the legislature since it was comprised of legal principles and rules of action that relate to governance and security of persons and property, the authority of which was based solely on traditional usages and customs. Another source of common law came from the judgments and decrees of the courts recognizing, affirming, and enforcing such usages and customs, particularly the ancient unwritten law of England.

The early-nineteenth-century common-law courts assumed that judges were better suited to discover the law as it existed and apply it to fit the needs and circumstances of a given case or controversy before the court. Conversely, they viewed the legislature's function as merely to codify common-law precedents and correct any technical deficiencies.

The rise of legislation in Illinois, and elsewhere among the states, began around the mid-nineteenth century, and the reaction of the common-law courts to the surge of legislative policy making accounts for an inherent tension that naturally exists to this day between these co-equal branches of government. Initially, the courts reacted with hostility and protected common-law principles from legislative encroachment by narrowly interpreting new statutes. The balance of power between the legislature and the judiciary has since evolved into the modern doctrine of separation of powers. With the shift from common-law courts as the source of public policy to the modern age of statutes as the primary source of law, the courts have embraced their role of interpreting and applying statutes to the facts or circumstances of a case before the court or determining the constitutionality of a statute, a function known as judicial review.

In *Kunkel v. Walton,* the Supreme Court in 1997 noted that the "cardinal rule of statutory construction, to which all other canons and rules are subordinate, is to ascertain and give effect to the true intent and meaning of the legislature. *Solich v. George & Anna Portes Cancer Prevention Center of Chicago, Inc.*, 158 Ill. 2d 76, 81, 196 Ill. Dec. 655, 630 N.E.2d 820 (1994). In doing so the court should look first to the statutory language, which is the best indication of the legislature's intent. *Solich*, 158 Ill. 2d at 81. Where the meaning of an enactment is unclear from the statutory language itself, the court may look beyond the language employed and consider the purpose behind the law and the evils the law was designed to remedy. *Solich*, 158 Ill. 2d at 81. Where statutory language is ambiguous, it is appropriate to examine the legislative history. *People v. Hickman*, 163 Ill. 2d 250, 261, 206 Ill. Dec. 94, 644 N.E.2d 1147 (1994). However, when the language is clear, it will be given effect without resort to other aids for construction. *Hickman*, 163 Ill. 2d at 261; *Solich,* 158 Ill. 2d at 81."[40]

The plain meaning of the statute in the *Kunkel* case required that personal injury plaintiffs give written and signed medical release forms, but it was silent about judicial safeguards against abuse. The statute as written and enacted by the legislature required unlimited disclosure of medical information, and the court declared that as a matter of statutory construction it was "not at liberty to depart from the plain language of a statute by reading into it exceptions, limitations or conditions that the legislature did not express."[41] Yet the court then reviewed the constitutionality of the statute and declared that it violated the constitution.

Another example of judicial review is another 1997 case in which the Illinois Supreme Court invalidated the state's sex offender notification statute because it violated the state constitutional requirement that bills be confined to a single subject.[42] According to the high court, "What the Framers sought to do was avoid legislation being passed which, standing alone, could not muster the necessary votes for passage."[43]

Prior to the *Johnson v. Edgar* case, the court had construed single-subject challenges liberally. So long as the various parts of the bill in question related to the overriding subject of the bill, then the court deemed the single-subject proviso to have been met. As an illustration, consider a bill whose subject was transportation or schools, and all the elements of the bill related to those subjects, respectively; that bill fulfills the single-subject requirement.[44] In *Johnson,* however, the court departed from its precedent and instead examined whether each part related to the others, rather than each part to the bill's overall purpose or subject. Consequently, legislation that the court once would have deemed properly drafted had become vulnerable to constitutional challenge.[45]

The bill under challenge in *Johnson* amended twenty-three existing statutes, most with provisos that were in some way related to criminal law or criminal procedure. But the bill also created an Environmental Impact Fee Law, which imposed a fee on refiners and manufacturers of fuel. Proposed earlier in the legislative session as an independent bill, the impact fee had failed. The Cook County Circuit Court, which had been the trial court in the case, declared the many-faceted bill "a textbook case of the situation that Article IV of the Illinois Constitution was enacted to prevent, that is, attaching an unpopular bill to a popular one to circumvent legislative input or scrutiny."[46] The supreme court affirmed the trial court ruling that the legislation was unconstitutional.

Subsequent single-subject decisions by the state high court have reinforced the *Johnson v. Edgar* decision.[47] Because of the sudden turnabout in the court's interpretation of the single-subject proviso, Michael J. Kasper, a former top aide to House Speaker Michael Madigan, asserted that "the Supreme Court has greatly limited the legislature's flexibility in combining even tangentially related matters during the legislative process."[48]

Interest groups also turn to the courts to seek judicial review. In the *State Chamber of Commerce v. Filan,* an Illinois business trade group sought in 2005 to invalidate higher fees imposed by the governor on employers who utilized the Industrial Commission, which adjudicates claims of injury under the Workers' Compensation Act.[49] The chamber of commerce contended that the increased fees bore no relation to the cost of operating the commission; therefore, the increase violated various provisions of the state constitution. Although the supreme court declined to decide whether increasing to balance the state budget violated the constitution, it returned the case to the Cook County trial court for further proceedings.[50]

The consequences of a decision that is favorable to the state chamber would be significant because the decision would call into question similar fee increases in about three hundred different programs and funds of state government that total several hundred million dollars annually.

Illinois Courts Shun Progressive Role

One of the most far-reaching potential roles for a court system is to interpret the state constitution in a manner that attempts to engineer societal change. There have been trends toward doing so in other states, for instance, in the name of protecting citizens' liberties and individual rights on the basis of broadened interpretation of state constitutions rather than merely imitating federal constitutional law. The Illinois courts, on the other hand, are generally conservative and defer to the legislature when it comes to making public policy.

One area in which other state courts assumed a progressive role in recent years has been in the revamping of school financing formulas, especially where large disparities existed between poor and wealthy districts. For example, courts in California, Kentucky, Texas, Montana, and New Jersey have declared school funding provisions unconstitutional.[51] Because Illinois has similar disparities, thirty-seven school districts, twenty-two children and their parents, and an education rights group filed a lawsuit. In the 1992 case of *Committee for Educational Rights v. Edgar,* plaintiffs sought a declaratory judgment that the statutory scheme governing the funding of public schools violated the Illinois Constitution. The trial court dismissed the complaint for failure to state a cause of action, and plaintiffs appealed.[52]

The crux of the *Edgar* case was the state's overreliance on local property taxes for school funding. Plaintiffs argued in the supreme court that the statutory school finance scheme and the failure of the state to provide sufficient state aid violated the state's equal protection clause[53] and the education article.[54]

The supreme court in *Edgar* held that disparities in educational funding that resulted from differences in local property wealth did not violate the Illinois Constitution's education article or the equal protection clause.[55] Moreover, the court held that the question of whether the educational institutions and services were of "high quality" as required by the constitution was "outside the sphere of the judicial function" and that the "legislature was the proper forum to undertake education reform."[56] The court affirmed the dismissal of the lawsuit.

Justice Charles E. Freeman dissented, and he focused his opinion on the "high quality" aspect of the education article.[57] In his analysis Freeman acknowledged that the basic sovereign power of state resides in the legislature—in theory, there is no need to grant any power to the legislature—and limitations written into the Illinois Constitution were restrictions on legislative power and were enforceable by the courts. For this reason, according to Justice Freeman, constitutional directives to the legislature were mandates or commands to the legislature to act.[58]

He first examined the education clause in the 1970 constitution and then compared it with the one in the 1870 constitution. Section 1 of article 10 of the Illinois Constitution of 1970 provided:

A fundamental goal of the People of the State is the educational development of all persons to the limits of their capacities.

The State shall provide for an efficient system of high quality public educational institutions and services. Education in public schools through the secondary level shall be free. There may be such other free education as the General Assembly provides by law.

The State has the primary responsibility for financing the system of public education."[59] (emphasis added)

Justice Freeman focused on plaintiffs' allegations that an educational funding system was not an efficient system when some children had quality educational resources and others had minimal resources. He rejected the majority's conclusion that the high-quality education requirement in the education clause of the Illinois Constitution is not judicially enforceable.[60] The lynchpin of his argument was the 1870 education clause, which states: "The *general assembly* shall provide a thorough and efficient system of free schools, whereby all children of this state may receive a good common school education" (emphasis added).[61]

The 1870 constitution, Freeman noted, contained an education clause that was directed to the "general assembly"; on the other hand, the 1970 constitution's education clause is expressly addressed to the "State"—not the legislature only. Freeman concluded that the provision in the 1970 version is a constitutional directive to all three branches of state government to fulfill their duties in accordance with their traditional roles under the principles of separation of powers.[62]

He then addressed the plaintiffs' contention that the state cannot provide a high-quality education to some students and not to others. According to him, the plaintiffs clearly alleged that children in poor school districts receive an inferior education. He stated that educational resources and services in poor school districts are so inferior to those provided to enriched school districts as to violate the education system provision.[63]

Justice Freeman concluded: "Unfortunately, by holding that the high quality aspect of the education system provision is nonjusticiable [outside the sphere of the judicial function], the majority today abandons its responsibility to interpret the Illinois Constitution. The judiciary joins the legislative and executive departments in failing to fulfill our state government's constitutional responsibility of providing for an efficient system of high quality public education."[64]

In 2008 the Chicago Urban League and the Quad County Urban League in the Chancery Division of the Circuit Court of Cook County filed a lawsuit

(Case No. 08CH30490) that once again challenged the way Illinois funds its public schools.[65] The gist of the plaintiffs' case concerned documented achievement gaps among schools and funding disparities among school districts. The trial court dismissed all counts of the complaint except for Count I, in which plaintiffs alleged that the public school funding scheme violated the Illinois Civil Rights Act of 2003.

Section (a) (2) of the Civil Rights Act provides that "no unit of State, county, or local government in Illinois shall . . . utilize criteria or methods of administration that have the effect of subjecting individuals to discrimination because of their race, color, national origin, or gender."[66] Under Illinois law, in order to plead a cause of action under the Civil Rights Act, plaintiffs must allege membership in a protected class and a causal link between the use of criteria or methods of administration by units of state, county, or local government and the plaintiff's injuries. The trial court concluded that the complaint sufficiently alleged that "the school funding system adopted and implemented by the Defendants has the effect of subjecting African American and [Latino] students to discrimination because they attend schools in 'Majority Minority Districts.'"[67] This designation refers to schools where the majority of the student populations are members of an ethnic or racial minority group.

The plaintiffs seek an order that declares the current state statutory school finance scheme to be in violation of the Illinois Civil Rights Act and that enjoins the Illinois State Board of Education from using it to finance public schools. The court order could compel the General Assembly to enact legislative reform concerning the way Illinois funds education, including the provision of adequate funding to provide access for all students to high-quality education. The outcome of this case has the potential to affect public education in Illinois in the decades to come.

The Perfect Storm

The arrest of Rod Blagojevich in December 9, 2008, set in motion a dynamic collision among the powers that be in Illinois, including the state supreme court.[68] Within a week, Attorney General Lisa Madigan had filed a petition in the supreme court seeking an order compelling the removal of the governor from office because of pending federal corruption charges. The unprecedented case, filed pursuant to Supreme Court Rule 382 and article 6, section 3, of the Illinois Constitution, challenged "the ability of the Governor to serve."[69] The court, on December 17, 2008, swiftly dismissed the petition without comment.

Notwithstanding the federal charges, the governor intensified the already raging storm by offering to Roland Burris the appointment to the U.S. Senate seat about to be vacated by Barack Obama. In a press conference with Blagojevich on December 30, 2008, Burris accepted his nomination. The U.S. Senate refused to seat Burris, however, without a document signed by the Illinois secretary of state attesting to the validity of the appointment. The secretary of state refused to countersign and affix the seal of the state to the document because of the scandalous circumstances surrounding the nomination.

Despite the court's apparent efforts to stay out of it, Roland Burris pulled it back in to the pounding storm. Burris filed a petition for a writ of mandamus on January 2, 2009, in which he demanded that the supreme court order the secretary of state to sign the validating documentation. On January 9, 2009, the court denied the petition. On January 15, 2009, the U.S. Senate relented, and Vice President Dick Cheney swore in Roland Burris as a U.S. senator.[70]

On January 26 the full force of the gathering storm struck in the state senate with the impeachment trial of Blagojevich, which, as provided by the state constitution, was presided over by Chief Justice Thomas R. Fitzgerald. The designated prosecutor was Speaker of the House Michael J. Madigan's legal counsel, and the fifty-nine state senators acted as the impeachment tribunal, each of them having sworn an oath to "do justice according to law."[71] All three co-equal branches had now joined in a precedent-setting political trial[72] that resulted in the conviction of the governor and his removal from office.

It had been the perfect political storm. Thus, although many have argued over the years that Illinois judges must keep their distance from the legislative and executive branches of government and remain independent and above the fray, in reality, politics has always inextricably entangled the courts.

8.

The Intergovernmental Web

• • • • • • • • • • • • •

In our federal system, powers are formally divided between the national, that is, federal government, and the state governments. The local governments are, in contrast, creatures of their respective state's constitutions and laws. In the real world, however, the federal government heavily influences, even controls many state-administered programs, because of superior revenues and aggressive policy making by Congress, the president, and the federal bureaucracy. Even the creatures of state government at the local level exert strong pressures on state government through organized lobbies and local political power centers. This chapter provides an overview of Illinois local governments and of the relationships among the federal, state, and local governments.

Illinois has more units of government than any other state.[1] With 6,039 local governments in 2005, Illinois far surpassed Pennsylvania and its 5,032 units. With 1,292 municipalities, Illinois leads all states. With its 876 school districts it ranks high in total numbers among the states as well. Illinois has 1,433 townships that serve as active governments in most but not all of Illinois's 102 counties; the township is not found in most eastern states. Illinois also leads in numbers of special districts (discussed below), at 2,220.

Several factors contributed to the growth of local governments in Illinois. First, as noted in chapter 1, Illinois platted townships as part of the Northwest Ordinances of 1785 and 1787. Township governments continue to function in

Illinois, primarily to maintain rural roads. Most states outside the Midwest operate without township government.

Second, the 1870 constitution limited the debt of each local government to 5 percent of assessed property valuation. Local civic leaders, therefore, simply created special district local governments, with their own debt capacity, to overlay on the cities, townships, and counties. Third, Illinois has always had a large number of school districts, though the 876 districts that existed as of 2006 represent a continuing decline from the 12,000 districts, most of them one-room districts, that existed prior to World War II (see table 8.1).

Table 8.1. Number of Taxing Districts by Type, 1996–2005

Type of district		Year		
		1996	2000	2005
Counties		102	102	102
Townships[1]		1,433	1,433	1,433
Road districts[2]		92	91	77
Cities, villages, & incorporated towns		1,286	1,287	1,292
School districts	Elementary	389	383	377
	Unit	407	408	397
	High	105	102	101
	Non-high	1	1	1
	Community college	40	39	39
	Total school districts	942	933	915
Special districts	Fire protection	826	830	836
	Park	351	359	362
	Multi-twp. assessment	345	345	341
	Library	312	328	337
	Sanitary	144	142	127
	Cemetery	31	34	33
	Airport authority	28	28	28
	Street lighting	25	26	26
	Mosquito abatement	21	21	21
	Hospital	20	18	18
	Water authority	17	17	16
	River conservancy	14	14	14
	Forest preserve	13	13	13
	Mass transit	11	11	6
	Other	39	39	42
	Total special district	2,197	2,225	2,220
Total—all types		6,052	6,071	6,039

Source: Illinois Department of Revenue, 2006.
1 Townships include road and bridge districts.
2 Commission counties only

This bewildering array of governments gives Illinois and metropolitan Chicago the distinction of being the nation's largest experiment in decentralized government.[2]

The maze of overlapping jurisdictions is so thick that most Illinois residents live under the jurisdiction of eight or more local governments. Fairly typical are residents of Urbana, who could, if they had the time and energy, become active in the nine governments they purportedly control: the city, county, township, school, Urbana park, and community college jurisdictions and the Champaign-Urbana sanitary, public health, and mass transit districts. The first six of these have elected boards, and the last three have appointed boards. Residents pay property taxes to each of these.

Each local government is either a general- or special-purpose government. General-purpose governments include municipalities and counties and, to a lesser degree, townships. Townships are controversial, and their elimination is proposed from time to time because, with their generally narrow functions, they are considered by many reformers to be an unnecessary layer of government. Seventeen counties, mostly in southern Illinois, have historically operated without townships under the commission form of county government, which elects three commissioners to conduct their business, including functions that are otherwise the purview of townships.

Special or limited-purpose governments provide a particular service to a particular geographic area; they include school, fire protection, mosquito abatement, and sewer districts, as well as authorities organized to operate exposition halls, convention centers, airports, ports, and mass transit systems.

The large number of government units in Illinois, some argue, provides an opportunity for many persons to participate in democracy. Indeed, by one estimate there are sixty-five thousand elected and appointed local officials in Illinois.[3] Because power and decision making are broken down into small and distinct areas, the argument goes, citizens have more "public choice" and "local option" in the type of government they want and can pick and choose which functions their area needs or desires.

Although this may be so, the multiplicity of governments also provides a shield for weak performance, uncoordinated regional planning, and lack of accountability to citizens. The same functions that are managed in unified fashion in other states or regions are often fragmented and duplicative in Illinois. Instead of one bureaucracy, there are several; instead of one or two arenas of power, there are five or seven or ten. The extreme case is the seven-county metropolitan Chicago area, which comprises 1,450 governments with taxing powers. Here, regionwide problems of transportation, land-use planning, and flooding are solved piecemeal or not at all.

With so many governments, public oversight is necessarily limited, and lines of authority between one local government and another are blurred. As a result, featherbedding, favoritism in contract awards, and other forms of corruption have surfaced repeatedly among local governments in Illinois. As far back as 1928, officials at the Chicago-area Metropolitan Sanitary District "looted the public till through payroll padding, phony expense accounts, nepotism, mismanagement, and improper favors, among other malpractices," writes the historian Robert P. Howard.[4] In 1994 the daughter of a former Chicago alderman admitted to taking paychecks—without actually working—from three separate local government agencies: the Cook County clerk's office, the Cook County sheriff's office, and the city council's Finance Committee.[5] Similar stories have emerged from forest preserve districts, park districts, school districts, and other subunits of Illinois government.

Despite these difficulties, the multitudinous local governments and their citizens have in general fiercely defended the current structure, beating back most efforts to merge or eliminate government units. Officials for the municipal, county, township, and special district units each have one or more strong statewide lobbying organizations in Springfield such as the Illinois Municipal League and more than twenty area municipal councils. Special district lobbies include the Illinois Association of Park Districts and similar organizations for library, fire protection, civic center, forest preserve, and mass transit districts, among others. County officers such as sheriffs, treasurers, and clerks also have their own lobby organizations. In addition, more than one hundred units of local government hired sixty-five lobbying firms in 2007 to push for particular objectives, spending more than $5 million in the efforts.[6] The Regional Transportation Authority of metropolitan Chicago alone spent $223,600 on four separate lobbying contracts. The authority was successful in 2007 in winning an increase of one-quarter of a percentage point in sales tax revenues for its operations.

Some of the resistance to consolidation comes from the fact that local governments are the "farm teams" for membership in the state legislature and for the major political parties, sometimes providing patronage positions for the parties.

With the exception of the school districts, where the teachers' unions have more power than the Illinois Association of School Boards, these local government lobby groups can usually defeat legislative efforts to make changes. The concept of local control and local accountability—however difficult it may be to wield—remains a cornerstone of Illinois's individualistic culture.

Citizens have an argument in support of the state's multiplicity of governments, on the basis of the low ratio of government employees to overall population. Although it is counterintuitive to most observers, the Illinois governments rank among the lowest of all the states in number of employees per unit of population. Illinois had 637,000 state and local government full-time-equivalent employees in 2005, or 499 employees per 10,000 residents, making Illinois forty-eighth in the nation, versus a national average of 537 per 10,000 population.[7] About 500,000 of the total are strictly local government employees.

Good local leadership can help cut through the tangle of local governments, but even conscientious citizens might have trouble keeping track of candidates at the local elections, which in Illinois are a strange mixture of partisan and nonpartisan races. In nonpartisan elections, there are no party labels on the ballot. In partisan elections, the national party labels (Republican and Democrat) or local party labels (for example, Peoples and Citizens) appear on the ballot. The local parties in some places are fronts for the national parties; in other places they represent local groupings of citizens concerned with one or more issues. In still other places, local party labels are simply devices for getting candidates' names on the ballot.

There is no consistency to this approach. In one of Illinois's twin cities, the elections are nonpartisan in Champaign and partisan, with national party labels, in Urbana.

Some persons would argue that all local elections should be partisan. Such a system would create political bonds between neighboring or overlapping governments, possibly improving cooperation across regions and boosting the strength of local and, over time, state parties as well. The "good government" element, however, argues for nonpartisan local elections because "there is no Republican or Democratic way to clean the streets." With no agreement forthcoming, the strange mixture of elections continues, possibly discouraging cooperation among governments.[8]

State Assistance to Local Governments

The large number of local governments complicates not only local-to-local relations but also those between local governments and the state. All local governments (except those with home-rule powers, discussed below) have to look to the state statutes for their authority to function. The superior position of the state in the state-local hierarchy is clear enough on paper, but in reality the legislature and the administrative agencies of state government simply cannot police six thousand governments directly.

The *2008 Catalog of State Assistance to Local Governments* identifies 230 state financial assistance programs and another 150 technical assistance programs for Illinois local governments.[9] Financial programs include grants for public library services for the blind and physically handicapped, soil and water conservation, housing, fire protection, museums, and drug enforcement, to name a few. Technical assistance services include computerized data, group health insurance information, and the provision of surplus property, among many others.

In 2007 grants and shared taxes distributed to local governments (not counting school districts) totaled $7.5 billion.[10] For example, the Department of Revenue distributes to cities and counties a percentage of the state income tax receipts as well as personal property replacement tax monies. Similarly, the state Department of Transportation distributes a portion of the motor fuel tax revenues to counties, municipalities, and townships. In addition, Illinois provides salary subsidies and bonuses to many local officials, including state's attorneys, assessment officers, county clerks, police, and probation officers.

Much of the state's business on a day-to-day basis, in fact, involves serving the needs of local communities. The Department of Children and Family Services licenses child care facilities; Commerce and Economic Opportunity consults with local governments on business; and Corrections establishes and enforces standards for local government sheltered care, detention, and correctional facilities. The Department of Public Health approves payment of state and federal funds to local health programs and services.

Most state departments must carry on regular relations with their local counterparts. But this does not mean that the state exerts a great deal of control. Local government discretionary authority in Illinois is high compared to other states. The now defunct U.S. Advisory Commission on Intergovernmental Relations ranked Illinois twelfth among the states overall and tenth for the relative authority of cities (because cities with more than twenty-five thousand residents have home rule authority in Illinois, unless they reject it).[11] Such rankings give credibility to the sentiment that Illinois local governments have considerable freedom from state government regulation.

Governor Richard B. Ogilvie in 1969 thought the answer to improving state-local relations was a new department, the Department of Local Government Affairs, a one-stop agency for local governments to interact with state government. At that time, the department received much federal money that was to be distributed to local governments. The department was also interested in improving local government management, particularly in fiscal affairs.

The agency as conceived did not last. A reorganization report titled *Orderly Government*, prepared for Governor James Thompson in 1977, recommended that the department be abolished and its functions transferred to other agencies. Thompson implemented the recommendation in part when he created the Department of Commerce and Community Affairs by executive order in 1979. That agency is now the Department of Commerce and Economic Opportunity, with no mention in its name of local government or community services.

For Bigger Players, Home Rule

True to the individualistic culture of the state, Chicago and many smaller cities had bristled under the state's authority since the nineteenth century. They wanted home rule—the ability to make their own decisions, raise their own revenues, and in general be able to make decisions without first asking the state for permission. They got what they wanted when the 1970 constitution went into effect on July 1, 1971.

The constitution established home rule for Cook County and all municipalities with more than twenty-five thousand residents. Unlike other states, where voters have to approve a charter in a local referendum to receive such powers, the grant of home rule was automatic in Illinois. Municipalities with fewer than twenty-five thousand residents can also secure home rule by a vote of the people, and larger cities can vote out home rule by the same referendum process.

Home-rule units in Illinois "may exercise any power and perform any function pertaining to its government and affairs including, but not limited to, the power to regulate for the protection of the public health, safety, morals and welfare; to license; to tax; and to incur debt." Some limitations are spelled out in the constitution, but the courts are admonished that the "powers and functions of home rule shall be construed liberally."[12]

The 1970 constitution also provided that county governments with an elected chief executive automatically became home-rule units. Cook County was the only county to qualify for this power, and though other counties can qualify by adopting the chief executive office by referendum, all such referenda have failed. The state's second-largest county, DuPage, debated whether it qualified for home rule. The full-time chairman of the DuPage County Board is elected on an at-large basis. The issue was whether he is a chief executive officer as prescribed in the constitution. The *Chicago Tribune* said in an editorial in 1990: "Jack Knuepfer [the board chairman] committed political suicide when he insisted on the eve of the March [1990] primary that the county, like Cook, had 'home rule' power—the right to govern itself."[13] The editorial concluded: "With home rule authority, DuPage would have the power to manage its own affairs and chart its own future. Knuepfer understands that. Someday, the voters of DuPage may understand that, too. For now, they at least should appreciate that someone with nothing more to lose is trying to point the way for a county with a lot to gain." Knuepfer was defeated in the March 1990 primary.

In 1987 James Banovetz and Thomas Kelty surveyed ninety-five Illinois municipalities and found that home rule was used in a wide variety of ways to change local conditions. In descending order of importance, the uses were new debt (89 percent), regulations (72 percent), regulatory licensing (61 percent), intergovernmental agreements (58 percent), new taxes (57 percent), property transactions (43 percent), new sources of nontax revenues (36 percent), changes in government structure (28 percent), and consolidation of property tax levies (26 percent).[14]

Banovetz and Kelty found that once this power is used, most municipalities prefer to keep it; when the question to retain home rule was put to the voters in twenty-five municipalities, twenty-one voted for its retention. The four municipalities abandoning home rule were Lisle, Villa Park, Lombard, and Rockford. The Illinois Supreme Court also has been "pro-home rule," according to Banovetz and Kelty. They classify thirty-one court decisions handed down between 1972 and 1987 as favorable to home rule and twenty as unfavorable. Last, the General Assembly has reacted cautiously to bills that preempt home rule; only a handful of such bills have been approved since 1972.

Two-thirds of the state's population is now governed by home rule because, with a few exceptions, it is in place for the state's largest municipalities and its most populous county. Still, that leaves a lot of downstate and suburban counties and about six thousand other government units that remain subject to the common law principle known as Dillon's rule, the cornerstone of municipal law since 1872, which holds that a local government has only that authority specifically granted by the state constitution and its statutes.

"State mandates," which direct local governments and school districts to provide a benefit or service, represent the flip side of home rule. For example, the state legislature from time to time increases pension benefits for local government employees—without providing the funds to pay the benefits. A 2008 compilation listed 105 mandates that school districts must fulfill, including instruction in AIDS prevention, manners and etiquette, principles of free enterprise, and pride in work. In addition, statutes also require Illinois school districts to collect data about obese students, provide pregnancy counseling, and close school for selected ethnic and national holidays, among many other mandates.[15] In 2008, a propos of the sub-prime mortgage crisis, another mandate was added that requires instruction on "the basic process of obtaining a mortgage" as well as the difference between fixed-rate and adjustable-rate mortgages. A State Mandates Act passed by the legislature in 1980 was intended to limit mandates and provide state assistance in paying for the mandates. In recent years, however, most school mandate legislation includes at the bottom of each bill a proviso that exempts the bill from the State Mandates Act.

Experiment in Decentralization

The wide freedom of choice in the way local government conducts its affairs remains at the philosophical core of the decentralized approach. Like all freedoms, this one carries responsibilities, the most prominent being the creation of local governments that can manage themselves well. At the most prosaic level, that means creating responsible recordkeeping systems, communicating well with other agencies, and remaining accountable to the taxpayer.

The very nature of the decentralized system makes it difficult to gauge how well local governments are doing these jobs. Local governments are not audited by any state agency. They are required to file either annual financial reports or audits with the Illinois comptroller, but that office lacks the staff to review the reports and the authority to cause a local government to change its financial practices. The comptroller does provide a summary financial document about each type of government—municipalities, counties, townships, and special districts. (The state board of education performs this function for school districts and has tighter control.)

The value of the reports filed with the comptroller has been questioned. A study by the Taxpayers' Federation of Illinois concluded, "As it is currently constituted, the annual financial reporting requirement set forth in Illinois law is a useless exercise because the data collected is inadequate to satisfy basic research. The reports appear to be relatively worthless for comparative tax purposes."[16]

Because of varying approaches to management and widely divergent agendas, it is no wonder that local governments have a difficult time presenting a common front in Springfield. Most government units in Illinois are organized into statewide lobbying groups—for cities, townships, and villages—with the overall aim of improving the local governments' authority vis-à-vis the state government. But even with a strong financial base, the Illinois Municipal League has a hard time representing the needs of the rapidly growing northeastern cities along with the problems of the many declining municipalities downstate. Chicago, East St. Louis, Aurora, and Naperville all have their own sets of problems. In order to address these differences, separate regional groupings of municipalities have been developed for lobbying purposes. For example, there are strong mayors' and managers' organizations in DuPage and Will Counties, in the southern Cook County suburbs, and in other regional groupings throughout the state.

Pushing for the expansion of such operations, the Metropolitan Planning Council in 1991 wrote that the council "helps members save money through joint purchasing, training programs for municipal employees, and joint testing of police and fire candidates. Special programs address issues that cross jurisdictional boundaries, including solid waste, cable franchising and storm-water management."[17]

The council's report on intergovernmental cooperation was based on interviews of fifty-seven political leaders, planners, and budget experts. Authors Deborah Stone and Joyce O'Keefe noted that many problems "leap jurisdictional boundaries." In addition, large-scale issues, most notably the dispersion of jobs away from areas with affordable housing, the disparity in spending by school districts, and the worsening problem of traffic congestion throughout the metropolitan area, beg for regional solutions. But better relations among governments will not be easy to create. "The region is extremely fragmented, and those regional efforts that do exist are themselves fragmented either by geography or policy area. There is a serious lack of trust between municipalities and counties, local governments and the state, and the city and suburbs."[18]

Trust may be increasing, if slightly, as a result of the 1997 creation by Chicago mayor Richard M. Daley of the Metropolitan Mayors' Caucus. Each of the nine metropolitan mayors' and managers' associations sends delegates to the caucus, which represents 273 municipalities. The caucus has worked on economic development, reliability of electricity, affordable housing, emergency preparedness, and other topics; the caucus agrees to avoid topics of certain conflict such as expansion of O'Hare International Airport and a possible third airport.

The Chicago Approach

Even if regional cooperation could be developed, the state is likely always to be affected by difficult relations between its biggest city and the state government. As by far the largest municipality in Illinois at almost 2.9 million people, Chicago as a geopolitical region wields a level of political power disproportionately greater than its numbers. Legally, Chicago is a subunit of the state, but politically, the city often tries to operate independently.[19] Prior to the provision of home-rule powers to cities by the Illinois Constitution of 1970, Chicago and its disciplined legislative bloc frequently were successful in generating special legislation for the city through classification; that is, ensuring that a state statute would either apply to or exempt cities of more than 500,000. This applied, of course, only to Chicago. Nonetheless the lack of home-rule powers spurred recommendations to make Chicago and the metropolitan area a separate state; in 1933, for example, a University of Chicago study said, "There is much to be said for the separate statehood of Chicago, especially in view of the inability of the city to obtain proportional representation in the state legislature, or a degree of home-rule adequate to deal with the needs of a growing metropolis."[20] The city has since gained the home-rule powers it sought, and in any case such proposals are not taken too seriously because Illinois without its only large city would be a much more modest state with a fraction of its current national profile.

The career ladder for Chicago politicians illustrates the confusion about the relation between local government and the State of Illinois. Several former legislators (plus one former congressman) have served in the Chicago City Council, but few former city aldermen have sat subsequently in the state legislature. In other parts of the state, the pattern of upward mobility for a local government official is to be elected to the legislature. In Chicago, the legislature has more often been a stepping stone not only to the City Council but also to more powerful local offices. Both the late Chicago mayor Richard J. Daley and his son Mayor Richard M. Daley served in the Illinois General Assembly early in their political careers. In 1979, powerful Illinois senate president Thomas Hynes resigned his office so that he could run for the office of Cook County Assessor (which he won).

Chicago uses its home-rule powers extensively. It started the home-rule movement in 1954, when Mayor Martin Kennelly created a Home Rule Commission. Kennelly's successor Richard J. Daley continued to carry the home-rule banner, and Richard M. Daley helped create the home-rule provisions as a member of the 1970 Constitutional Convention's Local Government Committee.

The home-rule authority has increased Chicago's bargaining power with the legislature and governor. Prior to 1970, Chicago had to present a laundry list of changes it wanted from the legislature and had to negotiate and make trades to achieve its aims. Not having to negotiate items that can be changed under home-rule authority increases the city's negotiating strength in matters not covered by home rule.

In theory, Chicago is a "weak mayor" city, with much power lodged in the city council and numerous other elected citywide officials. In practice, however, most recent Chicago mayors have had very strong political power. Richard J. Daley was chairman of the Cook County Democratic Central

Committee, which controlled thousands of patronage jobs at the time, as well as mayor, and as a result developed legendary power. The mayors who served after his death (Michael Bilandic, Jane Byrne, Harold Washington, and Eugene Sawyer) did not hold the party office and were not as strong, but they were often able to steer the city council.

Mayor Richard M. Daley also eschewed the party office. He has nevertheless been able to control the city council, largely by appointment of replacements for aldermen who have been favored with other jobs. In addition, the mayor maintains a large political war chest as a result of his authority to award contracts for business with the city.

For example, Mayor Richard M. Daley served fifteen years in that office before he had to exercise his veto power over the council. In 2007 the city council passed, over the mayor's objections, an ordinance requiring that "big box" retailers such as Wal-Mart pay a wage higher than the state minimum wage. The mayor was able to sustain his veto by convincing several aldermen to change their votes.

In 2008 the mayor faced a challenge from lakefront alderman Brendan Reilly, who opposed location of a children's museum in the new Millennium Park along Lake Michigan. Initially, several aldermen supported Reilly because of the strong tradition that aldermen controlled land use decisions in their respective wards. When push came to shove, however, the principle was set aside, and the mayor easily won the council's approval for locating the museum in the park.

The council is large. Aldermen are elected from each of the fifty wards on a nonpartisan ballot, as is the mayor, although the partisan affiliations of the aldermen are well known. In 2007 all but one were Democrats, though they came from different factions of the party. The wards are the building blocks for the county political organization, and in some instances the elected Democratic ward committeeman is also the alderman. This combination makes the alderman a very potent political actor because Chicago ward committeemen appoint party precinct captains.[21]

The Chicago City Council has the potential to wield great power, and it used it at the start of Mayor Harold Washington's first term in 1983. The majority of the council members at the time were not supporters of Washington, the city's first black mayor. By voting as a bloc for three years straight, the aldermen were able to prevent the bulk of Washington's program from being implemented. Called the "council wars" by the media, this conflict had strong racial overtones, with blacks generally supporting Washington and most of the council's white majority opposing him.

There have been calls to reform the city council, most recently a 1989 report titled "Chicago City Council Reform" by the City Club of Chicago. Some changes have been made in the council and its procedures. But the size of the council has not been changed, although it could be done using the city's home-rule powers. Apparently, the classic remark of colorful alderman "Paddy" Bauler, uttered with gusto in 1955, still prevails: "Chicago ain't ready for reform."

Efforts to reduce endemic corruption in Chicago's governments have not been successful. One of the most dramatic and revealing investigations of this institutionalized corruption was splashed on the front pages of the *Chicago Sun-Times* for a solid month in 1978, after the newspaper and the Better Government Association (BGA) had opened and operated a tavern named the Mirage less than a mile from city hall.

That Chicago's inspectors were on the take had been well known for decades, but because business owners needed licenses to operate and could cut a few corners with a fifty-dollar bribe, they rarely came forward to fight the system. Investigative reporter Pamela Zekman and the BGA's William Recktenwald decided the best way to gather hard evidence was to open a real business and let the inspectors walk in. As they prepared to open the tavern and during the four months it was in business, the purported tavernkeepers encountered repeated payoff demands. Plumbing, electrical, and fire inspectors and a sign inspector all looked the other way or hastened some paperwork in exchange for payoffs of ten dollars or more. The owner of a neighborhood delicatessen already knew the pattern. "The name of the game in Chicago is baksheesh. . . . That's Arabian. It means payoff, bribe. This is the city of baksheesh."[22]

More recently, from 2004 to 2007, the U.S. Attorney convicted forty-five persons, including City Clerk James Laski, in a "hired trucks" scandal in which private trucks were hired to do city business.[23] Laski pled guilty to receiving $50,000 in bribes to steer business to certain trucking companies. The federal investigation broadened to city hiring practices and resulted in the conviction of Chicago patronage official Robert Sorich for violating federal court orders concerning hiring practices.

Corruption aside, Chicago looks good when its spending is compared to that of other big American cities. This is possible because functions that would belong to the city elsewhere are performed by other governmental units in Chicago. These arrangements were made by the legislature and are in line with the decentralized nature of local governments throughout Illinois. Public hospitals are a county, not a city, function in Chicago. The public schools, as in other parts of the state, are a separate government unit with taxing powers. The Chicago Housing Authority has considerable independence. Public transportation is the purview of the Chicago Transit Authority and the Regional Transportation Authority. The park district, too, is fiscally independent of the city.

This decentralization helped Chicago, or at least masked its symptoms, during the 1970s, when New York City faced fiscal disaster. As one reporter noted, "Today the effect of these differences [between the two cities] is striking. Cook County, not the city of Chicago, operates the city's public hospitals and the state legislature picked up most of the city's transportation and social welfare costs. By contrast, New York is the only city in the country whose state legislature requires it to pay a substantial share of its own Medicaid and welfare bills."[24]

Although these Chicago agencies are legally independent and do not appear on the organization chart as city functions, the mayor can have considerable impact on their decision making. Recent mayors have exercised influence through their appointment powers. This is best illustrated by the Chicago Park District, for which the mayor appoints the board members and the top administrative officer. Legally, all of these separate governments are outside the jurisdiction of the mayor. In reality, their independence depends on whether the mayor has the political strength to control his appointees.

The city has fought hard to maintain control over the city's airports. When plans were made for developing O'Hare Airport in the early 1950s, the city carefully annexed a strip of land several miles long and the ground around the airport to make sure the airport was within the city limits. More logically, the airport should have been a part of one or more of the adjacent suburbs. Suburban Republican legislators have since introduced legislation that would bring all regional airports under an authority appointed by the governor, taking jurisdiction away from the city and the mayor. This legislation has always provoked fierce opposition from the city and has not passed.

The importance of the airport and its job base to the city was well demonstrated in the early 1990s, when decisions were being made about whether and where to build a third airport. Mayor Daley wanted to relocate a neighborhood so as to squeeze the airport onto former industrial and landfill areas on the city's southeast side. Governor Jim Edgar wanted a south suburban site. When Daley's plan could not win legislative approval, he withdrew it, putting the burden on the governor to push forward on the suburban airport without city support. In 2009 O'Hare International Airport's runways were being expanded, and planning for a south suburban airport was ongoing.

Hope Blooms in East St. Louis

Social communities such as cities are not static. No city better illustrates this point than East St. Louis, Illinois, across the Mississippi from its name-sake. A city of ninety thousand in 1950 but only about thirty thousand in 2008, East St. Louis is probably the most studied, analyzed, planned, and helped city in American history.[25] After World War II, it was predominantly white. By 1970, of eighty thousand residents, 70 percent were black; by 1990 the census showed about forty thousand, of whom nearly all were African American.[26] The 2010 census will show few more than thirty thousand, according to close observers of the city. It is at the heart of a great floodplain called the American Bottoms, where water and waste collect naturally, though whites living on the Bluffs above the city pay nothing for control of the water that drains down from their communities onto the floor of the Bottoms.

The city seemed programmed to fail from the first. Decades ago, industries created their own towns (for example, Sauget, originally Monsanto Town, and Alorton, for the Aluminum Ore Co.) around the edges of East St. Louis to avoid paying higher taxes. When industries and jobholders began leaving after World War II, they left behind old housing stock and an aging infrastructure. In the 1960s, when community college districts took shape in Illinois, Belleville Area College and Lewis and Clark College drew boundary lines up to East St. Louis and adjacent black towns, leaving them an island with neither the population nor the tax base to support a college.

By the late 1980s the world outside the city had basically taken over its management. The housing authority was run by a private company; state troopers frequently patrolled the streets because often all the city police cars were inoperable; state-created financial oversight teams ran the schools and the city government.[27] In 1990 the State of Illinois protected the city from bankruptcy by providing $34 million in state credit.[28]

Although many outsiders might want East St. Louis to continue wither-ing, the city won't go away—and it appears to be improving, as a result of cash infusions from a state-licensed gambling casino along the river in the city, continuing activist help and money from the outside, and morale build-ing from citizen-generated success stories. The casino's tax revenues and its foundation have helped reforge the police and fire departments. The state is spending about $100 million to rebuild most of the city's schools. Citizens in the Emerson Park neighborhood successfully fought for additional stops in East St. Louis by the 1998 MetroLink light rail service, which connects the city to St. Louis and its major airport hub; the Emerson Park citizens have also helped generate handsome new private housing in their neighborhood, the first private development in decades. The city has a new library and forty public access sites to computers. For a city that had basically no retail in 1990, a new downtown has been created around major supermarkets and a chain pharmacy store. Ten to fifteen active neighborhood improvement groups push for park, school, and infrastructure upgrades

And the always-struggling State Community College of East St. Louis has been absorbed into a regional Southwest Illinois Community College, a marriage that was impossible decades earlier.

The East St. Louis Action Research Project (ESLARP) of the University of Illinois at Urbana-Champaign is an illustration of the many outside helpmates developed for the city over the decades. The project was created in 1988 in response to a challenge from East St. Louis state representative Wyvetter Younge that the state's flagship public university provide some real public service to the city.

The project has morphed from a traditional, somewhat detached academic urban planning activity into a hands-on, activist organization. It provided training and support, for example, to the Emerson Park citizens' group, which has now taken on a life of its own. Each year, ESLARP leads more than five hundred University of Illinois students to the city to set up computer facilities, design parks, and paint community centers, among other activities.

Daunting problems remain. The water and sewer system is more than a hundred years old and operates within a water table that is just inches from the surface; the levee on the river needs upgrading. Property tax rates are by far the highest in the state, which hinders residential development. The hospital is moving out of town, and the dramatic loss of population has created gaping "urban voids," which isolate individual homes and make it hard to create neighborliness. And casino tax revenues and foundation support may plummet as the result of competition from a huge new casino directly across the river in St. Louis.

Still, much has changed, according to Bruce Wicks, director of ESLARP. "The city is a lot better than it was," says Wicks. "The infrastructure is being improved. Residents are shifting from concerns solely about their own plight to interest in seeing, for example, the parks improved."[29]

A city with a recent history of being helped by the outside has begun to help itself, by itself. Hope, indeed, blooms in East St. Louis.

Regional Planning

The expanding metropolitan Chicago region of 9.4 million people is one of the most vibrant in the nation. For example, one-third of the nation's rail and truck cargo moves to, from, or through the Chicago region.[30] Growth of 2 million persons and 1.2 million jobs is projected by 2030. The seven-county region (Cook, DuPage, Lake, Kane, Will, McHenry, and Kendall) also has 1,450 local governments. These independent-minded local governments also generally share the individualistic values discussed in this book, that is, they tend to be skeptical of or outright opposed to comprehensive, collective policies for the region that would override the objectives of the individual governments.

For decades, the Northeastern Illinois Planning Commission (NIPC) served the region as a toothless tiger that planned for the region yet lacked any enforcement authority. According to one business newspaper writer, "Such plans in the past have been routinely disregarded, as municipal officials exert their authority to make decisions about zoning and land use in their towns."[31]

Chicago Metropolis 2020, an organization of civic leaders, has been working in recent years to replicate planning for the region similar to that of the fabled Burnham Plan of a century ago, which preserved the lakefront and built wide boulevards and fine parks throughout Chicago. In 2005, Metropolis 2020 and many planning allies convinced the legislature and the governor to take a baby step in the direction of more prominent planning with enactment of a new Chicago Metropolitan Agency for Planning (CMAP), which consolidates NIPC and the Chicago Area Transportation Study, another longtime planning unit. As with the predecessor units, appointments to the seventeen-member CMAP board are carefully doled out in a balanced fashion to people from Chicago, Cook County, and suburban county sub-regions.[32]

The problem of lack of teeth remains, however. "The new agency faces the same legal obstacles as CATS and NIPC," declared one observer. "Under pressure from municipal officials, lawmakers in the spring (2005) insisted the bill creating CMAP avoid anything that could be construed as giving the new agency control over land use decisions."[33]

Chicago Metropolis 2020, CMAP, and a coalition of regional nonprofit organizations hope to persuade the legislature to provide CMAP with at least the powers of incentives and disincentives to encourage local governments to adhere to the regional plan. For example, municipalities that choose to disregard designated open spaces could lose state money for roads or other infrastructure projects.

"Does it make sense to spend state capital dollars for things that don't meet the regional plan?" asks CMAP executive director Randy Blankenhorn. "We think there are incentives out there . . . that can get communities to think twice."[34]

As of 2008, however, the planning proponents had failed to convince lawmakers to provide this power to CMAP. Cooperation and collaboration are fine, say lawmakers, but not coercion of their local governments. As a result, CMAP declares that it "will provide leadership by taking a comprehensive, collaborative approach that gives decision makers a new regional context for their choices regarding land use and transportation."[35]

It is not that Illinois residents and their leaders do not recognize the inefficiencies of the current system. Rather, they accept them as part of the state's personality and way of doing business. Instead of trying to dismantle something so integral—and in the process disrupting long-standing webs of jobs and allegiances—they develop mechanisms to fine-tune relations among the multitudes.

Lack of planning and cooperation are not peculiar to northeastern Illinois. The problem is statewide and is more intense in growing areas such as Champaign County, where uncontrolled urban growth forced a clumsy and inefficient reaction by three neighboring municipalities: Champaign, Urbana, and Savoy. Each recognized the need for an annexation agreement, but because each had its own interests, negotiations were prolonged and complex.

The three cities decided to sign agreements among themselves so that they could divide up unincorporated areas just outside their boundaries. But they needed the help of a fourth entity, the Champaign-Urbana Sanitary District, so that they could withhold sewer connections to developers in areas refusing to be annexed to a city. What was the advantage for the sanitary district? Champaign and Urbana would assume the district's liability for the frequent flooding of Boneyard Creek, which runs through the twin cities. When the district agreed to that approach, Champaign County had to be convinced because it appoints sanitary district board members. It came on board and the deal went through in 1993, but only after the three cities agreed to reimburse the county for sales tax on any commercial properties that they annex for an agreed number of years. All this negotiation was needed to address what would seem to be a simple matter of providing orderly growth.[36]

Beyond the Borders

States cannot afford to be shy in dealing with the national government in Washington, D.C. Nor has Illinois been, although dollar figures suggest otherwise, as we will see. Even before the state's incorporation in 1818, the territory's delegate to the U.S. Congress, Nathaniel Pope, was working hard in Washington, D.C. Through Pope's efforts, Congress pushed the northern border of Illinois forty-one miles up from Lake Michigan's southern tip, capturing the port of Chicago from Wisconsin and setting a precedent for aggressiveness that serves the state to this day.

Pope's advocacy beyond Illinois's original borders has been followed by a steady stream of leaders who went before the U.S. Congress, the federal bureaucracy, the president, and even foreign governments to assert the state's needs. Members of the congressional delegation played the lead roles, yet governors, mayors, state legislators, and business leaders also had parts in the ongoing efforts.

External relations are typically pursued for a simple reason: to bring back money or jobs. From the 1950s to the 1970s, Chicago mayor Richard J. Daley was a master of this art, trading his ability to generate votes for hundreds of millions of dollars' worth of building projects and federal human service programs. Governor Jim Thompson (1977–90) traveled frequently to foreign cities and helped generate thousands of jobs backed by export sales and foreign investments. Governor Rod Blagojevich maintained foreign trade offices in nine foreign cities, including Hong Kong, Shanghai, Warsaw, and Johannesburg. Former speaker of the U.S. House Dennis Hastert (R-IL, 1999–2006) continued to bring home the bacon, as has U.S. Senate assistant majority leader Dick Durbin (D-IL). With the election of Senator Barack Obama as president in 2008 and his appointment of the savvy Chicagoan Rahm Emanuel as his chief of staff, Illinois leaders have high hopes for increased largesse from Washington, D.C.

Washington is the focus of each state's external relations because that is where the money is. Federal payments to Illinois state and local governments in 2009 amounted to $13.1 billion and represented about one-quarter of the total state budget that year.[37] The money from Washington comes via 356 categorical grants (for specific purposes) and block grants (groupings of grant programs in a functional area such as health or community development). Other dollars flow directly to the research universities, particularly the University of Chicago, the University of Illinois, and Northwestern University via agencies such as the National Institutes of Health, the National Science Foundation, and the Department of Defense.

Federal aid to the states has been shifting. General, unrestricted revenue sharing with the states was terminated in 1980 and for local governments in 1986. There were reductions in numerous categorical aid programs to the states during the Carter and Reagan administrations in the late 1970s and early 1980s. But there have been massive infusions of federal dollars to Illinois since the late 1980s to match state dollars for the rapidly expanding federal-state Medicaid program, which provided health coverage for 2.5 million of Illinois's 12.8 million residents in 2007.

Although the amount of federal monies that come to the state is huge, the state ranks forty-fifth among the states in the amount of federal aid it receives on a per capita basis.[38] In 2006 Illinois received $1,250 per person, significantly below the national average of $1,516 per person and far below the amount received by other big states such as New York ($2,267) and California ($1,561). This is all the more reason that the state's political leaders feel pressure to increase Illinois's slice of federal funding.

Several factors explain the state's low ranking in terms of federal largesse. First, state social service program expenditure dollars are often matched by the federal government on formula bases—the more the state spends, the greater the match in federal dollars. In 2006, Illinois state and local governments spent $1,054 per person (including federal dollars) on public welfare programs, whereas New York spent $2,229 and California, $1,237.[39]

Illinois, along with New York and California, receives the lowest percentage match from the federal government for the immense Medicaid program, which provides health care for low-income residents. Because of a formula created in 1965 that was based on the wealth of the state and welfare needs at that time, Illinois receives only a 50–50 match from the federal government for Medicaid, while neighboring Indiana and Iowa receive 63 cents for each 37 cents expended by those states. If Illinois received the match of these neighbors, it would generate about $2 billion more in federal funds per year from that program alone. Because of the huge cost to the national government in increasing the match for states such as Illinois, New York, and California, even Illinois's well-placed members of Congress have been unable to achieve a higher federal match. The temporary federal stimulus funding from the American Recovery and Reinvestment Act of 2009 temporarily increased the reimbursement rate for Illinois to 61 percent.

Other factors include transportation and military expenditures. Illinois has a rich highway network, yet it ranks lower in miles of highway per person than sparsely populated states in the West. Illinois also has fewer military installations than do a number of southern and coastal states, so it receives fewer dollars than many states to support installation children in local schools.

With structural factors such as these working against the state, Illinois officials are expected to devote a significant part of their time to winning projects and funding for the state. For example, the Illinois congressional delegation holds monthly luncheon meetings that are chaired by Senator Dick

Durbin. The delegation works on a bipartisan basis to lobby for projects for their state. Illinois governors have maintained a state office in Washington for the same purpose, as does the City of Chicago. Many smaller cities and entities such as hospitals retain lobbyists in Washington to seek funding from the hundreds of grant programs sprinkled across the federal agencies as well as from special project "earmarks" of funding sponsored by individual members of Congress.

Friends in High Places

The most significant factor in external relations is the human one. Simply put, a state that provides effective political leaders will do better in Washington than one that does not. Prior to the 2008 election of Barack Obama as president, one other Illinois resident, Abraham Lincoln, has been elected president, defeating a fellow Illinoisan, Stephen A. Douglas, in 1860. Governor Frank O. Lowden was a leading candidate for president in 1920, losing out to Warren G. Harding at the Republican convention. Another governor, Adlai E. Stevenson, was the unsuccessful Democratic candidate for president in 1952 and 1956.

Illinois has also played an important role in presidential elections. In 1960, John F. Kennedy narrowly defeated Richard M. Nixon in Illinois on the strength of Richard J. Daley's organization. Daley knew that the downstate vote would be sufficiently pro-Nixon that he had to deliver a surplus of four hundred thousand or more votes to put his man in the White House. That was a tall order, even for Daley. "At no time . . . had the Democratic ward bosses been subject to the pressure he [Daley] applied for Jack Kennedy," wrote television commentator Len O'Connor. "There was not the slightest doubt in the minds of the ward bosses, in advance of the 1960 election, that the man who failed to deliver a massive vote was going to be permanently maimed politically."[40] Every vote counted. Daley delivered a plurality of 456,312 votes in Chicago, and Kennedy squeaked through by a margin of 8,858 votes out of 4.65 million cast. In appreciation, Kennedy was always responsive when Daley called for help.

Illinois is at the heart of a sticky web of governments, as well as other political actors. The federal and local governments constrain, support, complement, and frustrate the state government. Each level of government—federal, state, and local—tries to maximize and apply financial resources to achieve its respective objectives. In chapter 9 we turn to education, another arena in which the intergovernmental give and take is also rich and dynamic.

9.

Education

· · · · · · · · · · · · · ·

Education is arguably the most important function of state and local government. Illinois enrolls more than three million students from pre-kindergarten through higher education, about one in every four of the state's 12.8 million people. Illinois governments spend about $30 billion annually, about 5 percent of the state's gross domestic product, on education.[1]

After decades in which Illinois ranked in the middle or lower rungs among the states in financial support for kindergarten through high school (K–12) public education, the state and local school districts showed strong support for public education from the 1990s to 2005. In 1992, for example, Illinois state and local governments spent $4,866 per pupil versus a national average of $5,097 and ranked twenty-third among the fifty states. By 2008 Illinois spending per pupil had jumped to $11,428, fourteenth in the nation, and significantly higher than the national average of $10,259.[2] The figure is misleading, however, because spending for Illinois schools is spread unevenly across property-rich and property-poor districts; as a result, two-thirds of Illinois school districts actually spend less than the national average.[3]

From 1998 to 2006, in contrast, state general funds spent for higher education actually declined, breaking a tradition in Illinois budgeting in which state increases for the two sectors of education went together.

These two issues—uneven spending for K–12 and weak support for higher education—are central to understanding the dynamics of the politics of education in Illinois, including regional differences, individualistic as opposed to collective approaches to spending, and state budgetary constraints imposed by the demands of health care and pension obligations.

If politics is about who gets what, how, and why, then clearly education funding is political. Other educational issues that are clearly political include that of who governs education (the local, state, or national government), whether children and parents should have choices in the schools they attend, and whether all children should have equal educational resources.

This chapter provides an overview of the state's education system and profiles some of the major players, showing how their work, though highly effective in some areas, has been inadequate to resolve fundamental financing problems. We begin with sketches of the elementary, secondary, and higher education systems, and then look at the political tugs-of-war that characterize the state's education communities.

"Fourth Branch" and Competition for Dollars

Many educators like to think of education as an independent fourth branch of government, and in many ways it is. In 1941, public university employees in Illinois were placed in their own civil service system, and job openings have been mostly exempt from the political patronage pressures that have affected state government otherwise. University and school employees have their own separate retirement systems, and on the organization charts, education is distinctly separate from other state agencies.

Governors and lawmakers traditionally viewed education as a major responsibility, but they did not consider it as important politically as transportation, regulation, criminal justice, and capital spending for a lawmaker's district. Since the 1970s, education has become more important politically because it has been linked to economic development and workforce quality. The growth since World War II of the twelve public universities and thirty-eight public community colleges has also made higher education a part of pork barrel politics because a lawmaker seeking reelection can pick up votes by delivering an auditorium or law school to his or her district. The trend toward full-time service by lawmakers has played a role as well. It increased the amount of time legislators and their staffs could devote to education and encouraged a tendency to keep constituents happy by addressing parochial needs rather than trying to institute comprehensive statewide change.

The Illinois Constitution of 1970 devotes only three short sections to education, but a few clauses are often quoted and debated hotly. "The State shall provide for an efficient system of high quality public educational institutions and services," the constitution says, and the state "has primary responsibility for financing the system of public education."[4] Varied critics have charged repeatedly that state government neither provides an efficient system of high quality nor fulfills its primary responsibility for financing schools, which we discuss below. There is no mention of higher education in the state charter, in contrast to most other state constitutions.

Public school enrollment reached a high of 2.37 million pupils in 1972, declined to 1.93 million in 1994, and stood at 2.1 million in 2008.[5] Minorities represented 28.8 percent of enrollees in 1981, yet a generation later, in 2005, nonwhites represented 43.4 percent, with blacks and Latinos each representing about 20 percent of total enrollment. Nearly three in every ten public school students came from low-income families in 1991; by 2007, four in ten public school students were classified as low-income.

Many families eschew the public system. Private schools play a large though declining role in educating children. Private schools enrolled 14 percent of all elementary and secondary students in 1994 but only 11.2 percent in 2008. Private school enrollments have declined sharply from 320,290 in 1994 to 265,276 in 2008.[6] Still, in 2007 the Catholic Archdiocese of Chicago alone enrolled 98,000 students in 257 schools, and there were 1,250 private schools throughout Illinois.

The number of families educating their children at home has grown sharply in recent years, although no one seems to know by how much. Illinois requires only that families who homeschool register their children with their regional office of education; there is no assurance that all do so. As a result, the Illinois State Board of Education (ISBE) is unwilling to hazard a guess as to how many children in Illinois are schooled at home. At the national level, about 1.1 million students are homeschooled, according to a 2003 survey. If Illinois is close to the average, the state would have about 40,000 students who are schooled at home.[7]

Illinois public schools are organized into a tangle of state, intermediate, and local administrative units. The governor appoints the nine-member board of education from the state's five appellate court districts; the ISBE in turn appoints a state superintendent of education who oversees a staff of five hundred in Springfield, Chicago, and Mt. Vernon. In addition, forty-one independent, elected regional office of education superintendents throughout the state support the ISBE and operate their own independent programs in support of local school districts. At the local level, 873 school districts elect seven member boards, which operate K–12, elementary, or high school districts.

In 1942 there were 12,000 elementary school districts in Illinois, most with a single one-room schoolhouse per district.[8] Some counties had more school board members than teachers. Increased state aid and persistent efforts by groups including the Illinois Farm Bureau cut the number of districts in half by 1948. Consolidation continued in the 1950s with the total falling to 2,000 districts, and this number fell to 870 in 2008, still far more districts than in most states.

Who Governs?

"Local control" of schools is the mantra of elected officials at all levels, because that plays best with voters, who generally treasure their local schools. In fact, control of the schoolhouse is a continuing struggle among the local, state, and national governments, as well as the business community and education unions, among other interests. Since early in the twentieth century, control of local schools has been eroding, first shifting from the local school districts to the state and, since the 1980s, moving to the federal government.

Today, the State School Code, located at Chapter 105 of the *Illinois Compiled Statutes,* is almost 600 pages of dense, small type on large double-columned pages. The School Code is replete with 105 mandates about what the schools must do.[9] For example, instruction must be provided in patriotism, honesty, kindness, consumer education, the Holocaust, prevention of steroid abuse, and the avoidance of abduction. The state mandates that driver training be made available to both public and nearby nonpublic students and, for drivers' education, that precisely "thirty clock-hours of classroom instruction and six clock-hours of behind the wheel instruction" are provided, including instruction on how the Litter Control Act pertains to auto use. Legislative efforts to remove instructional mandates, such as the requirement of four years of physical education in high school, are quickly buried as the unions rally teachers to the cause. Even efforts to reform education tend to create new mandates; the 1985 requirement of "learning assessments" and school improvement plans created lengthy exercises in paperwork that may or may not translate into better schools.

In the 2009 session of the legislature, lawmakers added several new mandates including instruction on teen dating violence, disability history, deportation of Mexican Americans during the Great Depression, and the U.S. Congressional Medal of Honor, among others.[10]

National elected officials have been catalysts for change since the 1980s, when *A Nation at Risk,* published by the U.S. Department of Education in 1983, decried deteriorating educational performance and triggered a national school reform movement.

In the 1980s business leaders across the country, including those in Illinois, became deeply involved in school improvement. Corporate chief executives probably have more potential to cause fundamental change in education than any other group, including school leaders and elected officials. When aroused, CEOs can raise the necessary funds to generate pressure for change, as they did in the case of Chicago school reform in the late 1980s, discussed below.

Jim Broadway, an observer and advocate of Illinois education, saw strong influence by business in education policy making in the 1990s, especially from the Illinois Manufacturing Association (IMA), Illinois Business Roundtable, and the Illinois State Chamber of Commerce. "For three or four years, Blouke Carus [head of the IMA education committee] owned education in Illinois," declared Broadway. "He brought in the German model. And in 1993–94, Jeff Mays [Roundtable] and Robb Karr [IMA] basically ran the Senate Education Committee."[11] Broadway considered the federal No Child Left Behind Act (NCLB) to be the most far-reaching of the neoconservative business community's education efforts.

In 2002 President George W. Bush signed NCLB into law. According to one observer, it is "the most comprehensive federal education law ever written and one that imposed serious sanctions for states and schools that failed to abide by its provisions."[12] The act requires states to improve performance of students so that by 2013–14 a full 100 percent of students are scoring at least "proficient" on required annual state-developed exams. If schools fail to make "adequate yearly progress" (AYP), sanctions are imposed. These include providing students in underperforming schools the right to transfer to a better public school within the district and to receive special after-school tutoring. Schools that fail to reach AYP after five consecutive years are to be restructured and new staff hired, all decisions that have heretofore been the province of state statute and local school district management. Because the federal government provides less than 10 percent of total school funding in America, the authors observe that 10 percent of the money is telling 90 percent what to do.

Because of the strong sanctions and the natural desire not to be seen as underperforming, local school districts are focusing on the required annual testing that is also part of NCLB, often to the consternation of educators who feel that comprehensive education is about more than teaching to the math, reading, and science tests. As Kewanee school board member Martin Hepner lamented, half seriously: "The only thing we have left is the power to set school district boundaries and they'll probably try to take that away from us."[13]

Possibly because it is assaulted from all sides, the state and local education community in Illinois tend to be cautious, protective, and resistant to change.

The issue of choice in school attendance illustrates the resistance to change. Although there is a serious scholarly debate about the merits and shortcomings of choice, a 1989 Gallup survey found that the public favored choice by a proportion of two to one.[14] The ISBE spent 1988–89 developing a statewide policy regarding choice, but it was not much of a policy; the ISBE recommended that any choice in Illinois be limited to choice within a school district, which limits the concept dramatically. The recommendation produced no significant change, but it served its purpose by allaying the fears of teachers' unions and the associations of administrators and school board members. The issue surfaced again in 1993, when Governor Jim Edgar proposed creating fifteen public charter schools that would be exempt from most state regulations. This modest proposal was defeated in the legislature by the teachers' unions, but forty-five schools were authorized the following year when Republicans gained control of the legislature for the first time in more than two decades, and the influence of teachers' unions was trimmed.

Charter schools proved to be popular. In 2005, fifteen thousand children applied to the state's twenty-nine charter schools, yet only five thousand students could be accepted because of space limitations.[15] As of 2007, state law authorized sixty charter schools in Illinois, with one-half of these in Chicago.[16] The city operates twenty-eight charter schools, some of which operate on more than one campus. Opponents of charter schools tried to prohibit this practice in 2007.[17] There are only two charter schools in the suburbs, and there are five downstate. Because charter schools are allowed to operate without certified instructors, resistance to rapid expansion of a popular concept comes from the strong teachers' unions.

The charter schools in Chicago appear to have been generally effective. According to *Catalyst Chicago,* a school watchdog publication, school graduation rates have continued to rise and drop-out rates have fallen in the six Chicago charter high schools in operation since 2002. In addition, the group reported that "charters are outperforming neighborhood schools where their students would likely have landed if the charters didn't exist."[18]

Unions Show Their Muscle

The strength of the education unions should not come as a surprise, but it was not always so. Until the 1970s, Illinois education policy tended to be shaped by small groups of education elites and legislators.[19] Teacher organizations were passive. Governors were not closely involved, except in setting overall budget limits, nor was the federal government active. Most funding came from the local taxes. Those days are over. Today the state and national governments have greater funding at risk, and the U.S. Congress and the Illinois legislature have large and active education staffs. Governors now see education as central to economic prosperity. Most important, the teachers' unions have become assertive and highly protective of their gains.

The Illinois Education Association is a teachers' union with 130,000 members in suburban and downstate school districts that dominate the politics of education outside Chicago. The other major union is the Illinois Federation of Teachers/Chicago Teachers Union (IFT/CTU), with 90,000 members in Chicago and in several downstate cities, including Champaign and East St. Louis.[20]

Beginning in the late 1960s, the IEA transformed itself from an apolitical, milquetoast group of teachers and administrators into a political powerhouse that can strike terror into a lawmaker. Ken Bruce served as director of government relations for the IEA for more than two decades, stepping down in 1993. "When I started, we would not take a stand on any—not any—piece of legislation," recalls Bruce. "In 1989, we tracked seven hundred bills, and not just education bills, but bills on pension issues and school bonding and other matters, and we took positions on most of those bills."[21]

The IEA contributes to favored candidates, sends staff professionals to help manage campaigns, and organizes teachers to get involved in local races. The IEA endorsed Republican governor James R. Thompson early in his first campaign in 1976 and contributed $80,000 to his candidacy (about $300,000 in 2009 dollars), more than any other group that year. Its teachers were active in each of Thompson's four successful campaigns. Not surprisingly, Thompson's first assistant for education reported that he consulted with the IEA on education issues as a matter of standard operating procedure.[22] The deputy governor for education under George Ryan (1997–2000) was herself an IEA activist prior to joining the Ryan administration.

The IEA has become involved in judicial contests as well, endorsing and providing contributions to candidates for the appellate and supreme courts. It makes sense to see friends of the IEA succeed to the state's high courts, according to Bruce, because many issues of importance to teachers are resolved by lawsuits.

The IEA has had more influence than other education interests because the union has invested heavily in Illinois elections. It assesses each of its 130,000 members $20 per year for dues for its political action committee. Between 1993 and 2006, the IEA contributed $12.8 million to statehouse candidates, and the IFT/CTU donated $8 million. Of all political contributors, the IEA ranked first in contributions and the IFT/CTU third, ahead of trial lawyers, manufacturers, bankers, and utilities.[23] The IFT/CTU has increased its giving in recent election cycles and now equals the IEA in that regard. Part of the motivation was the fact that the CTU was shut out in the 1995–96 Chicago schools reforms, when it was stripped of its power to strike, which has only recently been restored.

Nonmonetary contributions were made as well, typically by local affiliates for rallies and other campaign activities. Attracting hundreds of teachers to a rally generates media coverage and increases enthusiasm among teachers to go out and do telephoning and other campaign work. This show of support increases credibility for the candidate, spurring support and contributions from elsewhere.

The IEA has long linked contribution decisions to legislative performance, according to analyst Kent D. Redfield.[24] Even legislators who are confident that they could beat an election challenge from the IEA would just as soon avoid the increased time, effort, and money needed to do so. Thus whenever a legislator can give the IEA a vote in committee or on the floor, he or she generally tries to do so. As a result, the IEA has dominated education action in the house and senate. Its five full-time lobbyists meet with committee members before every hearing, testify in committee, and organize teachers and specialists to provide testimony. Several observers of the legislative process say they have watched IEA lobbyists give "thumbs up" and "thumbs down" signals from the committee hearing room audience and house and senate galleries as cues to legislators about how to cast votes. The IEA has even provided written colloquies for legislators to read into the record on the chamber floor, thus establishing a record of legislative intent for use later when the resulting statute is being interpreted by lawyers and judges in court cases.

On the two hundred or more bills introduced each session that are specifically related to school matters, the IEA generally—but not always—gets what it wants. The IEA beats back with apparent ease efforts to reduce instructional mandates. The union has progressively restricted the authority of local boards. In 1987, for instance, it was successful in extending seniority protection to all nonteaching personnel, including bus drivers, food service workers, aides, and secretaries. Further, teachers are almost never successfully fired for incompetence. In an award-winning investigative series, Scott Reeder of the Small Newspaper Group found that between 1985 and 2005, on average only two teachers per year—of ninety-five thousand tenured teachers—were fired for incompetence.[25] The average cost in legal fees to school boards for each of the firings came to $219,000. Part of the reason for the small number of firings for incompetence is believed to be the unions' effectiveness at bargaining for detailed, protective procedural elements in the dismissal process.

The IEA played an important part in Governor Thompson's decision to support collective bargaining for teachers. Possibly as a result, Illinois teachers ranked fifth in the nation in average teacher salary in 2009, at $62,787 compared to a national average of $53,910.[26]

There are, nonetheless, limits to the union's power. On the one issue that most seem to agree is the most important facing the education community—state finance of education—the IEA has had little effect. State government provides only 29 percent of total funding for local school districts in Illinois, one of the lowest percentages in the nation. The IEA's lack of aggressiveness may be the result of its internal dominance by teachers from the collar counties, where schools generally have strong property tax bases and thus need relatively little state funding. The IEA also has had more influence on narrow education issues than on broader questions such as school funding, which involves taxes and thus transcends the education arena.

Management Fights Back

School management interests have had much less influence than the IEA, in part because of the fragmentation created by regional differences—primarily differences in wealth—across the 873 school districts. The Illinois Association of School Boards (IASB) and Illinois Association of School Administrators (IASA) find it difficult to represent all their members satisfactorily with regard to contentious issues such as funding and school consolidation. Thus many sub-state organizations have been created to represent categories of interests. These include the Large Unit District Association, Education Research and Development (an organization of 135 north suburban school districts), South Cooperative Public Education (representing 35 districts in southern Cook County), Legislative Education Network of DuPage, and FAIRCOM, an organization of school districts that have utility power plants in their boundaries and thus great property wealth coveted by other districts.

School management groups appear to have more potential than they have realized. Each district elects seven board members, so more than six thousand individual board members could conceivably be rallied to support issues. But this has not happened, perhaps because the board members serve as volunteers and thus lack the vested interests that spur teachers to action. In addition, the school board members often devote long hours to their local schools, leaving little time or energy for lobbying government.

The IASB staff nonetheless presents well-developed testimony in legislative committees and in other communications with lawmakers. The legislators and their staffs listen respectfully and sometimes act on the basis of a case well made. But because the group has not produced votes at the polling place, lawmakers do not fret much when they cast a vote against the IASB or the IASA.

In 1994 school management groups began to play political hardball. They forged the Illinois Statewide School Management Alliance, a single lobby representing the statewide organizations of board members, administrators, principals, and school business officials. They developed unified positions with regard to bills, coordinated their lobbying efforts, and created a political action committee to raise money for contributions to legislative candidates. Early in the 1994 election campaign, they endorsed Governor Edgar's reelection bid. This unprecedented endorsement was doubly appreciated by Edgar, who had just lost the endorsement of his previous ally, the IEA.

During the campaign, volunteers for the alliance walked precincts for Edgar and fourteen legislative candidates who were locked in contests with opponents backed by the IEA. Thirteen of the fourteen and Edgar won their races. Clearly the statewide school management groups had learned the lesson: if they wanted a seat at the table where education policy was shaped, they had to get into the trenches of electoral politics. During Edgar's second term in office, he rejected all school mandates bills that came to his desk. Still, the school management groups lack the clout of the IEA.

Several other players sometimes influence legislators. The Catholic Church has worked effectively to extend transportation, driver training, textbook, and other services to private schools. Small school districts are another force. In 1985, when legislation was introduced that would have required the smallest districts to consolidate, a group called Save Our Schools was organized literally overnight. It filled the Capitol with emotional adults and children opposed to the plan. Legislators and the governor quickly backed off.

Other players in education politics include the *Chicago Tribune* and State School News Service, an education policy and advocacy publication put out by former newspaper reporter Jim Broadway. The *Tribune* is as close to a statewide newspaper as can be found in Illinois. With the largest circulation and the largest editorial page staff in the state, the newspaper editorializes extensively and at length about education issues, which most legislators read. Broadway's State School News Service is read by most school superintendents and others interested in Illinois education politics.

The Illinois State Board of Education and its appointed superintendent served as important political players until the Blagojevich administration took office. The board submitted an independent budget to the legislature, and the superintendent was generally a strong advocate for education and on education legislation. Blagojevich tried unsuccessfully to have the board abolished in 2004 and replaced by a state agency under his control. He was successful in gaining authority to appoint all new board members, and during his tenure it appeared that the board and superintendent operated as wholly owned subsidiaries of the governor and his office. The only budget numbers or funding formula recommendations came from the governor's office, not from the state board of education.

Who Pays for Schools? Local Wealth and Inequities

Illinois spends about $20.6 billion per year in total on its public K–12 schools, which as noted at the beginning of this chapter is significantly higher than the national average on a per-pupil basis.[27] Illinois is, however, significantly different from national norms both in where the money comes from and in how the money is allocated. These differences have sparked decades-long efforts to reform the school finance system in Illinois, to no avail as yet.

School funding comes from state, local, and federal sources. In 2004–5, schools nationwide derived 47.6 percent of funding from state sources, 43.4 from local sources, and 9 percent from the federal government.[28] In fiscal year 2006, however, state revenues provided a much smaller share of school funding in Illinois than was the case in most states, with 29.6 percent coming from state sources, 62 percent from local school districts, and 8.4 percent from the federal government.[29] The share from the Illinois state government put the state in forty-ninth place, ahead of only Nevada on this indicator.

Property wealth, the primary source of local school revenue, is spread unevenly in Illinois. In 2005, median property taxes per household ranged from a high of $5,538 in Lake County to a low of $500 in Hardin County (see figure 9.1). As a result, districts with high property wealth can fund their schools extravagantly, without any state funding, while many property-poor districts fund their schools inadequately, even with significant state revenue assistance. For example, the per-pupil operating expenditures of elementary school districts in Illinois in 2006 ranged from $5,144 to $22,050, with a median of $8,298.[30] Even with the extremes taken out, some districts spent more than twice as much as others across the state. A random perusal of school districts using the Illinois School Report Card data shows that Aviston elementary school district in downstate Illinois spent $5,191 in 2005 while the Salt Creek district in suburban DuPage County expended $12,415, and Lake Forest High in Lake County spent $15,365 per pupil. (The Illinois School Report Card is an annual public report of test scores and related data about each public school in the state. The Report Card is easily available on the internet at the site of the Illinois State Board of Education.)

Illinois state government attempts to reduce the differences between the richest districts and the poorer ones by funding the difference between what property wealth provides and a "foundation level" of support. Determining this difference is accomplished by means of a complicated formula. Property-

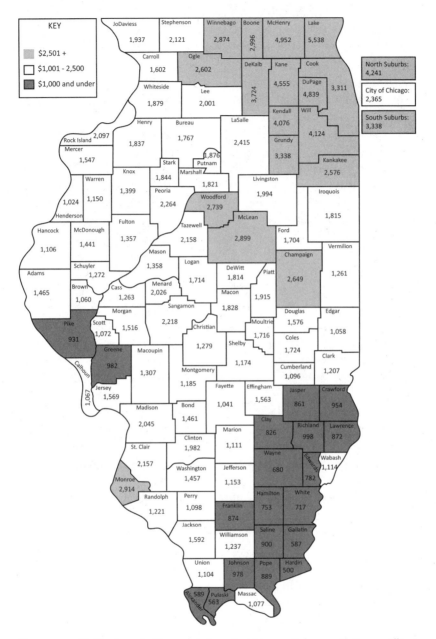

Fig. 9.1. 2005 Median household property taxes (paid in 2006), by county. Source: Illinois Department of Revenue Income Tax Statistics of Homeowner Property Tax Credit.

poor districts, generally those downstate, cannot reach the foundation level with their property taxes alone, so they receive significant monies from General State Aid[31] to bring their funding up to the foundation level. Property-rich districts, generally those in the Chicago suburbs, can generate more than the foundation level, often much more, from local property taxes alone, so they receive little from the General State Aid formula. For example, in the 2008–9 school year, the property-poor East St. Louis school district received $5,277 per pupil from the foundation formula whereas the Hinsdale district in suburban Chicago received only $218 from the formula.[32]

In 1997 the state board of education created the Education Funding Advisory Board (EFAB), made up of school experts, for the purpose of establishing an objective level of per-pupil funding that would be adequate to provide a minimally acceptable education. The idea was that the "adequacy level" would become the foundation level, which would still not eliminate the big disparities between the poorer and the richest districts.

In recent years, however, state aid has fallen short of the recommended adequacy level. In April 2005, EFAB set the adequacy level at $6,405, yet the actual amount funded by the state provided a foundation level of $5,334.[33] Adjusting for inflation to 2007, $2 billion more in state funding would be needed to reach the EFAB adequacy level, last set in 2005. Although EFAB recommended levels have not generally been achieved by the governor and legislature, the group's work provides a highly visible annual benchmark for elected officials to consider.

Speaking at a meeting of poor school districts, former University of Illinois education professor James Ward declared, "If you folks spent a couple of days in a top flight school in DuPage or Lake Counties and saw what they had that you don't, there would be a revolution."[34] No revolution occurred during the 1980s, when the per-pupil spending gap was widening, for two basic reasons. First, the fragmented education community could not agree on a course of action. Second, huge infusions of state funding for local schools would have been required to reduce the disparities significantly. The option of taking property tax money away from rich districts and giving it to poor districts was politically unacceptable. State lawmakers have appeared paralyzed by the magnitude of the action needed to reduce the variance: a shift the primary mechanism for funding schools from the local property tax to state sources such as the income tax, which would require a major statewide tax increase.

Efforts have been mounted to reverse the inequities, but none has been successful. The legislature in 1985 tried to institute a no-pain approach by passing a law requiring that all profits from the Illinois lottery go to education. The law turned out to be the equivalent of a shell game: the lottery profits replaced general revenue funds rather than supplementing them. Little additional money was apparently generated for education, and the public felt hoodwinked.

Low-property-wealth school districts organized in 1990 to mount a legal challenge to the school funding system. Thirty-six downstate school districts that were generally poor, joined by the Chicago Board of Education, organized the Committee for Educational Rights. They filed suit against the state of Illinois, alleging that the per-pupil expenditure variances violated the Illinois Constitution's mandate for "an efficient system of high quality public educational institutions and services." The suit was dismissed without a hearing at the circuit court level in 1992, and the group was rebuffed again in 1994 in the appellate court. The state supreme court did not take the appeal.

Another approach was tried in 1992, when the legislature put to a referendum a constitutional amendment that would have assigned the state "preponderant responsibility," as opposed to the current "primary" responsibility, for financing local schools. Opponents led by the Illinois Manufacturers Association and the Illinois State Chamber of Commerce targeted the collar counties and declared that adoption of the measure would require a doubling of the individual and corporate income taxes. The proposal garnered strong support in Chicago and downstate because those areas include the underfunded districts, but only 46 percent of voters in the collar counties were in favor of the change. Statewide the amendment received 57 percent of those voting, shy of the 60 percent required to ratify an amendment.

In 1997 Governor Jim Edgar backed an increase in the income tax to increase support for local schools. The bill passed the house but was blocked from coming to a vote in the state senate by its president, James (Pate) Philip, who felt the legislation would be bad for his suburban DuPage County voters. And this is true, in the sense that in any combination of income tax increase and property tax reduction, suburban residents would generally end up paying more in additional taxes than would downstate and Chicago residents.

More recently, a coalition of groups from across the state called A+ Illinois has generally backed an increase in the state income tax to reduce funding inequities, coupled with a reduction in property taxes. House Bill 750 proposed just such a tax restructuring, and the bill became a vehicle in the 2005 and 2007 legislative sessions for proponents of significantly increased state funding of schools, but the legislation never passed. In 2008, Senate Bill 2288 fulfilled the same objective as HB750, yet it also languished in the legislature, primarily because of Governor Blagojevich's promised veto. In 2009 the "750" legislation passed in the senate but never came up for a vote in the house.

In 2008, civic leaders created another high-profile group called Advance Illinois, which also has education and school funding reform at the top of its list. Obama confidant William Daley (brother of Chicago mayor Richard M. Daley) and popular former governor Jim Edgar co-chair the organization. On another front, the Chicago Urban League and the high-profile Chicago law firm of Jenner & Block filed another suit aimed at overthrowing the long-standing variances in financing between rich and poor districts. The suit contends that the civil rights of minority groups are being violated because these groups tend to be in districts that receive less in total school funding than do the generally white, more affluent school districts.[35]

The discussion above should make clear that finance is the most intransigent education problem in Illinois.

The Experiment in Chicago

Education reform came slowly to the Chicago Public Schools (CPS) system although its problems were evident to any who cared to look. But after years of teacher strikes, crumbling buildings, and declining performance, a major reform effort was mounted in the late 1980s.

The Chicago system is the third-largest in the United States, with 421,000 pupils in 623 schools.[36] Many of the city's white residents and those with the means to afford private schools have fled the system, so by 2009 the CPS student body was 46.2 percent African American, 41.2 percent Latino, 8 percent white, and 6 percent Asian and other. Eighty-five percent of the students were from low-income families.

Traditionally, Chicago Democratic political leaders have declared this huge system and its 44,400 employees to be out of bounds for education policy makers. The schools have been the province of local politicians, the Chicago Teachers Union, other AFL-CIO unions that represent nonteacher employees, and the central bureaucracy of the Chicago Board of Education.

In 1988 state policy makers were forced to deal with the Chicago public schools in response to intense local and national pressure and to an energized—and anxious—business community. In a scathing multipart series about the schools, the *Chicago Tribune* declared: "Chicago public schools are hardly more than daytime warehouses for inferior students, taught by disillusioned and inadequate teachers, presided over by a bloated bureaucracy, and constantly undercut by a selfish, single-minded teachers union."[37] Former Secretary of Education William Bennett spread the stain nationally by repeatedly calling Chicago's schools the "worst in the nation."

There was reason for concern. Thirty-five of the sixty-five Chicago high schools ranked in the bottom 1 percent of all high schools in the United States in achievement test scores.[38] Fewer than one-half of students who entered high school graduated; in several schools only 10 percent made it. In 1984 the system graduated only ninety-five hundred African American and Latino young people of twenty-five thousand originally enrolled as ninth graders. Only two thousand of those who did graduate could read at or above twelfth-grade level.

Until then few Illinois leaders and elected officials cared about the Chicago public schools. Their children for the most part did not attend them; only one of Chicago's eighteen state senators had a child enrolled in a Chicago public school in 1988. The segregated ghettoes, in which the worst schools are located, were outside the field of vision of most Illinois business and political leaders.

Money was not the most obvious problem. The Chicago Board of Education spent more money per pupil than the average school in Illinois (about $6,031 in 1991–92 compared to a statewide average of $5,327), but it was getting no results. The system's bureaucracy was partly to blame—a great deal of waste at the central office was suspected—but the fundamental problem was a feeling of defeatism. Many of the schools were embedded in the social pathologies of the areas they served—poverty of money and spirit and an absence of family, parenting skills, and good role models. Children with signs of potential were often "skimmed off" by private or public magnet schools, and in the city's worst neighborhoods, many stronger families moved out when they were financially able to do so.

The bureaucracy and the teachers responded exactly as organizational theorists would have predicted. Because the problems seemed beyond fixing, the teachers and staff often displaced the goal of good performance with the pragmatic objective of protecting themselves with good pay and the privileges of seniority. The catalyst for almost every negotiation over these matters was a strike, one every other year, on average, for two decades.

By 1987, when the walkout extended to nineteen days, Chicago parents and the business community had had enough. In addition to the embarrassing national attention, businesses were having increasing difficulty finding qualified entry-level employees. In a major effort to generate school reform, chief executive officers of leading companies joined forces with education activists and school reform groups such as the Chicago Panel on Public School Policy and Finance. They soon made history.

It was a remarkable period of civic involvement in Chicago as community interests gained strength and found common ground with the business leaders. After Mayor Harold Washington convened an education summit in the fall of 1987, bank presidents and corporate executives sat down to hash out a plan with community activists, young mothers, and university professors. More than half a dozen groups and coalitions developed various reform structures, most of them similar in their emphasis on shifting power from the central bureaucracy to school-based councils. In the spring of 1988, the reformers went to Springfield. Mary O'Connell, a journalist and mother of two students in the system, documented the process in *School Reform Chicago Style:*

> [The legislative campaign] featured continual assault waves of reformers, parents and community members, business leaders, and other "interested parties" descending on Springfield. They didn't just come on one designated day; they came day after day, week after week throughout June, forming what one experienced legislative observer calls "a consistent vigil" for school reform. UNO [United Neighborhood Organization] organized "five to ten" busloads of people; the People's Coalition sent six busloads. . . . The Campaign for School Reform . . . organized car pools and four busloads of people. The PTA estimates it sent "300 to 400" people. . . . At the same time, the business leaders organized by Chicago United came down by corporate jet and met with every legislator who would see them.[39]

The constant pressure by so many parties triggered an unusual collaborative process for hammering out reform legislation. In Speaker of the House Michael Madigan's office, Representative (later state senate president) John Cullerton and an ad hoc committee consisting of Senator Arthur Berman and Representative Anthony Young led a series of meetings that spanned, as Cullerton remembers it, "sixty hours, the last two weeks of the session, twelve hours a day."[40] In the room were parents, business leaders, union leaders, principals, and representatives of reform groups and community organizations.

The product of these efforts was the Chicago School Reform Act of 1988, whose reforms were called revolutionary for their scale and for the level of control given to parents and local communities. The act mandated a 25 percent cut in the central school bureaucracy and set elections to establish 540 decentralized local school councils.[41] These councils, each consisting of six parents, two community members, two teachers, and the principal, were charged with hiring the principal, approving the school budget, and creating a school improvement plan. Corporations encouraged their employees to run for the councils and provided training for the candidates. In the October 1989 elections, there were 17,000 candidates for the 5,400 council positions and 312,000 voters; Senator Berman called it "the most democratic election in the history of this country."[42]

The first dose of reality for the new councils came from the building engineers' union. The engineers, not the principals, controlled the school buildings. The councils were told that according to union rules no one could use a school in the evening unless a building engineer was present—at a cost of $162 per night in overtime pay. The central board of education had little money for such payments. Incredibly, therefore, some school councils were forced to hold meetings outside their schools. This glitch was overcome, and in a few months the councils were meeting inside their school buildings.

There were other frustrations for the councils as they jousted with statutes, rules, and central office staff to carve out some authority over their schools. But as education writer John Camper noted, reform was not to be discouraged easily: "In the struggle between the amateurs on the local councils and the 'experts' on Pershing Road [central school system headquarters at the time], most of the public is likely to sympathize with the amateurs."[43] Since their inception, however, local schools councils have frequently become mired in community politics and have sometimes become divisive rather than unifying forces for their schools.

By 1994, five years into the reform, no clear verdict had been rendered on the process. Anecdotal information and several surveys by reform organizations showed that many schools had gained ground through addition of new programs, intensive teacher training, and more flexible use of some school funding. But test scores showed only marginal or no improvements in many schools, and the Board of Education faced a potential deficit of $300 million going into the 1995–96 school year.

Exasperated by the continuing problems in the Chicago public school system, in 1995 the suburban-dominated Republican legislature and Governor Edgar enacted a sweeping reorganization of the system. The legislation gave the Chicago mayor power to appoint a five-person board and chief executive officer, prohibited Chicago teachers from striking, and provided local budgetary and regulatory flexibility. In other words, it's your problem, Mr. Mayor; you fix it. With lightning speed—and to the amazement of most—Mayor Daley and his appointed team balanced the budget, negotiated a multiyear contract with teachers before school opened, and infused the system with newfound enthusiasm and hope. Ironically, because of political fiefdoms in Chicago, these changes could have been imposed only by outsiders, that is, the suburban Republican legislative leadership and a Republican governor from downstate.

After 1995, Chicago school superintendents Paul Vallas and Arne Duncan (who became U.S. Secretary of Education) took the lead in shaking up the school system.[44] Vallas instituted a centralized, structured curriculum and extensive summer schooling for struggling students. Duncan developed twenty-eight charter schools on forty-eight campuses and created small schools within big high school structures, among other changes.

Still, the system struggles. Although the district has recorded gains on achievement tests, in 2005 the National Assessment of Educational Progress reported that low-income students in Chicago scored significantly lower than low-income students in other large urban districts on the eighth-grade science test.[45] On the other hand, graduation and drop-out rates have improved in recent years. Among blacks, for example, graduation rates increased from just 46 percent in 2002 to 51 percent in 2006, and graduation rates for Latino students improved from 51 to 59 percent in the same period.

Statewide, Illinois had a graduation rate in 2007 of 73 percent, higher than the 69.3 percent national average, and placing it twenty-ninth among the states.[46] Illinois is also in the middle range among the states on national tests generally; for example, in 2007 on the National Assessment of Educational Progress test, Illinois eighth graders ranked twenty-eighth among the states in reading, with 30 percent scoring at the proficient level or higher. Eighth graders ranked thirtieth in mathematics, with 31 percent scoring at or above the proficient level.[47] The "most average state" is also performing around average in its K–12 education system.

Decline of Higher Education Funding

In 1989 education expert Harold Hodgkinson wrote of Illinois, "While the schools are in some difficulty, there is no doubt that Illinois has, over the years, built a major system of higher education, diverse and of high quality, including both public and private institutions."[48] In the face of a series of state funding reductions between 2002 and 2008, leaders in the area of higher education have begun to worry that the quality of the diverse system may be in jeopardy.

Nor does the Illinois public appear to share Hodgkinson's enthusiasm for the high quality of the overall system. A 2008 opinion survey found that only 11 percent of the respondents considered the public four-year universities to be doing an "excellent" job, and most (77 percent) thought the quality of the public institutions was "about the same" as the quality of those across the nation.[49] Fifteen percent thought Illinois public universities were better than those in the rest of the nation, and 8 percent thought them worse.

In 2005, more than 805,000 students were enrolled at 12 Illinois public university campuses, 50 community college campuses, 111 private, nonprofit colleges and universities, 33 for-profit colleges, and 15 out-of-state institutions offering programs in Illinois or online.[50] Almost half the total enrolled in the two-year community college system, and two-thirds of those students attended part-time. The public and private four-year institutions roughly divided up the other half of the enrolled students. In full-time equivalent enrollments, each of the three sectors—public universities, private colleges and universities, and community colleges—enrolled roughly one-third of the total.

In 1947, before expansion of the public system, two-thirds of Illinois students attended private institutions. By 1992, private students made up 29 percent of the total. Since 1992, however, private nonprofit and for-profit institutions have once again surpassed the number of students enrolled in public four-year institutions; as of 2007, private institutions enrolled 219,000, compared with 202,000 in the public four-year category.[51]

Following strong funding increases in the late 1990s, Illinois General Revenue Funds support for public universities decreased 17.9 percent between 1998 and 2008, on an inflation-adjusted basis (see figure 9.2).[52] During the same period, support for elementary and secondary education increased by 46.8 percent. Between 2002 and 2006, state funding for colleges (other than student tuition payments) declined from $2.94 to $2.62 billion.[53] In 2006 state and local funding for higher education stood at $582 per capita, less than the national average of $643.[54]

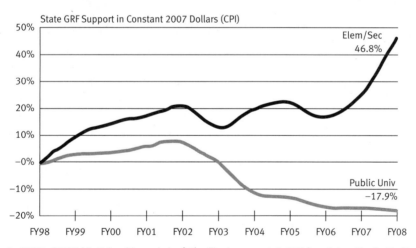

State GRF Support in Constant 2007 Dollars (CPI)

For FY02 to FY08 Public Universities excludes $45 million in payments to CMS from Universities for Health Insurance. Sources: Illinois State Budgets, ISBE and IBHE. FY08 is from Governor's Budget as proposed before initiatives and revolving funds. FY08 GRF funding based on Governor's proposed budget.

Fig. 9.2. Support for education in Illinois, 1998–2008. Source: Institute of Government and Public Affairs, University of Illinois, Urbana.

James D. Nowlan recalls being told as a young member of the Illinois house appropriations committee in the late 1960s that "we" (lawmakers) always provided one dollar for the "big kids" in higher education for every two dollars that went to the "little kids" in K–12 education. In contrast, for fiscal year 2008 Governor Rod Blagojevich proposed increasing spending for K–12 education by $1.5 billion and that for higher education by less than $50 million, a ratio of 30:1.

Illinois also exports more of its best students to out-of-state colleges and universities than any state other than New Jersey. According to a recent study by Illinois State University, Illinois exported 66,000 more students than it imported from other states during the decade from 1992 to 2002.[55] Most of these exports went to top-rated schools with average ACT scores of 27 or above, such as neighboring flagship public universities in Iowa, Indiana, Wisconsin, and Michigan.

Politics has played a part in the development of higher education in Illinois since 1863, when the Illinois General Assembly accepted 480,000 acres of land from the federal government through the Morrill Land Grant Act for the establishment of programs of higher learning.[56] Presidents of the sectarian colleges immediately lobbied to seek division of the proceeds among a select number of private institutions. This approach was resisted by legislators, however, and the communities of Lincoln, Bloomington, Kankakee, Jacksonville, and Urbana entered into competition as prospective sites for the new institution, each city bidding for the prize. Urbana's $285,000 was a low bid, but through political manipulation, it garnered the campus, which would become the University of Illinois.

From 1867 until World War II, the University of Illinois was the sole state university. There were five teacher education, or "normal," schools that struggled with whatever appropriations were left after the university had been funded. After the war, public higher education in Illinois blossomed into five multi-campus systems coordinated at the top by a statewide Illinois Board of Higher Education (IBHE).[57]

Since the great European universities were established in the Middle Ages, higher education has, above all else, valued autonomy, or at least relative independence, from the outside world. This status has become increasingly difficult to sustain in recent decades as state lawmakers have more actively demanded accountability for their appropriations. In 1961 the legislature created the Illinois Board of Higher Education to provide comprehensive planning and to reduce what had become blatant political logrolling by the legislative patrons of the two dominant universities, the University of Illinois and Southern Illinois University. Conceived to be independent of both elected officials and higher education institutions, the IBHE quickly came to be seen as a fair and relatively impartial advocate for higher education.

Executive directors of the IBHE sought unity among the five higher education systems in support of its budgetary recommendations to the governor and legislature. They maintained a strategy of recommending annual budget growth that was relatively balanced among the public systems as well as the private college sector. That is, if the governor's annual budget proposed, say, a 4 percent increase for higher education, the IBHE staff would allocate increases of around 4 percent to each of the five systems. Under this approach, although no system got everything it wanted, all systems—certainly the smaller ones—are thought to be better off than they would be with a return to raw political bargaining.

During the 1960s the fair share system worked rather well. Public enthusiasm for higher education was strong and money was plentiful; the universities' program and budget recommendations were usually accepted by the IBHE, and in turn by the governor and legislature, with little change.

When revenues for higher education tightened during the 1980s, cracks appeared in the wall of solidarity. Northern Illinois University went directly to the legislature to request a new law school. Over the strong objections of the IBHE and expressions of concern from the other systems, the legislature and governor agreed to establish the new school.[58] In a similar move, University of Illinois president Stanley Ikenberry negotiated directly with Governor Thompson on establishment of new research facilities. These projects required funding that was outside the capital construction priorities established by the IBHE; nevertheless, the university received the governor's blessing and garnered the funding.

Lawmakers representing NIU pushed legislation that would create an independent board for NIU and free it from the perceived constraints imposed by the regents system. Albert Somit, retired president of the Southern Illinois University (SIU) system, proposed compressing the present five systems into two, with SIU to become a part of the University of Illinois system. The IBHE has vigorously opposed such changes, defending the "system of systems" as working well for Illinois. But in 1992 Governor Edgar proposed the abolition of the boards of regents and governors and the creation of separate appointed boards for each of their universities. (This included Eastern Illinois University, Edgar's alma mater, which the governor felt suffered within the constraints of the Board of Governors system.) The legislature adopted the proposal in 1995, also merging Sangamon State University in Springfield with the University of Illinois.[59]

In recent decades, the struggle for funding between the public and private sectors has been civil but sometimes intense. In the 1980s the private sector received total state revenues (primarily in the form of financial aid to students) of about 8 percent of general revenue appropriations for all of higher education. In an effort to increase that amount in 1989, the Federation of Independent Illinois Colleges and Universities convinced a legislator to introduce a bill that would require the IBHE to "fully fund" the monetary award program of the Illinois Student Assistance Commission. This program helps needy students pay tuition at either private or public institutions, but underfunding mean that it did not meet all the financial needs of its applicants. To do so in 1990 would have required about $100 million in additional state funding.

The bill was opposed vigorously behind the scenes by IBHE, which tried without success to get the federation to withdraw the proposal. The staff of IBHE did not fear that the bill would pass, only that the effort represented a serious breach in the agreement among sectors to support the fair-share allocation approach. Indeed, the bill generated open conflict between the public and the private sectors, and though ultimately defeated easily on the house floor, it violated two of the norms of higher education politics in Illinois: do not propose anything that would take funding away from another sector within higher education, and do not impose on legislators the task of resolving conflict that higher education ought to resolve within its own community.

In 1995 the community college sector successfully advocated legislation that would take their system out from under the umbrella of the IBHE, but Governor Edgar vetoed the legislation at the urging of IBHE leadership. In 2007, Harper Community College in the northwestern Chicago suburbs challenged the IBHE with a proposal, ultimately unsuccessful, to authorize Harper to award four-year baccalaureate degrees. If such an idea did succeed, the authorization would open a Pandora's box of similar offerings by others among the thirty-eight community colleges in Illinois. The IBHE has approved centers in the Quad Cities (Moline, East Moline, and Rock Island, Illinois, and Davenport, Iowa) and Gray's Lake in Lake County, where multiple colleges and universities may offer courses, programs, and degrees.

With regard to matters of capital construction projects for higher education, the IBHE has provided a priority listing of projects based on objective criteria of need and appropriateness to the missions of the respective public colleges and universities. This process has also broken down. For example, in 2007 state senator Mike Jacobs (D-East Moline) and Governor Blagojevich agreed to fund a $75 million appropriation for a Western Illinois University campus in the Quad Cities on the Illinois-Iowa border.[60] The governor later threatened to veto any such appropriation, should it reach his desk, because he felt that Jacobs had double-crossed him on a vote. Although the IBHE had recommended planning monies for the project, clearly the elected officials in this case had no trouble playing politics with the project outside the IBHE process.

Even small private colleges have in recent years been hiring individual lobbyists to advocate for "member initiative" appropriations for building and renovation projects for their respective campuses, far outside the strictly public institution appropriations by the IBHE.

The IBHE has been put in an uncomfortable, some would say almost impossible, position by the erosion of respect for its decision-making role, which was always about keeping higher education outside politics. Its executive director holds a position that lacks the visibility and institutional prestige that comes with presiding over a flagship public university system, and the organization has no built-in constituency of faculty and alumni. As former executive director Richard Wagner has commented, "I'm a general without an army, and that makes leadership difficult, to say the least."[61]

With the governorship of Democrat Rod Blagojevich (2003–9), the influence of the IBHE eroded further. Instead of being an independent body, it became almost an arm of the governor's office.

Facing Stagnation: New Markets, New Players

When enrollment demand is strong, growth comes easily and all can benefit, as happened in Illinois between 1951 and 1967, when total college enrollment grew from 127,000 to 344,000 students.[62] During the 1980s, however, full-time-equivalent enrollments were basically flat for public universities, community colleges, and private colleges, and state appropriations grew at less than the rate of inflation. This combination created understandable concern within the world of higher education and forced private colleges and public universities to seek additional markets to ensure stability or growth.

The old system had been slow to respond to rapid growth in the largest, richest, and best-educated region in Illinois, that is, the suburban ring around Chicago. Other than Governors State University in the south suburbs, there is no public university campus in the collar counties. With bureaucratic and political hurdles slowing public expansion into this student-rich area, the private universities rushed ahead of their competitors into the new market. In the 1990s, Roosevelt University and the Illinois Institute of Technology (IIT), both headquartered in Chicago, opened suburban campuses. Northern Illinois University, located in DeKalb at the far western metropolitan fringe, sought IBHE approval to open a satellite campus in Hoffman Estates, on the grounds of the Sears corporate headquarters. This move was opposed, unsuccessfully, by the Federation of Independent Colleges and Universities on the grounds that its member institutions could fill the need without constructing expensive new public facilities.

In 1990 the IBHE recommended an appropriation of $27 million to construct a University of Illinois–DuPage County Center that would offer courses primarily at the graduate level and in high technology. The Illinois Institute of Technology saw this as unnecessary duplication of its own $15 million campus in the county, then under construction. It hired a lobbyist and, joined by the private college federation, mounted opposition to the appropriation. State senator Patrick Welch (D-Peru), whose district included NIU in DeKalb, killed the plan by amending the bill to exclude the UI appropriation.

Similar conflicts have been waged elsewhere. After two decades of on-and-off agitation, legislators in Rockford in 1989 won an appropriation of $500,000 to establish a branch of NIU in their city. This was achieved with the encouragement of NIU but over the objections of the private colleges' interest group, which counts Rockford College among its members.

Higher education is also undergoing something of a revolution as for-profit and out-of-state online universities have become aggressive in marketing their wares to Illinois students. For-profit colleges and universities more than tripled their enrollments between 1992 and 2007 in Illinois, from 13,500 students to 45,000. DeVry University alone doubled its enrollment from 7,000 to 14,000 students on three campuses. In 2007, out-of-state institutions enrolled 6,500 students in Illinois. The University of Phoenix, the largest university in the nation, enrolled 1,569 students in the state in 2005, primarily in online, internet-based degree-granting programs. So although the traditional college experience won't go away, a student today could well be sitting in a college dormitory taking an online course from another university thousands of miles away.

The increasing competition between the public and private institutions comes as the two sides become more like each other. Corporate grants to public universities have been growing such that by 1989 public and private institutions received roughly equal shares of corporate donations.[63] Public institutions have also become more aggressive in generating support from alumni, as the private colleges have been doing since their origins. This makes up somewhat for the recent decline in state funding, which, for example, dropped at the University of Illinois at Urbana-Champaign from 49 percent of total 1979 revenues to only 19 percent in 2005.[64]

Tuition charges have been outpacing inflation at both public and private institutions since the 1980s, striking fear in the hearts of parents and students alike. Tuition charges are set by the individual university governing boards, in contrast to states where the legislature and governor have a hand in setting the rates. The Illinois Truth in Tuition Law (2003) may have made it easier for public universities to raise tuition and easier for state lawmakers to ignore the increases. The law requires that the tuition for entering freshmen not change during their four-year college enrollment. As a result, only one class of students and parents becomes upset each year, rather than all of them as was the case when everyone's tuition went up each year.

In order to remain competitive, the public universities fight to keep their tuition low but feel forced to increase student charges for such things as room and board and athletic fees in the face of declining state funding. Between 2003 and 2006, aggregate tuition charges at public universities in Illinois increased from $692 million to almost $1 billion.

At the University of Illinois at Urbana-Champaign, tuition and fees have increased from $4,374 in 1998 to $9,882 in 2007. Indeed, the 2008 State Report Card on Higher Education gave Illinois an F in "affordability," noting that the average share of poor and working-class family income needed to pay for Illinois public university student expenses rose from 25 percent in 1992 to 37 percent in 2008.[65]

Though their stated tuition rates are still significantly higher than at the public institutions, the private colleges try to structure financial aid packages that bring their costs close to those of the public ones. For example, when admissions officers at Knox College, a private college in Galesburg, find that their prospective students are considering both Knox and the University of Illinois at Urbana-Champaign, the college officials can often build packages of federal, state, and Knox financial assistance and loans to bring out-of-pocket costs for Knox prospects close to those for students at the University of Illinois.

In summary, K–12 education has been pushed to the center of the political agenda, whereas higher education sits on the periphery at best. With significantly more money per pupil than it had a decade earlier, albeit unevenly distributed, K–12 education in Illinois has yet to prove that it can improve its scores significantly on nationally administered exams. Illinois colleges and universities overall need to reclaim the importance their sector held for lawmakers in the glory days of the 1950s or face a decline not only in funding but also in quality relative to many other state systems of higher education and to those abroad as well.

10.

Taxing and Spending

• • • • • • • • • • • • • • •

Budgets are the scorecards of politics. The ponderous documents tally in dollars the winners and losers in the game of who gets what.[1] The politics of budgeting revolve not only around who gets what but also who pays, and how much. Elected officials have strong political incentives to do things *for* their voters (for example, more spending on programs) and avoid doing things *to* them (for example, imposing more taxes). As a result, budgets have a natural tendency to increase over time, often faster than revenues.

The only way to make up the difference, besides cutting back on spending, is to increase revenues. This is a tricky proposition that might be likened to the ritual mating dance of the wild turkey. The governor, who often must initiate the revenue search, preens and struts throughout the state, trying to make his tax package attractive. The legislature reacts coyly, waiting to see how well this statewide dance plays with their voters. All the major players in state politics join in the ceremony.

Educators, as major beneficiaries, orchestrate marketing efforts among their constituents. Business groups often, but not always, rally the opposition. Government and university economists weigh in with projections of the consequences, good and bad, for the state's business climate. Elected officials and their staff also read the analyses and recommendations coming from groups such as the Taxpayers' Federation of Illinois, a moderate business group, and the Center for Tax and Budget Accountability, a research and advocacy group.

Often the ritual is never consummated. A scaled-back budget is contrived, cuts are made in programs, revenue projections are inflated, the payment of bills is delayed, and the tax dance is put on hold for another year or two. In 2007, for example, Governor Rod Blagojevich advocated a major "gross receipts tax" on business at each stage of the production process. Opponents in business mounted a furious opposition campaign and convinced the legislature that the tax was a bad idea. The proposal never came up for a formal vote.

The Illinois Budget

The Illinois state budget is a plan for spending scarce financial resources, including revenues from taxes, fees, lottery profits, casino boats, interest income, the federal government, and borrowed money (see figure 10.1). The budget reflects an allocation of public values. Each spending item competes with all others because the dollars available are always scarce relative to demand. Aid to college students competes not only with spending for prisons and county fairs but also with programs for mentally retarded adults and poor children.

An appropriation adopted by the legislature and approved by the governor represents spending authority for the fiscal year (FY), which for Illinois begins July 1 and ends June 30. The state spends money from six hundred separate funds, such as the Cycle Rider Safety Training Fund, the Hazardous Waste Research Fund, and the Wildlife and Fish Fund. But more than half of all spending is allocated through four general funds known as General Revenue, Common School, Common School Special Accounts, and Education Assistance. Budget problems tend to occur in the general funds.

The nearly $50 billion Illinois budget for 2008 represents about $4,000 per every person in Illinois and has major impact on the lives of residents.[2] Budgets redistribute resources, generally from the better off to the less well off. For example, Illinois provides health care to more than 2.5 million low-income residents at a cost of $16 billion, or almost $6,400 per beneficiary on average. Almost three million state residents are enrolled in public schools and colleges and university, at a total cost to the state of $12.4 billion, or about $4,000 per student. Health care and education together represent 60 percent of all state spending.

Smaller groups of state government "beneficiaries" absorb even larger amounts per person. For example, Illinois had forty-two thousand adult male and twenty-nine hundred female incarcerated prisoners in 2007 and another thirty-six thousand were on supervised parole, at a cost in state budget dollars of $1.2 billion, or about $26,000 per adult inmate.

But as of 2008, the state budget was in trouble primarily because of what

Fiscal Year 2009 Operating Appropriations by Major Purpose/Percentage of Total

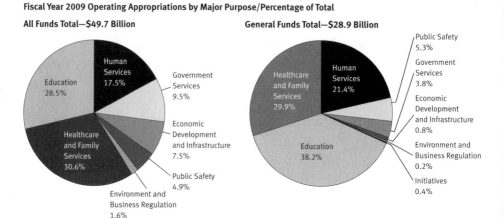

Fiscal Year 2009 Revenues by Source/Percentage of Total

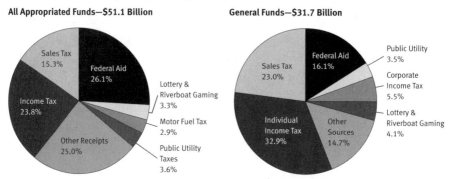

Fig. 10.1. Fiscal year 2009 appropriations and revenue for Illinois state government. Source: Illinois State Budget, Governor's Office of Management and Budget, Springfield, 2008.

economists call a "structural deficit," that is, perennial increases in spending that increase at rates higher than the annual growth rate of revenues. According to the Center for Tax and Budget Accountability, the difference between the costs of maintaining current programs and future obligations and what the state's revenue system produces (the structural deficit) is about $3 billion per year in a $50 billion budget.[3] This is a deficit that occurs without adding any new programs.

In the short term, these deficits can be hidden by underfunding long-term obligations to the state's pension and health care systems. In other words, because future retiree benefits don't have to be paid for this year, state government can appropriate (invest) less this year than will be needed to pay future obligations.

At the end of 2006, the Civic Committee of the Commercial Club of Chicago, a respected business group, conducted an extensive analysis of the state budget and declared, "Illinois is headed toward financial implosion. It annually spends or makes commitments that vastly exceed its revenues. The total of its debt and unfunded obligations now exceeds $100 billion."[4] Future state employee pension and health benefits make up most of the unfunded obligations, which reflects an unfortunate principle of political budgeting—spending for current operations is almost always preferred to saving for deferred obligations to be paid at a later date.

These unfunded obligations have developed in large part because the state has been spending and obligating more each year than it generates in revenues. According to the Civic Committee, the FY2007 Illinois budget included obligations and commitments of almost $6 billion more than actual spending, an amount equal to about 20 percent annual state General Funds revenues.[5]

How can the state get so far behind? Because rates of growth for major state programs are higher than those for state revenues, and because of understandable reluctance on the part of governors and legislators to increase taxes. For example, pension obligations and employee health benefits have been growing at about 12 percent per year for some years and Medicaid has grown at a rate of about 9 percent per year. Unfortunately for the state budget, state revenue growth has been about 4 percent per year on average.[6] Thus the structural deficit.

The Civic Committee's report concluded by identifying areas for cost savings in the budget but contending at the same time that increased taxation would be the only way to restore balance between spending (and obligations) and revenues.[7]

Searching for Pain-Free Revenues

As noted at the beginning of the chapter, elected officials enjoy doing things for people such as appropriating money for programs that benefit voters. They do not like to do things to people, in particular to levy taxes on them. But the bills have to be paid and the operating cash budget has to be balanced. To meet this responsibility, public officials search for revenues that are

- voluntary payments, as in taxes on gambling and tobacco usage;
- least painful (for example, a quarter-percent increase in the sales tax would add only a small amount to each purchase);
- tied to use of a product (such as the motor fuel tax);

- nontax revenue, such as a state lottery ticket (33 cents of each dollar gambled is net profit for the state); and
- big one-time payments from the lease of assets such as the state lottery and tollways. (Investment groups have offered billions of dollars up front in return for the rich cash flow generated by lotteries and tollways.)

The issue of who should pay becomes complicated. Should governments impose taxes on property, income, goods, services, gasoline, utilities, or the "sins" of consuming tobacco and alcohol? If it is to be property, should farmland, residential, and business property be treated the same, or differently, and if so, why? Who should bear the greater burden—individuals or corporations, the wealthy, middle class, or poor? These are tough questions for governors and lawmakers who want to be reelected.

Twenty-five taxes are listed in the 2008 edition of the *Illinois Tax Handbook for Legislators* including taxes for car rentals, pinball machines, and pull-tab and jar games.[8]

Fees for services and for the privilege of doing business make up another significant category of revenue, including university tuition charges, drivers' licenses, carnival amusement ride inspection fees, fishing and hunting licenses, and professional licenses for physicians, architects, and beauticians. In FY2006, the State of Illinois collected $5.6 billion from 1,349 fees administered by eighty state agencies, which represented about 8 percent of overall revenues.[9] If fees were tracked as a single revenue source, they would constitute the fourth-largest in the state.

Rod Blagojevich increased most fees significantly in his first year in office and subsequently transferred balances in many of these fee funds annually to the General Revenue Funds. Because many of the fees are imposed on small business and occupations that need licensure to operate, small business complained that this was in effect a new tax on business.

The main sources of state and local taxation come from taxes on what we buy (sales), what we earn (income), and what we own (property). The sales and income taxes are collected by the state government, and slices of these receipts are shared with local governments. The property tax, long ago the primary source of Illinois state government revenue, has become the primary tax of Illinois local governments. As can be seen in figure 10.1, after the federal government, income and sales taxes represent by far the largest specific sources of revenues for all the appropriated funds.[10]

Governors and lawmakers try to be sensitive to the impact that taxes might have on politically important groups such as senior citizens and on the state economy. Pension income of retirees was exempted from the state income tax, for example, although it is taxed by the federal government. In efforts to boost the economy, the tax on the purchase of manufacturing machinery was phased out in 1985, and farm machinery sales were exempted as well. The tax handbook lists sixty-seven types of items exempted from the sales tax, including newsprint and ink, coal gasification machinery, and goods sold to not-for-profit music or dramatic arts organizations.[11] These exemptions are called "tax expenditures" by public finance specialists because they represent the expenditure, or loss, of tax revenue that would otherwise be generated. In FY2005, these tax expenditures totaled $6.6 billion, more than enough to eliminate the state annual deficit and provide significant additional money for health care and education.[12]

During the same period, other taxes went up. To build and maintain the

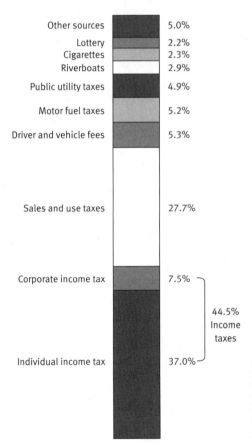

Other sources	5.0%
Lottery	2.2%
Cigarettes	2.3%
Riverboats	2.9%
Public utility taxes	4.9%
Motor fuel taxes	5.2%
Driver and vehicle fees	5.3%
Sales and use taxes	27.7%
Corporate income tax	7.5%
	44.5% Income taxes
Individual income tax	37.0%

Fig. 10.2. Percentages of revenue collected by major state taxes, FY 2007. Source: Illinois Tax Handbook for Legislators, June 2008, from the Legislative Research Unit, Illinois General Assembly, Springfield.

state's 137,000 miles of roads and 25,000 highway bridges, the state motor fuel tax on gasoline rose from 11 cents per gallon in 1983 to 20.1 cents in 1996, where it has remained.[13] The flat-rate income tax on individuals and corporations was increased in 1989 from 2.5 percent to 3 percent for individuals and from 4 percent to 4.8 percent for corporations. In 2009 Governor Pat Quinn made a major push to increase the state income tax.

In the quest for relatively painless revenue sources, policy makers in Illinois have been attracted by sin and gambling. The state tax on cigarettes rose from 20 to 30 cents per pack in 1990 and to 98 cents in 2002.[14] The lottery was the big revenue success story of the 1980s. Created in 1974, it got off to a slow start, generating net revenue of only $33 million in 1979, but by 2008, with steady promotion and regular introduction of new types of game cards, the lottery was netting $657 million on sales of $2 billion annually. This was more net revenue than the amount brought in by the income tax on corporations. If we think of Illinois as having four million families of three persons each, then the average family in Illinois spends about $500 per year in lottery tickets.

Riverboat gambling was approved in 1989. By 2007 riverboat revenues paid to the state had surpassed those from the lottery, reaching $813 million, plus additional revenues for the municipalities where the boats were docked.[15] A "drop" (total amount of wagering) of more than $25 billion, as was the case in 2007, represents about $2,000 for every man, woman and child in Illinois; this is misleading, however, because each dollar bet returns about 90 cents on average, so the same dollar can be wagered several times, on a declining basis, before becoming lost.

Legal gambling does not come without other costs to the state. It is widely assumed that poor families spend higher percentages of their income than the wealthy on the lottery and other state-sanctioned games. Jack R. Van Der Slik contends that the biggest negative is that the state legitimizes the making of new gamblers: "The state's slick television ads sustain hope among many, especially the poor, of a big hit, a jackpot, and then let the good times roll. Forget hard work. Saving is for suckers. Why sacrifice for the future when the future is now? And, like alcohol, widespread gambling reveals more and more people for whom it is an addiction. What a regressive way to serve the public."[16] Indeed, state-authorized and -operated gambling is the only function of state government in which its citizens must lose overall in order for the state to win.

With the structural deficit becoming evident to most state policy makers by 2007, three major approaches to increasing state revenues were proposed that year. Plans offered by the Cook County Assessor and by the Center for

Tax and Budget Accountability both proposed to increase the individual and corporate income taxes, expand the sales tax to include services (generally untaxed in Illinois), and provide property tax relief. True to his pledge not to increase income or sales taxes, Blagojevich trumpeted a plan that instead would tax the gross receipts on nearly all transactions by Illinois business.

The General Assembly rejected the governor's tax increase. Blagojevich tried in 2008 to gain passage of three revenue-generating proposals—lease of the lottery, borrowing, and awarding of a gambling license to the City of Chicago. Each of these would have provided revenue for the FY2009 budget as well as for longer-term purposes.

The concept of leasing the lottery to a private company is that the company could operate the gambling game even more successfully than the state. On that premise, a private company would pay from $10 to 12 billion up front for the right to operate the lottery for, say, thirty years. The company would pay off its debt from the cash flow from the lottery and presumably make a profit as well. The state would have the money up front and could use part of it to help fill the hole in the 2009 budget and also have investment income on an ongoing basis. This income might or might not be as great as the state would have earned annually from continuing to operate the lottery. In 2009 the General Assembly enacted legislation to lease the lottery as well as legalize video poker in taverns and veterans' clubs.

The proposal to borrow up to $16 billion to reduce the unfunded liability in the pension systems had a similar attractiveness. If the state sells the debt at a low rate of interest and earns a higher rate of interest from investing the $16 billion, then the state receives a net income. This is called "arbitrage," that is, a difference in interest rates that benefits the borrower. Of course, the opposite could occur, in which case the state would be a loser. If the borrowing proposal had been successful, which it was not in 2008 or 2009, the governor also planned to use part of the proceeds to help fill the FY2009 budget hole. In 2008 a gambling license was sold to Midwest Gaming for a casino in DesPlaines, near O'Hare Airport in the Chicago suburbs. DesPlaines paid $125 million up front to the state and pledged to pay an additional $10 million per year for thirty years. In 2009 Pat Quinn proposed a 50 percent increase in the state income tax rate, from 3.0 per cent to 4.5 percent.

Instead, legislative leaders crafted fiscal year 2008, 2009, and 2010 budgets without the governor's input and without any tax increases. We should note that the budgets have in recent years been crafted almost wholly by the legislative leaders and a few lawmakers who specialize in the state budget. Rank-and-file legislators are basically left out of the process, except when they vote on a final budget, which is presented to them without time for analysis.

At the end of the 2009 spring session of the General Assembly, legislators had enacted General Funds appropriations of $21 billion to serve programs that cost $28.4 billion in fiscal year 2009 (which ended June 30, 2009). Clearly, the growing mismatch between inadequate revenues and spending levels will require continuing work by lawmakers and governors in the years to come.

Budgeting: Simple Math, Difficult Decisions

According to Robert L. Mandeville, budgeting is a simple five-step process: (1) find out what you have in the bank; (2) estimate your receipts for the budget period; (3) decide what you want to have in the bank at the end of the budget period; (4) subtract item 3 from the sum of the first two items; and (5) allocate the remaining amount among programs.

"That's all there is to it. That's the truth," says Mandeville, who served as director of the Bureau of the Budget from 1977 to 1990.[17] Simple, perhaps, but never easy, because of step 5.

There are several fundamental points to keep in mind about budgeting in Illinois. First, major changes are difficult because most funding is already committed. Second, demands will always outstrip resources, and third, the growth generated primarily by inflation will not be enough to cover new programs.

A balanced budget is required by the Illinois Constitution, which says that "proposed expenditures shall not exceed funds estimated to be available for the fiscal year as shown in the budget."[18] This means that unless some new revenue stream is available, most of the spending for the coming year's budget will mirror that of the previous year. Education, transportation, health care, assistance to the poor and abused, and state agencies consume most of the budget every year and leave little room for dramatic changes.

Budgeting frustrates a new governor, who wants to do for his constituents all the good things he might have promised in his campaign. James D. Nowlan recalls a scene from the transition to office in 1976 of James R. Thompson, who had been holding sessions with his budget director, Robert Mandeville. As they prepared to review the education budget, Thompson looked at Mandeville and said, with some exasperation, "Okay, Bob, how much *can't* I spend today?"[19]

There are always more demands than available resources can satisfy. As Mandeville explained in 1990:

> Working on the budget is like spending an afternoon watching "Poltergeist II" and the "Attack of the Killer Bees." Just as Carol Anne yelled, "They're Baaack!!" so lobbyists and advocates will soon descend upon Springfield ar-

guing for a bigger piece of the budget pie. . . . Killer bees have not yet reached Illinois, but the KILLER P'S have. Pensions, Public Aid (health care), and Prisons have all made their assaults on the state's programs.

These programs are not killers in themselves. They are legitimate program needs that deserve as high a level of funding as possible. They can be budget killers because they require large increments to make changes. . . . Full funding of the pension systems is a noble goal. Cutting the funding from the poor to pay for state pensions is not. Restructuring Medicaid to make poor children healthier is a noble goal. Cutting the funding for poor children's education to fund Medicaid restructuring is not. If passing tough sentencing laws to put criminals behind bars is a noble thing to do, providing taxes to build the prisons and pay the guards is a noble thing.[20]

Under this pressure from areas of growing need, lawmakers must seek other ways to fund their pet projects, and they often latch onto inflation-induced "natural growth" in revenue. This growth is the revenue increase that occurs even when there is no change in the tax rates. It is generated primarily by inflation and generally does not represent a windfall, for the costs of salaries and health care and goods purchased by state government also increase with inflation.

Although it might seem self-evident that natural growth is not a dependable source of new money, Thompson in his FY1989 budget book listed twenty-one new initiatives adopted either by the legislature or by administrative action of the governor since 1985. They included education reforms, expanded probation services, expanded circuit breaker (property tax) relief for the elderly, searches for missing children, AIDS research, and asbestos removal in schools.[21] There had been little change in the state's tax structure during this period; Thompson and the legislature were counting on inflation-induced natural growth to carry the budget forward. Finally, in 1989 the legislature found it necessary to increase the individual income tax from 2.5 percent to 3 percent to accommodate increased spending for both "the Killer Ps" and new programs.

Natural growth might suffice to fund new initiatives if simultaneous minor cutbacks in various program areas were considered a normal part of budgeting. In reality, the opposite is true: the tendency is for programs to cost a little bit more each year. Governors, budget staff, and legislative leaders basically accept what was spent during the preceding year, on the assumption that it was reasonable—after all, they voted for it. Then they focus on how much of an increase, or increment, is proposed for the coming year. Specialists in public management have criticized this "incremental" approach as less than rational, saying that it lacks comprehensiveness and leaves most of the budget outside review.

Yet the time pressures of an annual budgeting cycle and the size and complexity of the budget induce this focus. As budget analyst Raymond F. Coyne pointed out, incremental budgeting has the consequence of limiting political conflict.[22] If the whole budget were opened up and the budgeteers were allowed to start from scratch each year, they might feel compelled to joust over the whole budget pie, rather than just the small slice represented by the increment. It would be politically treacherous and impractical given the limited legislative session time available, and thus it is almost never done.

The Other Budget: Capital Projects

In addition to expenditures for immediate purposes, the state makes long-term investments in highways, university laboratories, wastewater treatment plants, prisons, and other projects that will last many years. The 162-page Illinois Capital Budget for FY2008 proposed authorizing $11 billion for various projects, most of them for transportation projects, an amount equal to almost one-quarter of all proposed appropriations dollars.[23] The capital budget was not implemented, however, because no source of revenue was identified to support the debt.

Just as individuals pay for a home with a mortgage, the state borrows money and retires the debt by paying off principal and interest over the course of ten to thirty years. Illinois has authorized a number of agencies to borrow money by issuing bonds. The primary authorities are the Capital Development Board and the Illinois Finance Authority. Others include the Metropolitan Pier and Exposition Authority (for Chicago's McCormick Place and Navy Pier) and the Sports Facilities Authority (which built the White Sox stadium).

Although capital spending is separate from operating expenses, the two budgets are nevertheless in competition because state borrowing generally requires the identification of a revenue source or sources to make principal and interest payments. And sometimes the revenue source is insufficient. For example, a special tax on used cars was to be a primary source of revenue for the Build Illinois bonds, but in FY1990 that source generated only $41 million of the $83 million needed. As a result, an additional $42 million in general revenues was deposited in the Build Illinois account, money that might otherwise have been available for education or child care services.[24] Similarly, in 2007 the Metropolitan Fair and Exposition Authority took $30 million from general revenue funds to meet annual payments on bonds because the designated revenue sources for new capital projects of the authority, such as the new McCormick Place West building, were inadequate.[25]

Bonds cannot be sold to investors without assurances that streams of revenue are in place to pay the principal and interest for up to thirty years. During the Blagojevich administration (2003–9), most capital projects went unfunded because of a lack of an identified stream of revenue to meet bond obligations.

Although not part of capital spending, pension funding provides another illustration of the competition between current expenditures and long-term deferred obligations. Each year the state appropriates monies into retirement system funds for state employees, judges, legislators, schoolteachers, and university faculty and staff. The pension funds currently have balances large enough to pay for the current year's obligations, so it is possible to reduce the annual appropriation for pensions without shorting anyone *at the moment*. This often happens when money is tight, as in the FY1991 budget, when the legislature authorized the Chicago Board of Education to take $66 million that was to be invested in the Chicago teachers' pension system and appropriate it instead for teachers' salaries. The practice had become so widespread across the system that by 2007, the state pension systems had unfunded future liabilities of $49 billion, almost $4,000 per person in the state, which placed the state last among the states in amount of unfunded pension liabilities.[26]

Politics of "Shift and Shaft"

The politics of federalism can be seen in large part as a serious game in which each level of government—federal, state, and local—tries to expand its authority over programs while inducing the others to pay for the changes. Chapter 9 shows how, with the No Child Left Behind Act, the federal government asserted extensive authority over local education while paying only part of the bill. The State of Illinois has also imposed mandates for the way its local schools must operate while imposing the costs of compliance on local property taxpayers. Local government leaders are also skilled at playing the game. In 1993 municipal leaders negotiated an increase—from one-twelfth to one-tenth—in the share of state income tax revenues automatically distributed to cities and counties, thus reducing the amount available to be spent in the state budget. This game has been aptly labeled the politics of "shift and shaft."

One argument for shifting money from one government to another is that the receiving government can deliver the service more effectively. These monies can also act as a carrot to induce state or local governments to initiate or change programs. Prominent examples of the 356 federally supported but state-administered programs in Illinois include Medicaid, education, Temporary Assistance to Needy Families, and highway construction.[27] In FY2009, $13.1 billion in federal funds was directed to Illinois state government, more than half in the form of grants for health care and social services.[28] The $13.1 billion represented about one-fourth of total state appropriations.

Nevertheless, Illinois will continue to receive less from the federal government on a per capita basis than do most states, because many federal programs allocate funds on the basis of per capita wealth, and poorer states receive more support. Being above average in wealth, Illinois receives less per capita for many programs. Illinois is required, for example, to provide 50 percent of the cost of the Medicaid program, whereas neighboring Indiana and Iowa pay only 37 percent. In FY2008, federal grants to Illinois represented 3.1 percent of all federal grants, whereas Illinois's population represents 4.3 percent of the nation's population.[29]

There is a close working relationship between Illinois and its local governments on matters of finance, with the state government collecting local sales tax revenues and distributing them back to the local governments; the state also shares with local governments part of the income, sales, and motor fuel taxes. Major state appropriations are made for local education and social services; about 60 percent of all state expenditures are distributed in the form of grants and awards to school districts, nongovernment social service agencies, and individuals.[30]

The single largest source of revenue for Illinois governments continues to be the local property tax. In 2007 the property tax generated $21 billion for local governments, more than was generated that year for state government by the personal income tax, the state sales tax, and lottery profits combined.[31] Schools receive almost 60 percent of total property tax revenues; municipalities about 16 percent; special districts, 12 percent; counties, 8 percent; and townships, 3 percent.

The property tax has been a revenue mainstay since the state and its local governments were established, and today Illinois relies somewhat more heavily on the property tax to fund local services than do most states. In 2005 Illinois property tax revenues came to $1,469 per person, while the average was $1,134 for the nation.[32]

Heavy reliance on the property tax has caused problems. First, citizens consider the property tax the least fair tax in Illinois, according to an annual opinion survey by Northern Illinois University.[33] The tax is, for example, generally paid in two large lump-sum payments each year, which can mean two payments of up to $6,000 *each* on a half-million dollar home. Second, property wealth is not spread evenly across the state. In 2005 median household property taxes ranged from $5,538 in Lake County and $4,839 in DuPage

"AW, THAT'S NOT A GHOST—THAT'S SOMEONE OPENING THEIR PROPERTY TAX BILL".

Fig. 10.3. Cartoon by Bill Campbell (Courtesy of Carl Sandburg College)

County (two of the collar counties) to less than $500 and $563 in Hardin and Pulaski Counties, respectively, in deep southern Illinois[34] (see figure 9.1).

Political Dynamics of Budgeting

In the 1960s the political scientist Thomas Anton saw budgeting in Illinois as a ritualized game in which each interested party played its part and, if all went well, everyone came out a winner.[35] The agencies would request more than they needed, and the governor and legislature would each make some cuts. The final budget would provide the agencies what they actually wanted—sometimes more than expected—and the politicos could claim to have cut the budget.

Players in the budget game still anticipate the actions of others. Since the 1960s, however, the process has become more professional with the addition of the Governor's Office of Management and Budget (GOMB), legislative staffing, the Illinois Board of Higher Education (which recommends university budgets), and the reduction veto provided to the governor by the 1970 constitution. As a result, the state agencies probably have less influence than they had in an earlier era, and the legislature has become more involved in the substance of budgeting negotiations.

In simplified form the process is as follows. State agencies make budget requests to the GOMB, which makes its recommendations for each agency to the governor. If an agency head feels strongly that the budget level recommended by GOMB is unreasonably low, the agency head might be able to appeal directly to the governor, who resolves the differences. The final budget document, often up to seven hundred pages in length, is presented in March via a formal budget address by the governor to the General Assembly.

Throughout the process, the interest groups and beneficiaries of state spending press their claims. If budget recommendations are seen as inadequate, cries of catastrophe erupt. University presidents cite a brain drain of faculty who are leaving for higher salaries elsewhere. The rhetoric often heats up, as in this 1989 statement in a press release from the state school superintendent: "School districts are going down the financial tube; Chicago school reform is jeopardized before it gets underway. . . . We are in disgraceful condition and it's time for the people of this state to say we've had enough."[36]

The governor generally dominates the budget process because he constructs the original budget and later can impose line-item and reduction vetoes on spending requests outside his budget that are sent to him by the legislature. The legislature has, however, shown the capacity to impose its own spending priorities. As noted above, in 2007 the legislature basically took over the task of crafting a final state budget, although the governor had the final word.

Possibly because the rank-and-file lawmakers sometimes chafe at playing such a small role in budgeting, legislative leaders in the 1990s began a program of "member initiatives," in which each lawmaker was allocated an amount of money for projects identified by the lawmaker for his or her district. This is similar to the ear-marking process in the federal budget. The amount of money, often $1 million or more per lawmaker, has varied from year to year; in FY2009 the member initiative program was halted because of inadequate budget revenues. The member initiatives also increase the power of leaders over their members, because lawmakers can be punished or rewarded by the allocation process.

In summary, the budget represents accommodation. Seldom does any participant—agency head, GOMB analyst, governor, lawmaker, legislative staffer, lobbyist—see his or her budget agenda fully satisfied. Each uses influence and power, whether it is expert information, a key vote in committee, veto action, campaign support, or editorial comment, to pursue budget goals. The final appropriations, after the legislature responds to the governor's vetoes, roughly approximate the will and values of the political society of Illinois.

Workings of the Governor's Office of Management and Budget

After the annual budget process is complete, the chief executive has the responsibility of matching spending with revenue. Budgeting at this stage is basically cash management, and it is a challenging task. The monthly balance in the state's general funds "checkbook" has often fallen into the fiscal "danger zone" of less than $200 million, sometimes for a year or more at a time. Management of the budget falls to the GOMB, which must ensure that budget commitments are being met, and to the state comptroller, who holds the state checkbook and must often delay payments of valid claims to avoid overdrawing the accounts. As former budget division chief Craig Bazzani put it: "The [office of management and budget] is also something of an 'efficiency engineer.' As a protagonist in the budgeting process, it is GOMB's job to help departments find a more efficient way to 'build a better mousetrap'—that is, educate more students at less cost, improve management, or save more agricultural land."[37]

The GOMB requires a quarterly spending allotment plan of the agencies. Each agency under the jurisdiction of the governor is required to identify planned expenditures for each line item for each quarter. This forces an agency to refine its internal budget and gives the GOMB analyst assigned to work with that agency a plan to monitor.

The checkbook balance of cash on hand generally gives a misleading picture of the state's fiscal situation because the balance is subject to manipulation.[38] For example, the governor and his GOMB often find it necessary to hide the true budget deficit situation by delaying payment requests for nursing homes, hospitals, and school districts and by speeding up collections of certain taxes. In 2008, for example, health care providers were owed $3.8 billion that was deferred from one fiscal year to the next.

Politics of Taxation

As the old saw goes, "The only good tax is one you pay, and I don't." In 1978 James Thompson was running for his second term as governor, shortly after a property tax limitation known as Proposition 13 was adopted by California voters. To show his concern about taxes, he led a petition drive to put a nonbinding advisory referendum on the ballot. This so-called Thompson Proposition asked voters whether they favored ceilings on their state and local taxes. As might have been expected, 82 percent favored the idea.

Yet voters can be convinced to support tax increases. In elections held between 1972 and 1993, from one-fifth to one-half of all referendums for school tax rate increases were passed by the voters. Many rejected issues went back to the voters again and again until they were ultimately passed.

Illinois state finance is a cyclical affair, according to budget expert Michael D. Klemens: "Spending increases have preceded gubernatorial elections; then tax increases followed elections. Tax increases have prompted spending increases; then revenues have lagged and more tax increases are needed."[39] In a display of candor, Governor Thompson acknowledged in 1987 that he had signed into law dozens of programs without funds to pay for them: "Many of them I signed against the advice of my director of the Bureau of the Budget [Robert Mandeville], who for 11 years has stood for fiscal integrity and 'don't sign a bill unless you can pay for it, regardless of how good it is.' And I'd say to him, 'Doc, this is a good idea.' And he'd say, 'You can't pay for good ideas with no money.' . . . And I'd sit and say to myself, well, maybe the economy will pick up. Maybe they'll [the legislature] do the right thing next year. Maybe prosperity is around the corner. Maybe, maybe, maybe. . . . I should have listened to Dr. Bob."[40]

In part as a result of his actions, Thompson sought tax increases in 1987 and 1988, each time leading the ritual dance with legislators and interest groups. For two years, the legislature rejected the governor's pleas for more revenue. In 1989, however, following the lead of Speaker of the House Michael Madigan, lawmakers enacted a temporary 20 percent increase in the state income tax. It was less than Thompson wanted and in a different format, but he signed the bill and moved on, the crisis averted for the time being.

In more recent years, such outside groups as the Center for Tax and Budget Accountability and some lawmakers have been calling for tax increases, but Governor Blagojevich vowed to veto any that reached his desk. This dampens interest among lawmakers in possibly supporting a tax increase, because they would be making the politically tough vote for increases that probably would never become law because of the veto power of the governor. Votes for tax increases almost always become grist for commercials by opponents in the next election.

In 2009, however, Governor Quinn proposed an income tax increase that failed to pass the house in the spring session. For reasons noted above in the discussion of the structural deficit, the issue of increasing taxes will be with the legislature in the years to come.

Illinois as a Moderate Tax State

A consistent characteristic of Illinois tax policy is the moderate tax burden imposed on residents, at least relative to other states. State and local taxes in Illinois represent a slightly smaller percentage of personal income than they do for the nation as a whole. In 2006 state and local taxes in Illinois represented 10.6 percent of personal income; the national average was 10.9 percent. Revenues generated per person from state and local sources were $5,605 in 2006, less than the national average of $5,811.[41]

Advocates in Illinois for higher taxes seek to address education reform, health care, and infrastructure issues. There are equally intense opponents to tax boosts. Each side makes its arguments, one on behalf of improving workforce quality and social justice, the other in the interests of maintaining an attractive business climate.

For better or worse, the levels of taxation and performance in Illinois are probably reflections not so much of governors and legislators as of the individualistic attitudes and values that Illinois citizens bring to government. They consider government not as an instrument for doing good but, rather, as a necessary evil. Good services and great schools everywhere would be nice, the voters and their leaders seem to say, but if it means a consistently higher tax effort, perhaps the current system will be good enough after all.

11.

Illinois: Strong but not Achieving

● ● ● ● ● ● ● ● ● ● ● ● ●

Illinois is a relatively wealthy state with a huge, diverse economy. The state is richly endowed with natural resources of fertile farmland and enviable water supplies. As the great American Heartland's metropolis, Chicagoland continues to be the pulsing heart for rail, air, interstate highway, and waterway traffic probably unsurpassed in the nation. Yet the state suffers from a dispiriting culture of corruption and a "we're just average" complex that seems to restrain leaders and citizens from aspiring to distinctive high achievement as a state. Possibly affecting the complex is a severe lack of state identity, with Chicagoland and southern Illinois having stronger identities than the state itself.

As Illinois moves into the second decade of the new century, the landscape continues to tilt strongly toward the expanding metropolitan frontier. Citizens of the megalopolis anchored by Lake Michigan will continue to prize the wide-open spaces on the metropolitan frontier and the jobs in the suburban collar. Once-freestanding cities such as Aurora, Elgin, and Joliet are being leap-frogged by developments that reach out toward Rockford, DeKalb, and Ottawa, cities about ninety minutes from Chicago's Loop.

Under this relentless tide, the old downstate region will become physically smaller and politically weaker. As the suburban frontier envelops them, the residents and their leaders will face new problems. They will build streets, schools, sewers, and waste treatment facilities, cope with an influx of newcomers, and try to hold down their property taxes.

As longtime suburbanites move farther outward, urban dwellers of lesser means will replace them, especially in the older suburbs, where the problems of urban America were already evident in the 1990s. In a grand and ironic illustration of the urban development cycle, the inner core will continue its rejuvenation as old commercial and industrial sites are rehabilitated as condominiums and retail meccas.

In 1993 Chicago mayor Richard M. Daley created a stir by moving from the family's longtime political base in the working-class, now gentrifying, neighborhood of Bridgeport into a posh residential complex called Central Station, built on railroad property not far from the Loop in downtown Chicago. Nearby, former printing and manufacturing plants were transformed into loft apartments for young professionals, and west of the Loop new public facilities, commercial buildings, and residential developments were reclaiming decrepit industrial buildings.

Like a beating heart pumping vitality into the surrounding tissue, the expanding downtown area was creating a new ripple of middle-class expansion into once-struggling neighborhoods, pushing poorer blacks and Latinos and ethnic whites outward. As the middle-class population grew in the central city, it reinforced the role of Chicago's Loop as a magnet that draws the powerful, including political leaders, into its grasp. As in 1900, two players will dominate, but instead of the city and downstate, they will be two uneasy neighbors: the city and its own suburbs.

Winners and Losers

Since the origin of Illinois, political leaders have bargained for funding and benefits for their respective regions. In the 1830s Abraham Lincoln and eight fellow legislators from the Springfield area (they were known as the "Long Nine" because each was more than six feet tall) worked as a bloc to move the state capital from Vandalia in southern Illinois to Springfield in the rapidly growing center of the state. In return they supported canals, plank roads, and railroads for all who would vote their way on moving the capital.

The state's leaders have since distilled the bargaining process into a fine art of regional quid pro quo that takes in everything from school aid and transportation to state university campuses and construction of civic centers. Compromise is key, as is sharing the wealth. In 1984 the Chicago public school system requested $22 million from the legislature to end a strike. Leaders of the other two regions stepped forward, stated their price, and increased the tab to $75 million, providing something for everyone.[1] When the Chicago

Transit Authority sought an increased state subsidy in 1985, the legislature took care of it after arranging for similar boosts for several downstate transit districts.[2] But two decades later, in 2007, the legislature provided new taxing authority for mass transit in Chicago and the suburbs yet failed to enact a highways and buildings program demanded by downstate lawmakers. This may be a reflection of the declining power of downstate Illinois.

As in any negotiation, the uncomfortable question is who gets the better part of the deal. Downstaters have long believed that Chicago drains resources from the hinterland, especially funds for social services spending. Chicagoans complain that downstaters waste money to build highways in sparsely populated areas. Collar county leaders, citing the tax load, whine that the other regions take advantage of the hard-earned wealth of the suburban middle class.

The Legislative Research Unit found in 1987 that the suburban collar counties paid more proportionally in taxes than either downstate or Chicago and received less back in spending for state programs. That did not surprise the political economists James Fossett and Fred Giertz. Governments are, after all, in the business of taking in taxes and redistributing the resources, generally from the more prosperous to those less so. Even greater redistribution might well be in order, said Fossett and Giertz: "Considering the severity of their problems, Chicago and other hard-pressed areas are receiving relatively less state funds from a number of program areas, while the prosperous areas are receiving relatively more."[3]

But that shift will not happen without a fight, in part because many suburban legislators, indeed, most lawmakers in Illinois, have come to see political work as full-time careers. To help their reelection chances, they have become more intent on showing the home folks that they bring in their fair share of money and projects. This tends to perpetuate the status quo and constrain redistribution from one region to another.[4]

Whatever its faults, the individualistic culture shows a remarkable degree of resilience. The market-driven political culture by its very nature helps strong economic players become stronger and encourages the weaker players to find the right allies and develop the tactics needed to grab a piece of the action.

Downstaters and their city cousins have already begun to realize that they have more in common than previously thought. In 1990, when poor rural school districts were joined by the Chicago Board of Education in a lawsuit concerning school spending disparities, the Chicago Urban League and the Illinois Farm Bureau were additional unlikely allies. Two years later, when a proposed constitutional amendment sought increased school funding, the chief sponsors were a Chicago Democratic senator and a Republican senator-farmer from central Illinois. The business coalition that successfully opposed the measure targeted its media campaign at the suburbs.

By 2008 the struggle for education funding reform (read: more state money through an income tax increase) took the form of a large coalition of school district and tax reform advocates called A+ Illinois. Members include the Chicago Public Schools as well as the Marion school district in deep southern Illinois and several labor unions, among scores of partners. That year, business interests created a new advocacy group called Advance Illinois that targeted education reform as its highest priority as well.

The school aid formula provides a lens that reveals where the greatest needs are in Illinois. The formula bases allocations on property values in each school district and the numbers of poor children. It consistently shows that Chicago and downstate would almost always receive more resources than would the suburbs from increases in school aid formula funding. In the 1994 gubernatorial campaign, Democratic candidate Dawn Clark Netsch proposed (unsuccessfully, it turned out), a state income tax increase that would be tied to property tax relief and increased state school aid. Confirming the obvious, the Legislative Research Unit showed inquiring legislators that in the aggregate Chicago and downstate would be net beneficiaries, at the expense of the collar counties.

Downstate is becoming isolated from metropolitan Chicago, which dominates the state in wealth, political influence, and media attention. As the newspapers' "news hole" shrinks, there is less coverage of state issues. The state capitol has largely been abandoned for Chicago by state officers, agency directors, and policy makers whenever the legislature is not in session. Former governor Rod Blagojevich traveled infrequently and with little relish to the capital, even during legislative sessions.

There is little to bring the three regions together, as there is little sense of statewide community. Residents of metropolitan Chicago tend to vacation in Wisconsin and Michigan, not downstate. The Cubs and the Bears draw downstaters, yet the visitors seldom venture far from the buses parked near the stadiums. It is not unknown for a newly elected legislator from Chicago to make his first-ever trip downstate on the day he or she is sworn into office in Springfield.

Illinois has no unifying themes. There is no "Eyes of Texas" or "My Old Kentucky Home" to arouse sentiment. The fight song of the University of Illinois is little known outside the campus and alumni community.[5] This lack of unity may help explain why disparities in per pupil spending between the poorest schools (generally downstate) and the richest (in the suburbs) continue to be among the greatest in the nation. There is no emotional connection from region to region, except perhaps wariness.

Corruption: A Stain on Illinois's Reputation

In recent years, the authors have been struck by the continuing, indeed, unrelenting stream of allegations, indictments, and convictions for public corruption that fill the news media. Convictions and hefty prison sentences do not appear to have quelled the felonious behavior of some public officials and their co-conspirators such as Antoin (Tony) Rezko and Christopher Kelly in their abuse of the public trust.

Of course, it is not only fair but also crucial to say unequivocally that not every government official is corrupt. In Illinois, for the most part politicians and government officials are honest, hard-working public servants who want to do what is right for the people they represent. Rather, the problem is subtler and more insidious. A contagious mind-set infects the body politic that wears down citizens and officials or lulls them into expecting and tolerating corruption in government. Worse yet, it leads them to lose heart and take for granted that government has always been run that way and they cannot change it. Rather than quash corruption, the majority of otherwise law-abiding citizens and officials end up tolerating corrupt practices as "business as usual" in state and local government.

For that reason, a key message of this chapter is that the scandalous and criminal behavior in Illinois politics and government is recurrent and systemic, and far too many citizens and public officials tolerate it.

Costs of Corruption

The cost of corruption goes beyond the concerns of the political arena. The Illinois-based Sunshine Project warns that political corruption may threaten a loss of legitimacy of the political process—if politicians are corrupt, then citizens might reject their authority to govern.[6] Moreover, pervasive corruption may lead a citizen to conclude that if everybody else is trying to use the political system to his advantage, I am a fool not to do so as well. In addition, a corrupt political system may result in a weakening of the talent pool for government; the perception that government is corrupt destroys the notion that politics is a clear path to moral and social improvement, a civic mechanism for those who want to make things better. Finally, corruption brings deterioration of the quality of public services. Do-nothing jobs, make-work contracts, and inflated no-bid contracts take resources away from doing the real job of state and local government.

The Illinois Campaign for Political Reform advocates that citizens take on

Illinois political corruption, yet the group is aware that changing the culture will be difficult: "Illinoisans tend to think of politics primarily as a profession people take up in order to pursue personal interests. We are taught at our dinner tables, in our classrooms and churches, and by the media that politics is a business; we learn that it is a dirty business. The public expects that politicians will cut corners to win and that they will place the interests of those who supported them above the interests of the public. *Our standards for politics are very low and our politicians live up to them.*"[7] Although corruption in Illinois has been front-page news nationwide in recent years, citizens lack the sense of urgency and outrage that would otherwise move them to vote to rid the body politic of its rot. Citizens have yet to show that they will demand real reform from Illinois government officials.

A State Mired in the Middle

As noted in chapter 1, in 2008 the Associated Press named Illinois "the most average state" in the nation, based on state rankings on twenty-one indicators such as demographics, education achievement, and economic mix.[8]

The authors have also been struck by just how average Illinois is in terms of its performance with regard to numerous educational, health, social welfare, and infrastructure indicators. We evaluated Illinois's rank among the states on thirty performance measures such as crime rates, education performance on national tests, and infant mortality rate.[9] In no case did Illinois rank near the best or near the worst among the states. It ranged from eleventh to forty-third among the states in these areas, with most rankings in the mid-range.

This is understandable because the state is indeed about average on the key "input" indicators of population diversity and per capita income. Yet we also sense that being average is good enough for many if not most public officials and citizens of Illinois. There is nothing shameful about being average, yet we believe a state filled with boosterism, which Illinois apparently is not, would strive to be at or near the top on at least some performance indicators.

It is possible that the combination of our individualistic culture and the dispiriting blemishes caused by unusual levels of public corruption contribute to our generally average performance as a state. By definition, our prevailing culture focuses on the individual rather than the commonwealth.

We do not want to end on a negative note. Instead, we see these observations about a culture of corruption and of being mired among the middle ranks of the states as challenges for those who would seek the political leadership of this major State of Illinois, which we affectionately call our home.

Notes

● ● ● ● ● ● ● ● ● ● ● ● ● ●

Preface

1. Stephen Olemacher, "Early Presidential Primary States Are Far from U.S. Average," Associated Press, Washington, D.C., May 17, 2007.

Chapter 1: Illinois in Perspective

1. Stephen Ohlemacher, "Early Presidential Primary States Are Far from U.S. Average," Associated Press, Washington, D.C., May 17, 2007.

2. Daniel J. Elazar, *Cities of the Prairie* (New York: Basic, 1970), 282–316.

3. See Daniel J. Elazar, *American Federalism: A View from the States* (New York: Crowell, 1966), generally.

4. Elazar, *Cities of the Prairie,* 286.

5. Robert Sutton, "The Politics of Regionalism Nineteenth Century Style," in *Diversity, Conflict, and State Politics: Regionalism in Illinois,* ed. Peter F. Nardulli (Urbana: University of Illinois Press, 1989), 97.

6. Cullom Davis, "Illinois: Crossroads and Cross Section," in *Heartland: Comparative Histories of the Midwestern States,* ed. James H. Madison (Bloomington: Indiana University Press, 1988), 133.

7. For a good discussion of the internal improvements effort, see Robert P. Howard, *Illinois: A History of the Prairie State* (Grand Rapids, Mich.: Eerdmans, 1972) chap. 9.

8. Richard J. Jensen, *Illinois: A Bicentennial History* (New York: Norton, 1978), chap. 2.

9. Ibid., 86.

10. For an excellent discussion of the settlement of Illinois, see Frederick M. Wirt, "The Changing Social Bases of Regionalism: People, Cultures, and Politics in Illinois," in *Diversity, Conflict, and State Politics: Regionalism in Illinois,* ed. Peter F. Nardulli (Urbana: University of Illinois Press, 1989) 31; Davis, "Illinois: Crossroads."

11. James Simeone, *Democracy and Slavery in Frontier Illinois* (DeKalb: Northern Illinois University Press, 2000).

12. Jensen, *Illinois: A Bicentennial History,* throughout.

13. Ibid.,

14. Ibid., 53–54.

15. Ibid., 49–49.

16. William Cronon, *Nature's Metropolis: Chicago and the Great West* (New York: Norton, 1991), chap. 8.

17. Kristina Valaitis, "Understanding Illinois," *Texas Journal* 14 (Fall–Winter 1992): 20–22.

18. Cronon. *Nature's Metropolis,* 208–9.

19. Cronon (ibid., chap. 7, "The Busy Hive") provides an assessment of the business dynamics of Chicago and the Midwest.

20. As cited in ibid., 3, citing Frank Norris, *The Pit,* 1903.

21. Howard, *Illinois: A History,* chap. 21.

22. Cronon, *Nature's Metropolis,* 347. A few years after the 1893 fair, the architect Daniel Burnham produced "The Chicago Plan," a design for a city of wide boulevards, spacious parks, and an unobstructed lakefront. Much of the audacious plan was implemented.

23. Jensen, *Illinois: A Bicentennial History,* 162.

24. Nelson Algren, *Chicago: City on the Make* (New York: McGraw-Hill, 1951), 56.

25. Illinois General Assembly Commission on Government Forecasting and Accountability, *A Comparative Study of the Illinois Economy,* Springfield, September 2007; see also J. Fred Giertz, "The Illinois Economy," presentation at the Institute of Government and Public Affairs, University of Illinois at Urbana-Champaign, March 8, 2007; "The World in Figures," special issue of the *Economist,* 2007 ed.

26. Giertz, "Illinois Economy."

27. Geoffrey J. D. Hewings, "Economic Challenges for the Illinois Economy," presentation at the Institute of Government and Public Affairs, University of Illinois at Urbana-Champaign, March 8, 2007.

28. Ibid.

29. Center for Tax and Budget Accountability, *The State of Working Illinois: Executive Summary* (Chicago: Center for Tax and Budget Accountability, 2005).

30. Mid-America Institute on Poverty of the Heartland Alliance, *2007 Report on Illinois Poverty* (Chicago: Mid-America Institute on Poverty of the Heartland Alliance, 2007).

31. Daniel J. Elazar, "Series Introduction," in *Illinois Politics and Government: The Expanding Metropolitan Frontier,* Samuel K. Gove and James D. Nowlan (Lincoln: University of Nebraska Press, 1996), xi.

32. See the map in Robert Sutton, ed., *The Prairie State: A Documentary History of Illinois,* 2 vols. (Grand Rapids, Mich.: Eerdmans, 1976), 1:369.

33. Davis, "Illinois: Crossroads," 147–48.

34. For a lyrical essay on the diversity of people in Illinois, see Paul Gapp, "Chicagoans All—Our 'Melting Pot' Is Really a Savory Stew," *Chicago Tribune Sunday Magazine,* September 25, 1988.

35. Robert Howard, *Illinois: A History of the Prairie State* (Grand Rapids, Mich.: Eerdmans, 1972), 103.

36. Elazar, *Cities of the Prairie,* 181.

37. St. Clair Drake and Horace R, Clayton, *Black Metropolis: A Study of Negro Life in a Northern City* (Chicago: University of Chicago Press, 1993), 47. The material that follows is based in part on chapters 2–5 of this book.

38. U.S. Census Bureau, "State and County QuickFacts," http://quickfacts.census .gov/qfd/states/17000.html (accessed September 5, 2008).

39. Extrapolation by the authors from Cheng H. Chiang and Richard Kolhauser, "Who Are We? Illinois' Changing Population," *Illinois Issues,* December 1982, 6–8.

40. U.S. Census Bureau, "State and County QuickFacts."

41. Chicago's 1950 population is given as reported in *Illinois Blue Book, 1951–52* (Springfield: Illinois Secretary of State, 1952).

42. U.S. Census Bureau, "State and County QuickFacts"; Samuel K. Gove and James D. Nowlan, *Illinois Politics and Government: The Expanding Metropolitan Frontier* (Lincoln: University of Nebraska Press, 1996), chap. 1.

43. Charles N. Wheeler, "Growing Population and Shifting Demographics Should Cheer Illinois Republicans," *Illinois Issues Online,* http://illinoisissues.uis.edu/politics/ population.html, accessed June 10, 2008.

44. This is as recalled by Nowlan, who represented Bureau, Carroll, Henry, Stark, and Whiteside Counties in the Illinois House of Representatives from 1969 to 1972.

45. Bocce ball is a lawn game enjoyed by many Italian Americans. Bud Billiken is a mythical hero of blacks on the South Side of Chicago who is celebrated each year in a parade that is obligatory for local and some statewide politicians.

46. Gapp, "Chicagoans All."

47. Gregory D. Squires, Larry Bennett, and Philip Ryder, *Chicago: Race, Class, and the Response to Urban Decline* (Philadelphia: Temple University Press, 1987), 98.

48. *Segregation in Chicago in 2006: Executive Summary* (Chicago: Center for Urban Research and Learning, Loyola University, 2006).

49. Ibid.

50. See Lawrence J. McCaffrey, Ellen Skerrett, Michael F. Funchion, and Charles Fanning, *The Irish in Chicago* (Urbana: University of Illinois Press, 1987), 90.

51. Edward R. Kantowicz, *Polish-American Politics in Chicago* (Chicago: University of Chicago Press, 1975), 41–42.

52. Milton Rakove, *We Don't Want Nobody Nobody Sent: An Oral History of the Daley Years* (Bloomington: Indiana University Press, 1979), 318.

53. Michael B. Preston, "Political Change in the City: Black Politics in Chicago, 1871–1987," in *Diversity, Conflict, and State Politics: Regionalism in Illinois,* ed. Peter F. Nardulli (Urbana: University of Illinois Press, 1989), 180–87.

54. Figures concerning the council are from Paul Green, interview by James D. Nowlan, Chicago, July 10, 2008.

55. Rich Miller, interview with James D. Nowlan, Springfield, July 8, 2008.

56. Within the legislature, the luck of the draw in winning the right to redistrict has

been with the Democrats three in four times the draw has been employed. (If decennial redistricting reaches an impasse within the legislature as well as in a subsequent commission that is balanced evenly between the parties, then the two parties draw from a hat to pick a Democratic or Republican name that in effect determines which party controls redistricting.) If Republicans were to control redistricting, they could increase their numbers in the General Assembly and thus conceivably win control of one or both houses of the legislature.

57. University of Illinois at Springfield Survey Research Office Statewide Telephone Survey, August 2007. The survey had more than one thousand respondents.

58. John Herbers, *The New Heartland* (New York: Time Books, 1986); "Look Out, Wasco, Here Comes Suburban Sprawl," *Chicago Tribune,* March 18, 1994.

59. Census *Quickfacts.*

60. Interview with Paul Green, April 4, 1994.

61. *1993 Metro Survey Report* (Chicago: Metro Information Center, 1993).

62. Mary Patrice Erdmans, "New Chicago Polonia: Urban and Suburban," in *The New Chicago,* ed. John Koval et al. (Philadelphia: Temple University Press, 2006), 125.

63. Mid-American Institute on Poverty of the Heartland Alliance, *2007 Report on Illinois Poverty.*

64. Patrick D. O'Grady, *Taxes and Distribution by Region of the State* (Springfield: Legislative Research Unit, Illinois General Assembly, March 9, 1989).

65. Email discussion with Kent Redfield, week of June 29–July 5, 2008.

66. The quotation is from a speech delivered by Ted Sanders in 1987, as recorded by James D. Nowlan.

67. Rich Miller, CapitolFax, Springfield, May 19, 2009.

68. Sutton, "Politics of Regionalism," 113.

69. For purposes of our discussion, we define *corruption* as "any personal gain at public expense."

70. Robert J. Schoenberg, *Mr. Capone* (New York: William Morrow, 1992), 40.

71. Ibid., 40. For a general discussion of the Yerkes era, see James D. Nowlan, *Glory, Darkness, Light: A History of the Union League Club of Chicago* (Evanston, Ill.: Northwestern University Press, 2005), 41.

72. Nowlan, *Glory, Darkness, Light,* 51.

73. Ibid., chap. 7, "The Buying of a U.S. Senate Seat—as Revealed at the Union League Club."

74. Schoenberg, *Mr. Capone,* 40.

75. Ibid.

76. Ibid., 41.

77. Kenneth Alsop, *The Bootleggers* (New Rochelle, N.Y.: Arlington, 1961), 239.

78. Schoenberg, *Mr. Capone,* 41.

79. Ibid.

80. "Report to Congress on the Activities of the Public Integrity Section for 2005," Criminal Division, United States Department of Justice, Washington, D.C. The South-

ern District of Florida recorded the highest number of convictions in the period: 576.

81. Political Diary, *Opinion Journal,* October 16, 2006.

82. *Chicago Sun-Times,* October 12, 2006.

83. *Chicago Tribune,* December 10, 2008.

84. *Chicago Tribune,* January 22, 2006.

85. Douglas L. Whitley, "Promoting Prosperity for Illinois," Heartland Institute, October 5, 2006.

86. Center for Governmental Studies, *The 2007 Report on the Illinois Policy Survey* (DeKalb: Center for Governmental Studies, Northern Illinois University, 2007).

Chapter 2: Power, Parties, Groups, and the Media

1. Quoted in Peter J. Wilson, *The Domestication of the Human Species* (New Haven, Conn.: Yale University Press, 1988), 117.

2. For a discussion of power and influence in politics, see Roger Scruton, *A Dictionary of Political Thought* (London: Macmillan, 1982), 224; Dennis Wrong, *Power: Its Form, Bases, and Uses* (Oxford: Oxford University Press, 1979).

3. John Camper and Daniel Egler, "Democrats Find It Pays to Be on Madigan Team," *Chicago Tribune,* April 16, 1989. Much of the discussion of Madigan is drawn from this lengthy profile.

4. Figures for campaign contributions and expenditures are from the Illinois State Board of Elections campaign disclosure Web site at www.elections.state.il.us/campaigndisclosure (accessed June 15, 2008).

5. Camper and Egler, "Democrats Find It Pays to Be on Madigan Team."

6. Ibid.

7. For an illuminating brief history of parties in Illinois, see Paul M. Green, "History of Political Parties in Illinois," in *Illinois: Political Processes and Governmental Performance,* ed. Edgar Crane (Dubuque, Iowa: Kendall-Hunt, 1980), 167–76. The discussion that follows is drawn primarily from this article.

8. Kent D. Redfield, "Limited Role of State Political Parties in Financing Illinois Campaigns," *Illinois Issues,* November 1992, 16–19.

9. The illustration is provided by Edwin Dale of Champaign, former member of the Illinois House of Representatives, July 15, 1990.

10. Thomas Hardy, "Political Slatemaking Not What It Used to Be," *Chicago Tribune,* December 26, 1993, sec. 4, p. 8.

11. Aaron Chambers, "The Illinois GOP Puzzles Over Ways to Rebuild," *Illinois Issues,* http://illinoisissues.uis.edu/features/2007mar/gop.html.

12. Redfield, "Limited Role," 19.

13. Office of the Illinois Secretary of State, Index Division, Springfield, June 25, 2007.

14. Senate Amendment 1 to House Bill 7, Illinois General Assembly, 2009.

15. "Money and Elections in Illinois, 2006," Illinois State Board of Elections, Springfield, May 2007, 25.

16. Ronald J. Hrebenar and Clive S. Thomas, eds., *Interest Group Politics in the Midwestern States* (Ames: Iowa State University Press, 1993), 20–49.

17. Kent D. Redfield, "Raising Rod: Illinois Politics' $26 Million Man," http://illlinoisissues.uis.edu/papers/raising.html.

18. Sarah McCally Morehouse, *State Politics: Parties and Policy* (New York: Holt, Rinehart and Winston, 1981), 10.

19. Clive S. Thomas and Ronald J. Hrebenar, "Interest Groups in the States," *Politics in the American States,* 7th ed., eds. Virginia Gray et al. (Washington, D.C.: CQ Press, 1999), 137.

20. Kent D. Redfield, "Investing in the General Assembly," in *Almanac of Illinois Politics—1994,* ed. Jack Van Der Slik (Springfield: University of Illinois at Springfield), 4.

21. Office of the Illinois Secretary of State, Index Division, Springfield, 2009.

22. Aaron Chambers, "The Outer Office," *Illinois Issues,* September 2007.

23. As reported in Green, "History of Political Parties in Illinois," 170.

24. Morehouse, *State Politics,* 110.

25. These are the observations of James D. Nowlan, who was Percy's campaign manager in 1978.

26. The series ran between September 19 and December 1, 1985, and was collected into a book: *The American Millstone: An Examination of the Nation's Permanent Underclass* (Chicago: Contemporary, 1986).

27. The following discussion is drawn from James D. Nowlan, "Television Charts a New Campaign Map for Illinois," in *Occasional Papers in Illinois Politics,* no. 2, ed. Anna Merritt (Urbana: Institute of Government and Public Affairs, University of Illinois, November 1983).

28. This case study is taken from James D. Nowlan and Mary Jo Moutray Stroud, "Broadcasting Advertising and Party Endorsement in a Statewide Primary: An Illinois Case Study," in *Occasional Papers in Illinois Politics,* no. 4, ed. Anna Merritt (Urbana: Institute of Government and Public Affairs, University of Illinois, November 1983).

29. Kevin McDermott, *St. Louis Post-Dispatch,* November 11, 2006.

30. Rich Miller, CapitolFax, July 3, 2008. http://www.thecapitolfaxblog.com/.

31. Rich Miller, interview by James D. Nowlan, Springfield, July 8, 2008.

32. Ibid.

Chapter 3: Elections

1. For examples see the most recent Election and Campaign Finance Calendars for even- and odd-numbered years issued by Illinois State Board of Elections, www.elections.il.gov.

2. David R. Miller, ed., *1970 Illinois Constitution Annotated for Legislators,* 4th ed. (Springfield: Legislative Research Unit, 2005) 26, 41, and 57. www.ilga.gov/commission/lru.

3. See Illinois State Board of Elections, *Candidate Guide* (www.elections.il.gov), revised annually.

4. Justin Levitt, "The Truth About Voter Fraud," Brennan Center for Justice at the New York University School of Law, 2007.

5. See Kent D. Redfield, *Money Counts: How Dollars Dominate Illinois Politics and What We Can Do About It* (Springfield: Institute for Public Affairs, University of Illinois at Springfield, 2001); Kent D. Redfield, "Sunshine and the Shoebox: Money and Politics in the Unregulated State of Illinois," in *Money, Politics and Campaign Finance Reform Law in State Politics,* ed. David Schultz (Durham, N.C.: Carolina Academic Press, 2002), 55–98.

6. HB 824, Public Act 95-0971, 30 Illinois Compiled Statutes 500/50-37.

7. Justin Levitt, "A Citizen's Guide to Redistricting," Brennan Center for Justice at the New York University School of Law, 2008, 42–49.

8. Miller, *1970 Illinois Constitution,* 27–28.

9. See Milton Rakov, *Don't Make No Waves, Don't Back No Losers* (Bloomington: Indiana University Press, 1976); Mike R. Royko, *Boss: Richard J. Daley of Chicago,* (1971; reprint, New York: Blume, 1988).

10. Election outcomes and vote totals by county for statewide, legislative, and judicial elections are available from the Illinois State Board of Elections (www.elections .il.gov), as are campaign finance reports from statewide, legislative, and judicial candidates. The following summaries and analysis of campaign receipts and expenditures cited were compiled by the author for the Sunshine Project, which is funded by the Joyce Foundation. Analysis and campaign finance databases constructed for the Sunshine Project can be accessed through the Web site of the Illinois Campaign for Political Reform (www.ilcampaign.org).

11. Peter W. Colby and Paul Michael Green, "Burgeoning Suburban Power, Shrinking Chicago Clout: Downstate Holds the Key to Victory," *Illinois Issues,* February 1978.

12. See Paul Michael Green, "The 2006 Illinois General Election: A Vote Analysis," Institute for Politics, Roosevelt University, January 2007; Paul Michael Green, "2008—Illinois Primary: An Analysis," Institute for Politics, Roosevelt University, April 2008. Also see Rich Miller, The Capitol Fax Blog, "Two Views of the GOP's Future," February 13, 2007 (www.thecapitolfaxblog.com).

13. For sources of data from statewide elections, see note 10.

14. See note 12.

15. Kevin McDermott, "Blagojevich Outspent Topinka nearly 4 to 1," *St. Louis Post-Dispatch,* November 10, 2006.

16. Levitt, "The Truth About Voter Fraud"; Kent D. Redfield, *Show Me the Money: Cash Clout in Illinois Politics,* rev. ed. (Springfield: Sunshine Project), 2008.

17. See Kent D. Redfield, "What Keeps the Four Tops on Top? Leadership Power in the Illinois General Assembly," in *Almanac of Illinois Politics—1998,* ed. Jack R. Van Der Slik (Springfield: University of Illinois at Springfield, 1998), 1–8.

18. See Kent D. Redfield, "Living up to Low Standards: The Sad State of Political Ethics in Illinois," in *Almanac of Illinois Politics—2006,* ed. Amy S. Karhliker (Springfield: Center Publication/Illinois Issues, 2006), 23–31.

Chapter 4: Constitutions

1. Janet Cornelius, *Constitution Making in Illinois, 1818–1970* (Urbana: University of Illinois Press, 1972), 34. The sections about early constitutions rely heavily on this work.

2. Illinois allows for public initiative only for matters pertaining to the legislative article of the constitution. This petitioning process was used in the successful 1980 amendment that reduced the size of the house and eliminated cumulative voting in Illinois. Later, State Treasurer Patrick Quinn initiated a successful petition to require term limits for state legislators, but the Illinois Supreme Court in 1994 ruled that the petition was invalid because it did not address structural or procedural subject matter required by the constitution.

3. For further discussion of the slavery issue, see Cornelius, *Constitution Making,* 15–24.

4. Robert P. Howard, *Illinois: A History of the Prairie State* (Grand Rapids, Mich.: Eerdmans, 1972), 333.

5. Daniel J. Elazar, *American Federalism: A View from the States* (New York: Crowell, 1966), 20.

6. *Bachrach v. Nelson,* 349 Ill. 579, 182 N.E. 909 (1932).

7. Elmer Gertz and Joseph P. Pisciotte, *Charter for a New Age: An Inside View of the Sixth Illinois Constitutional Convention* (Urbana: University of Illinois Press, 1980), 6. This book provides a detailed and readable summary of the workings of the convention.

8. Elmer Gertz and Edward S. Gilbreth, *Quest for a Constitution: A Man Who Wouldn't Quit; A Political Biography of Samuel W. Witwer* (Lanham, Md.: University Press of America, 1984), 76–77.

9. Cornelius, *Constitution Making,* 124.

10. Quoted in Samuel K. Gove and Thomas R. Kitser, *Revision Success: The Sixth Illinois Constitutional Convention* (New York: National Municipal League, 1974), 15.

11. *Thorpe v. Mahin,* 43 Ill.2d 36 (1969). In this decision the Illinois Supreme Court overturned *Bachrach v. Nelson* (349 Ill. 579 [1932]), which states that the legislature was limited to enacting property taxes, occupation taxes, and franchise taxes.

12. *Cook County Republican Party v. Illinois State Board of Elections,* 378 Ill. App. 3d 752, 882 N.E.2d 93 (1st Dist. 2009).

13. Elazar, *American Federalism,* 20.

14. Daniel J. Elazar, introduction to *Illinois Government and Politics: The Expanding Metropolitan Frontier,* by Samuel K. Gove and James D. Nowlan (Lincoln: University of Nebraska Press, 1996).

15. Illinois Constitution, 1970, art. 1, sec. 8.1.

16. Quoted in James D. Nolan, "Con Con 30," personal files, n.d.

17. Neal R. Peirce, *The Megastates of America: People, Politics, and Power in the Ten Great States* (New York: Norton, 1972), 393–94.

18. *Klinger v. Howlett,* 50 Ill. 2d 242, 278 N.E.2d 84 (1972); *Continental Illinois Na-*

tional Bank and Trust v. Zagel, 78 Ill. 2d 387, 401 N.E.2d 491 (1979); *City of Canton v. Crouch,* 79 Ill. 2d 356, 403 N.E.2d 242 (1980).-

Chapter 5: The Legislature

1. Until the mid-1960s, the Illinois legislator had no office, no staff, no telephone, and insignificant pay. The constitution authorized only fifty dollars per biennium for postage for lawmakers, and they traditionally met only in the spring of odd-numbered years. For a thorough assessment of the Illinois General Assembly, see Jack R. Van Der Slik and Kent D. Redfield, *Lawmaking in Illinois* (Springfield: Office of Public Affairs Communication, Sangamon State University, 1986). An earlier yet still useful work is Samuel K. Gove, Richard W. Carlson, and Richard J. Carlson, *The Illinois Legislature: Structure and Process* (Urbana: University of Illinois Press, 1976).

2. Burdett A. Loomis reported in 1990 that the Illinois legislature ranked in the top ten among the fifty states on indicators of professionalism (staffing, compensation, and information capacity), percentage of full-time legislators, and low membership turnover. Burdett A. Loomis, "Political Careers and American State Legislatures," paper presented at the Eagleton Institute of Politics Symposium "The Legislature in the Twenty-First Century," April 27–29, 1990, Williamsburg, Virginia.

3. Amy S. Karhliker et al., *Almanac of Illinois Politics—2006* (Springfield: Center for State Policy and Leadership, University of Illinois at Springfield, 2006), 49–292.

4. *Illinois State Budget, Fiscal Year 2008,* Office of Management and Budget, Office of the Governor, Springfield, 2007.

5. Karhliker, *Almanac of Illinois Politics—2006,* 49–292.

6. See Illinois Constitution, 1970, art. 4, sec. 2, which requires that redistricting for all senate seats take place every ten years and that in the year following the redistricting all seats be up for election. After that, the seats go through two- and four-year terms in stages so there will be some senate seats up for election every two years. A statute divides senate seats into three groups, with the secretary of state to draw cards at random after each redistricting to determine which group of senators will have terms of four, four, and two years, which will have terms of four, two, and four years, and which will have terms of two, four, and four years. 10 Illinois Compiled Statutes 5/29C-5 ff.

7. As a result of rule changes that concentrate power in the leaders, since 2003, legislators have not been allowed to consider a "floor amendment" until the leader first assigns it for a hearing in committee. If the sponsor receives a favorable recommendation from the committee, it then goes back to the whole body for further consideration. Previously, legislators considered and voted on floor amendments *on the floor* without having to resort to committees.

8. Illinois Constitution, 1970, art. 14, sec. 2 provides for constitutional amendments by the legislature. The 1994 amendment to change the effective date of laws amended art. 4, sec. 10.

9. See Gove, Carlson, and Carlson, *Illinois Legislatures,* chap. 4, for a thorough discussion of lawmaking and legislative action relating to vetoes.

10. U.S. Constitution, art. 1, sec. 7: "If any Bill shall not be returned by the President within ten Days (Sundays excepted) after it shall have been presented to him, the Same shall be a Law, in like Manner as if he had signed it, unless the Congress by their Adjournment prevent its Return, in which Case it shall not be a Law."

11. House Rule 10 (b) (95th General Assembly).

12. Senate Rule 8-4 (a); House Rule 75 (95th General Assembly).

13. Illinois Constitution, 1970, art. 4, secs. 8–10.

14. Kent R. Redfield, "What Keeps the Four Tops on Top?" in *Almanac of Illinois Politics, ed. Mark Van Der Slik* (Springfield: University of Illinois at Springfield, Institute of Public Affairs, 1998), 2.

15. Illinoise State Board of Elections, *Money and Elections in Illinois 2006* (Springfield: Illinois State Board of Elections, 2006).

16. Alan Rosenthal, *Heavy Lifting: The Job of the American Legislature* (Washington, D.C.: CQ Press, 2004), 177, n. 36.

17. Elmer Gertz and Joseph P. Pisciotte, *Charter for a New Age: An Inside View of the Sixth Illinois Constitutional Convention* (Urbana: University of Illinois Press, 1980), 230.

18. See Charles N. Wheeler III, "Gov. James R. Thompson, 1977–1991: The Complete Campaigner, the Pragmatic Centrist," *Illinois Issues,* December 1990, 15: "It must have been tiresome to see his vetoes overridden with such impunity. Though it would have been difficult to compile statistics, it's probably a safe bet that Thompson was overridden more often than all his predecessors in this century combined."

19. See Charles N. Wheeler III, "Ends and Means: How Far Can the Governor Go in Rewriting Legislation?" *Illinois Issues,* September 2008, 37: "Madigan's concern about former Gov. Jim Thompson's prolific use of the veto pen led the House Speaker to engineer a 1989 revision in House rules intended to limit a governor's ability to make drastic changes in legislation. Under the revamp, still in effect today, before a sponsor can seek approval for an amendatory veto, the House Rules Committee must decide that the proposed changes do not alter the bill's fundamental purpose and are limited to the governor's objections to portions of a bill whose general merits he recognizes. Senate rules have included similar provisions since 2003."

20. Alan Rosenthal, *Governors and Legislatures* (Washington, D.C.: CQ Press, 1990), 205.

21. Rick Pearson and Ray Long, "'Present' Votes Emerging from the Past," *Chicago Tribune,* February 3, 2008.

22. This observation is provided by James D. Nowlan, who served in the House of Representatives from 1969 to 1972.

23. This section is drawn largely from James D. Nowlan, "Redistricting: The Politics," in the series A Media Guide to Illinois REMAP '91, no. 5 (Urbana: Institute of Government and Public Affairs, March 1991).

24. Illinois Constitution, 1970, art. 4, sec. 3 (b).

25. Jennifer Halperin, "The Walking Giant," *Illinois Issues,* December 1994, 24.

26. Daniel C. Vock, "Latino Power: A Rising Population Is Pushing for Political Change," *Illinois Issues,* May 2004.

27. *Blagojevich v. Madigan* (Circuit Court, Sangamon County, Ill. filed August 24, 2007).

28. Ray Long and Jeffrey Meitrodt, "Governor Picks and Chooses—Blagojevich Slashes $463 Million, Cuts Foes' Pet Projects," *Chicago Tribune,* August 24, 2007.

29. Doug Finke and Adriana Colindres, "Governor Moving Money / Will Veto $500 Million, Give $463 Million to Health Care," *State Journal-Register,* August 15, 2007.

30. *Caro v. Blagojevich,* 895 N.E.2d 1091 (1st Dist. 2008).

31. U.S. Constitution, amend. 17; 10 Illinois Compiled Statutes 5/25-8.

32. Jeff Coen, Rick Pearson, John Chase, and David Kidwell, "Feds Arrest Gov. Blagojevich to Stop a Political 'crime spree'"—Governor Faces Shocking Array of Charges—Topped by Accusations He Tried to Auction a U.S. Senate Seat," *Chicago Tribune,* December 10, 2008; "Final Report of the Special Investigative Committee," Illinois House of Representatives, 95th General Assembly, issued January 8, 2009.

33. John Chase and Ray Long, "Subpoenas Add Details of Probe—Grand Jury Looked at Early Hires for Blagojevich Staff," *Chicago Tribune,* December 30, 2008.

34. Ryan Keith, "Illinois House to Investigate Impeachment of Blagojevich," *State Journal-Register,* December 15, 2009.

35. Doug Finke, "Blagojevich Lawyer Genson Rips into Hearing," *State Journal-Register,* December 18, 2008.

36. "Final Report of the Special Investigative Committee," emphasis in original.

37. Ibid., 61.

38. Ibid., 56–60.

Chapter 6: The Executive

1. Rich Miller, "Recall Blagojevich?" www.illinoistimes.com/gyrobase/Archive, November 15, 2007.

2. Charles N. Wheeler III, "The Governor's Lawsuits Are the Latest Signs of a Toxic Environment at the Statehouse," *Illinois Issues,* October 2007, 33–34.

3. Taylor Pensoneau, "Rod Blagojevich," in *The Illinois Governors: Mostly Good and Competent Men,* rev. and ed. Taylor Pensoneau and Peggy Boyer Long (Springfield: Illinois Issues, 2007), 314–25 (update of the 1988 book edited by Robert P. Howard).

4. "Rod Blagojevich," http://en.wikipedia.org/wiki/Rod_Blagojevich. June 1, 2007.

5. Jim Fletcher, conversation with James D. Nowlan, Springfield, May 28, 2008.

6. Katherine Barrett and Richard Greene, "Grading the States 2008: The Mandate to Measure," http://governing.com/gpp/2008/index.htm, March 2008.

7. The quotations are in ibid.

8. This section draws heavily on the highly readable profiles of Illinois governors by Robert P. Howard, *Mostly Good and Competent Men: Illinois Governors, 1818–1988* (Springfield: Illinois Issues, Sangamon State University, and Illinois State Historical Society, 1988).

9. Ibid., 79.

10. Ibid., 21.

11. Ibid., 188.

12. Ibid., 340.

13. For Thompson's version of his years in office, see James R. Thompson, *Illinois, State of the State, 1977–1991: The Thompson Administration* (Springfield: State of Illinois, 1991).

14. "Political Hiring Out, Court Rules," *Chicago Tribune,* June 22, 1990.

15. *Rutan v. Republican Party of Illinois,* 110 U.S. 2729 (1990).

16. Chris Gaudet, "Financing Gubernatorial Campaigns," *Illinois Issues,* May 1987, 13–14.

17. Samuel K. Gove, "Illinois: Jim Edgar, the New Governor from the Old Party," in *Governing and Hard Times,* ed. Thad Beyle (Washington, D.C.: CQ Press, 1992), 107.

18. "For Governor: Jim Edgar," *Chicago Tribune,* October 23, 1994, sec. 4.

19. Dave McKinney, "Ryan's Paradox," *Illinois Issues,* November 2002, 15–19. This is an excellent summary of the career of Governor George Ryan.

20. "George Ryan," http://en.wikipedia.org/wiki/George_H. Ryan, May 22, 2007.

21. Kathleen O'Leary Morgan and Scott Morgan, *State Rankings, 2009* (Washington, D.C.: CQ Press, 2009), 359.

22. For more complete descriptions of the duties of the executive officers, see the *Illinois Blue Book,* published every two years by the Illinois Secretary of State. This is a comprehensive, though sometimes self-serving, guide to state government. For more balanced articles about the offices and the personalities and politics therein, see the annual index to *Illinois Issues,* a monthly magazine of public affairs published by the University of Illinois in Springfield.

23. David Miller, "Vetoes Could Cause Controversy," *First Reading* 4, no. 9 (October 1989): 11. This is a publication of the Legislative Research Unit of the Illinois General Assembly.

24. Ibid.

25. Alan Rosenthal, *Governors and Legislatures* (Washington, D.C.: CQ Press, 1990), 11.

26. Ibid., 15.

27. Anecdote related by James D. Nowlan from the period when he was a member of the Illinois General Assembly, 1969–73.

28. Rosenthal, *Governors and Legislatures,* 75–79.

29. Ibid., 113.

30. "State's Prison Population Surges," *First Reading* 5, no. 3 (March 1990): 1–6.

31. *Rutan v. Republican Party,* 497 U.S. 62, 110 S. Ct. 2729 (1990).

32. Rosenthal, *Governors and Legislatures,* 170.

33. Ronald D. Michaelson, "An Analysis of the Chief Executive: How the Governor Uses His Time," *Public Affairs Bulletin* 4, no. 4 (September–October 1971): 1–8. This is a publication of the Public Affairs Research Bureau, Southern Illinois University.

34. Governor's Office of Management and Budget, *Illinois State Budget, Fiscal Year 2008* (Springfield: Governor's Office of Management and Budget, 2007).

35. For an excellent overview of the style of Governor Rod Blagojevich, see David Bernstein, "Mr. Un-Popularity," *Chicago*, www.chicagomag.com/Chicago-Magazine/February-2008/February-2008–Table-of-Contents, February 2008.

36. Tom Berkshire and Richard J. Carlson, "The Office of the Governor," in *Inside State Government in Illinois*, ed. James D. Nowlan (Chicago: Neltnor House, 1991), 18–40.

37. For a full discussion of patronage practices in the Ogilvie administration, see James D. Nowlan, William S. Hanley, and Donald Udstuen, " Personnel and Patronage," in *Inside State Government in Illinois*, ed. James D. Nowlan (Chicago: Neltnor House, 1991), 51–64.

38. *Rutan v. Republican Party.*

39. Nowlan, Hanley, and Udstuen, "Personnel and Patronage."

40. Paul Craig, "A Matter of Character," *Illinois Issues*, June 2007, 27–28.

41. James D. Nowlan, "An Introduction to State Government," in *Inside State Government: A Primer for State Managers*, ed. James D. Nowlan (Urbana: Institute of Government and Public Affairs, University of Illinois, 1983), 5.

Chapter 7: The Courts

1. 2007 Annual Report of the Illinois Courts (Springfield: Supreme Court of Illinois, 2007), 12.

2. Illinois Appellate Court, http://www.state.il.us/court/AppellateCourt/default.asp (accessed July 2, 2009).

3. Illinois Circuit Court, http://www.state.il.us/court/CircuitCourt/default.asp (accessed July 2, 2009).

4. Ibid.

5. "Chapter VII. The Circuit Court of Cook County under the Judicial Article of 1964," http://www.state.il.us/court/SupremeCourt/Historical/judicialsystem.asp (accessed July 2, 2009).

6. Illinois Constitution, 1970, art. 6, sec. 16.

7. "State and Local Funding for the Illinois Courts," www.state.il.us/court/General/Funding.asp (accessed July 4, 2009).

8. James Tuohy and Rob Warden, *Greylord: Justice, Chicago Style* (New York: Putnam, 1989), appendix 2, p. 262; Illinois Supreme Court Special Commission on the Administration of Justice, *Final Report, Parts I and II*, Jerold S. Solovy, chairman (Chicago: n.p., 1993), pt. 2, 54–68 (hereafter *Solovy Report).*

9. Much of the detail recounted here is from Tuohy and Warden, *Greylord.*

10. Anne Keegan, "Inside Greylord," *Chicago Tribune Magazine*, December 17, 1989, 16.

11. Tuohy and Warden, *Greylord,* 26.

12. Ibid., 207–13.

13. See Robert Cooley and Hillel Levin, *When Corruption Was King: How I Helped*

the Mob Rule Chicago, Then Brought the Outfit Down (New York: Carroll and Graf, 2004), for Cooley's account of corruption in the Cook County courts.

14. The illustrations of Operation Gambat are from *Solovy Report,* 7–43.

15. Tuohy and Warden, *Greylord.*

16. Brockton Lockwood with Harlan H. Mendenhall, *Operation Greylord: Brockton Lockwood's Story* (Carbondale: Southern Illinois University Press, 1989), 156.

17. Illinois Constitution, 1970, art. 6, sec. 12 (d).

18. Nancy Ford, "From Judicial Election to Merit Selection: A Time for Change in Illinois," *Northern Illinois University Law Review* 8, no. 3 (1988): 665–707.

19. *Caperton v. A. T. Massey Coal Company,* 129 S. Ct. 2252, 173 L. Ed. 2d 1208 (2009).

20. Lawyers are encouraged to participate by canon eight of the American Bar Association code: "Generally, lawyers are qualified by personal observation and investigation to evaluate the qualifications of persons seeking or being considered for such public offices, and for this reason they have a special responsibility to aid in the selection of those who are qualified."

21. "Our Picks for Subcircuit Judges," *Chicago Sun-Times,* October 8, 1994.

22. Ford, "From Judicial Election to Merit Selection," 685.

23. Ray Gibson, "High Court Is in the Game—Illinois' Partisan Justices Are Asked to Rule on Blagojevich, *Chicago Tribune,* December 14, 2008.

24. Jesse Rutledge, ed., *The New Politics of Judicial Elections* (Washington, D.C.: Justice at Stake Campaign, 2004), 18.

25. Mike France And Lorraine Woellert, "*The Threat to Justice,*" *Business Week,* September 27, 2004.

26. Rutledge, *New Politics of Judicial Elections,* 18.

27. Christian W. Peck, "Attitudes and Views of American Business Leaders on State Judicial Elections and Political Contribution to Judges," Zogby International, May 2007. This was a national telephone survey of businesses conducted by Zogby International, http://faircourts.org/files/CED-ZogbyPoll2007.pdf (accessed July 3, 2009).

28. *Solovy Report,* pt. 1, 51.

29. Illinois Constitution 1970, art. 2, sec. 1. See *Kunkel v. Walton,* 179 Ill. 2d 519, 533, 689 N.E.2d 1047, 1053 (1997) (The separation of powers provision does not seek to achieve a complete divorce between the branches of government; the purpose of the provision is to prevent the whole power of two or more branches from residing in the same hands. . . . There are areas in which separate spheres of governmental authority overlap and certain functions are thereby shared [citation omitted]).

30. Illinois Constitution, 1970, art. 8, sec. 3.

31. Supreme Court of Illinois, "Amended Responses to the Financial and Compliance Audit Report" (State of Illinois, Springfield, October 4, 1989).

32. Ken Armstrong and Rick Pearson, "Heiple's Pyrrhic Victory—Panel Assails Him, Rejects Impeachment," *Chicago Tribune,* May 16, 1997.

33. Legislative Research Unit, "Articles Voted in 1833 Impeachment Proceedings"

(Research Response prepared by George Fox Rischel, staff attorney, File 10-833, April 22, 1997): "The only impeachment proceedings previously held in Illinois were the 1832–33 impeachment and trial of Theophilus W. Smith, a justice of the Illinois Supreme Court. The House of Representatives voted to impeach Justice Smith on January 5, 1833 and then prepared seven articles of impeachment and exhibited them on January 9, 1833 to the Senate (which failed to convict)."

34. Illinois Constitution, 1970, art. 6, sec. 14.

35. *Jorgensen v. Blagojevich*, 211 Ill. 2d 286, 811 N.E.2d 652, 285 Ill. Dec. 165 (2004).

36. James R. Thompson, State of the State Address, October 25, 1977, 855–56.

37. 730 Illinois Compiled Statutes 5/3-3-13.

38. *People ex rel. Madigan v. Snyder*, 208 Ill. 2d 457, 804 N.E.2d 546 (2004).

39. *People ex rel. Madigan*, 208 Ill. 2d at 480, 804 N.E.2d at 560.

40. *Kunkel*, 179 Ill. 2d 519, 533, 689 N.E.2d 1047, 1053 (1997). See generally Abner J. Mikva and Eric Lane, *An Introduction to Statutory Interpretation and the Legislative Process* (New York: Aspen Law and Business, 2002), 95–144 (chap. 3, "The Interpretation of Statutes"); William N. Eskridge, Philip P. Frickey, and Elizabeth Garrett, *Cases and Materials on Legislation: Statutes and the Creation of Public Policy*, 4th ed. (St. Paul: Thomson/West, 2007), 689–846 (chap. 7, "Theories of Statutory Interpretation").

41. *Kunkel*, 179 Ill. 2d 519, 533, 689 N.E.2d 1047, 1053 (1997).

42. *Johnson v. Edgar*, 176 Ill. 2d 499, 680 N.E.2d 1372 (1997).

43. *Geja's Café v. Metropolitan Pier and Exposition Authority*, 153 Ill. 2d 239, 606 N.E.2d 1212, 1220 (1992).

44. Michael J. Kasper, "Using the Single-Subject Rule to Invalidate Legislation: A Better Approach?" *Illinois Bar Journal* 87, no. 3 (March 1999): 146.

45. Ibid.

46. *Johnson v. Edgar*, No. 81019 (Cir. Ct. Cook Co. 1996).

47. *People v. Pitts*, 295 Ill. App. 3d 182, 691 N.E.2d 1174 (4th Dist. 1998); *People v. Reedy*, 295 Ill. App. 3d 34, 692 N.E.2d 376, 383 (2d Dist. 1998).

48. Kasper, "Using the Single-Subject Rule," 146.

49. *Illinois State Chamber of Commerce v. Filan*, 216 Ill. 2d 653, 837 N.E.2d 922 (2005)

50. *Illinois State Chamber v. Filan*, Case No. 2004-CH-06750, Circuit Court of Cook County, Illinois, https://w3.courtlink.lexisnexis.com/cookcounty/FindDock .asp?NCase=2004–CH-06750&SearchType=0&Database=3&case_no=&=&=&= &PLtype=1&sname=&CDate= (accessed July 4, 2009).

51. See generally Martin R. West and Paul E. Peterson, eds., *School Money Trials: The Legal Pursuit of Educational Adequacy* (Washington, D.C.: Brookings Institution Press, 2007), 55–74 ("Reinterpreting the Education Clauses in State Constitutions"), 345–58 ("Appendix: Significant School Finance Judgments, 1971–2005") .

52. *Committee for Educational Rights v. Edgar*, 174 Ill. 2d 1, 672 N.E.2d 1178 (1996).

53. Illinois Constitution, 1970, art. 1, sec. 2.

54. Illinois Constitution, 1970, art. 10, sec. 1.

55. *Edgar,* 174 Ill. 2d at 12–23, 672 N.E.2d at 1183–89 (efficiency requirement of education article); and 174 Ill. 2d at 32–40, 672 N.E2d at 1193–97 (equal protection clause).

56. *Edgar,* 174 Ill. 2d at 23–32, 672 N.E.2d at 1189–1193 (high quality requirement of education article not judicially enforceable).

57. *Edgar,* 174 Ill. 2d at 45, 672 N.E.2d at 1199.

58. *Edgar,* 174 Ill. 2d at 45–46, 672 N.E.2d at 1199–1200.

59. *Edgar,* 174 Ill. 2d at 44, 672 N.E.2d at 1198.

60. *Edgar,* 174 Ill. 2d at 45–58, 672 N.E.2d at 1199–1205.

61. Illinois Constitution, 1870, art. 8, sec. 1.

62. *Edgar,* 174 Ill. 2d at 45–52, 672 N.E.2d at 1199–1202.

63. *Edgar,* 174 Ill. 2d at 58–61, 672 N.E.2d at 1205–6.

64. The *Edgar* case was followed in *Lewis E. v. Spagnolo,* 186 Ill. 2d 198, 710 N.E.2d 798 (1999), where the supreme court also refused to consider the issue of whether the state inadequately funded its public schools, which was an argument of first impression in Illinois.

65. *Chicago Urban League et al. v. State of Illinois, et al.,* In the Circuit Court of Cook County, Chancery Division, Case No. 08CH30490, https://w3.courtlink .lexisnexis.com/cookcounty/FindDock.asp?NCase=2008–CH-30490&SearchType =0&Database=3&case_no=&=&=&=&PLtype=1&sname=&CDate= (accessed July 4, 2009).

66. 740 Illinois Compiled Statutes 23/5(a) (2).

67. *Memorandum Opinion* (Chicago Urban League et al. v. State of Illinois, et al., In the Circuit Court of Cook County, Chancery Division, Case No. 08CH30490), entered April 15, 2009, 2, http://www.thechicagourbanleague.org/7232108201329597/ lib/7232108201329597/CUL%20v%20ISBE%20Opinion%204-15-09.pdf (accessed July 4, 2009).

68. Chapter 5 of this book ("The Legislature") provides an account of the impeachment and removal from office of Blagojevich in 2009 from the perspective of the legislature.

69. Gibson, "High Court Is in the Game."

70. James Oliphant, "Burris Gets Senatorial Welcome—Blagojevich's Pick Sworn in as State's Junior Senator," *Chicago Tribune,* January 16, 2009.

71. Senate Impeachment Rules, Senate Resolution 6, 96th General Assembly. http:// www.ilga.gov/legislation/96/SR/PDF/09600SR0006.pdf.

72. Armstrong and Pearson, "Heiple's Pyrrhic Victory."

Chapter 8: The Intergovernmental Web

1. "Units of Government—We're Number 1," *Fiscal Focus* (a newsletter of the Illinois Office of the Comptroller), June 2006, 3.

2. "Regional Revenue and Spending Project," in *Seeking a New Balance: Paying for Government in Metropolitan Chicago* (Chicago: Regional Partnership, 1991). Executive Summary, 2.

3. James F. Keane and Gary Koch, eds., *Illinois Local Government: A Handbook* (Carbondale: Southern Illinois University Press, 1990), ix. Another estimate in the same book puts the figure at one hundred thousand.

4. Robert P. Howard, *Illinois: A History of the Prairie State* (Grand Rapids, Mich.: Eerdmans, 1972), 479.

5. Daniel J. Lehmann, "Payroll 'Ghost' Admits Scheme," *Chicago Sun-Times,* October 13, 1994.

6. "Governments Spent $5 Million to Lobby State Government," Illinois Campaign for Political Reform, press release, Chicago, April 21, 2008.

7. Kathleen O'Leary Morgan and Scott Morgan, *State Rankings 2007* (Lawrence, Kan.: Morgan-Quitno, 2006), 282–83. Data in the rankings are taken from federal government sources.

8. Samuel K. Gove, *The Illinois Municipal Electoral Process* (Urbana: Institute of Government and Public Affairs, 1964).

9. Illinois General Assembly, Legislative Research Unit, *Catalog of State Assistance to Local Governments 2008,* 12th ed. (Springfield: Legislative Research Unit of the Illinois General Assembly, 2008), xiii.

10. Ibid.

11. Advisory Commission on Intergovernmental Relations, *State and Local Roles in the Federal System* (Washington, D.C.: GPO, 1982), table 106, p. 262.

12. Illinois Constitution, 1970, art. 7I, sec. 6.

13. Editorial, *Chicago Tribune,* June 17, 1990.

14. James Banovetz and Thomas W. Kelty, *Home Rule in Illinois* (Springfield: *Illinois Issues,* Sangamon State University, 1987).

15. "Mandates Lists Suggest not Much 'Local Control,'" State School News Service, Springfield, Ill, September 16, 2008.

16. "Annual Financial Reports: Unused and Unusable," *Tax Facts,* October 1990, 7.

17. Regional Revenue and Spending Project, "Seeking a New Balance," Executive Summary, 25.

18. Ibid., 27.

19. An exception to this statement is found in Samuel K. Gove, "State Impact: The Daley Legacy," in *After Daley: Chicago Politics in Transition,* ed. Samuel K. Gove and Louis H. Masotti (Urbana: University of Illinois Press, 1982), 203–16. The political literature about Chicago is voluminous, but little attention is given to the city's relationship with the state because the authors do not believe that the relationship is important for an understanding of Chicago politics.

20. Charles E. Merriam, Spencer D. Parratt, and Albert Lapawsky, *The Government of the Metropolitan Region of Chicago* (Chicago: University of Chicago Press, 1933), 179.

21. In the suburbs of Cook County, township committeemen are elected to serve on the county central committee. Outside Cook County, precinct committeemen are elected and they then select the county chairmen.

22. Zay N. Smith and Pamela Zekman, *The Mirage* (New York: Random House, 1979), 39–40.

23. www.suntimes.com/news/metro/522594, CST-hired23.article, August 23, 2007.

24. Malcolm Gladwell, "Paring the Big Apple," *Washington Post,* national weekly edition, March 21–27, 1994, 33. The author relied heavily on the study by Ester R. Fuchs, *Mayors and Money: Fiscal Policy in New York and Chicago* (Chicago: University of Chicago Press, 1992).

25. See Mary Edwards and Laura Lawson, "The Evolution of Planning in East St. Louis," *Journal of Planning History* 4, no. 4 (November 2005): 356–82, for a thoughtful overview and rich set of written resources about East St. Louis.

26. James D. Nowlan, "Hope Still Blooms in East St. Louis," *St. Louis Post-Dispatch,* September 3, 1989.

27. Samuel K. Gove and James D. Nowlan, *Illinois Politics and Government: The Expanding Metropolitan Frontier* (Lincoln: University of Nebraska Press, 1996), 165–66.

28. Edwards and Lawson, "Evolution of Planning," 370.

29. Bruce Wicks, interview by James D. Nowlan, January 9, 2008. Also interviewed were senior ESLARP staff members Yanni Sorenson and Billie Turner.

30. *Regional Snapshot,* Chicago Metropolitan Agency for Planning, 2006.

31. Bob Tita, "Looking to Add Teeth to Planning," *Crain's Chicago Business,* October 16, 2006.

32. Chicago Metropolitan Agency for Planning, *About CMAP* (pamphlet), 2007.

33. Tita, "Looking to Add Teeth to Planning."

34. Ibid.

35. Chicago Metropolitan Agency for Planning, *About CMAP.*

36. Phillip Bloomer, *Champaign-Urbana News Gazette,* March 2, 1990.

37. Illinois General Assembly, Legislative Research Unit, "Federal Funds to State Agencies, FY 2007–2009," August 2008, xiii.

38. Kathleen O'Leary Morgan and Scott Morgan, eds., *State Rankings 2009* (Washington, D.C.; CQ Press, 2009), 301.

39. Ibid., 525.

40. Len O'Connor, *Clout: Mayor Daley and His Chicago* (Chicago: Henry Regnery, 1975), 150–57.

Chapter 9: Education

1. Kathleen O'Leary Morgan and Scott Morgan, eds., *State Rankings 2008* (Washington, D.C.: CQ Press, 2009), 143. Data in the state rankings book are from federal government sources, unless otherwise noted below, and sources are provided therein.

2. Ibid., 145.

3. Peter Mulhall, "Illinois K-12 Education," in *The Illinois Report 2007* (Urbana: Institute of Government and Public Affairs, University of Illinois, 2007), 24–29.

4. Illinois Constitution, 1970, art. 10.

5. Illinois State Board of Education, "Illinois Education QuickStats 2008" (Springfield, 2008); O'Leary Morgan and Morgan, *State Rankings 2009,* 124.

6. Illinois State Board of Education, "Illinois Education QuickStats 2008."

7. Homeschool statistics, "Let's Home School," www.letshomeschool.com/articles39 .html.

8. For an excellent discussion of education in Illinois before 1975, see Martin Burlingame, "Politics and Policies of Elementary and Secondary Education," in *Illinois: Political Processes and Governmental Performance,* ed. Edgar Crane (Dubuque, Iowa: Kendall-Hunt, 1980), 370–89. See also Cullom Davis, "Illinois Crossroads and Cross Section," in *Heartland: Comparative Histories of the Midwestern States,* ed. James H. Madison (Bloomington: Indiana University Press, 1988), 154.

9. James Broadway, "Mandates Lists Suggest not Much 'Local Control,'" State School News Service, September 16, 2008 (a subscription email service).

10. James Broadway, State School News Service, June 9, 2009.

11. James Broadway, interview by James D. Nowlan, February 13, 2009, Springfield.

12. Paul Kimmelman, *Implementing NCLB: Creating a Knowledge Framework to Support School Improvement* (Thousand Oaks, Calif.: Corwin, 2006), 22.

13. This remark was heard by James D. Nowlan while in the audience at a meeting of the Illinois Association of Schools Boards, n.d.

14. As reported in *First Reading, December 1989* (a newsletter of the Legislative Research Unit of the Illinois General Assembly).

15. "Charter School Tiff Attracting Friend, Foe," *Chicago Tribune,* March 22, 2007.

16. In 2009 the legislature increased to 120 the number of charters that can be created, 75 in Chicago and 45 in the rest of the state, but the governor had not signed the legislation into law as of July 2009.

17. "Charter School Tiff Attracting Friend, Foe."

18. "Separation Anxiety," a special supplement of *Catalyst Chicago* (Chicago: Catalyst Chicago, 2007).

19. Burlingame, "Politics and Policies," 370–89, provides a thorough discussion of the development and central role played by the School Problems Commission, which consisted of legislators and members of the public, from about 1950 until 1971.

20. Membership numbers provided by organizational officials via email to James D. Nowlan, July 5, 2007.

21. Ken Bruce, interview James D. Nowlan, February 1, 1990, Springfield.

22. Reflection of James D. Nowlan, who was special assistant to the governor in 1977.

23. Scott Reeder, "Teacher Unions Have A+ Clout," in a special reprint, "The Hidden Costs of Tenure," in the *Dispatch* (Moline, Ill.,) December 4–9, 2005.

24. Kent D. Redfield, "Investing in the General Assembly," in *Almanac of Illinois Politics—1994,* ed. Jack Van Der Slik (Springfield: Center for the Study of State Policy and Leadership, University of Illinois at Springfield, 1994), 8.

25. Reeder, "Teacher Unions Have A+ Clout."

26. O'Leary Morgan and Morgan, *State Rankings 2009,* 125, drawn from data provided by the National Education Association.

27. Ibid., 140.

28. National Education Association, *Rankings of the States and Estimates of School Statistics* (Washington, D.C.: NEA Research, 2006).

29. Data are from the National Center for Education Statistics, as reported in State School News Service, Springfield, August 6, 2008.

30. Toni Waggoner, PowerPoint presentation to the Budget Division of the Illinois State Board of Education, 2008. See also Deborah A. Verstegen, "Adequate Funding in Illinois Public Schools," in "Policy Research Brief," Department of Educational Organization and Leadership, University of Illinois at Urbana, May 2007, 1–7.

31. "Separation Anxiety," a special supplement of *Catalyst Chicago* (Chicago: Catalyst Chicago, 2007).

32. Commission on Government Forecasting and Accountability, Illinois General Assembly, "Education Funding," November 2008, 18.

33. Charles N. Wheeler III, "Illinois' Fiscal Health Is in a Sorry State," *Illinois Issues,* April 2007, 37–38. Also at illinois.uis.edu/features/2007apr/health.html.

34. James Ward, remarks before a meeting of Voice of the Prairie, Galesburg, Illinois, October 28, 1989.

35. *Chicago Urban League and Quad County Urban League, Plaintiffs v. State of Illinois and Illinois State Board of Education, Defendants,* complaint filed August 20, 2008 in the Circuit Court of Cook County, Illinois.

36. "Stats and Facts," Chicago Public Schools, http://www.cps.edu/AboutCPS/At-a-glance/Pages/Stats%20and%20facts.asp, accessed July 10, 2008.

37. Staff of the *Chicago Tribune, Chicago Schools: Worst in America,* special section of the *Chicago Tribune,* 1988.

38. Ibid.

39. Mary O'Connell, *School Reform Chicago Style: How Citizens Organized to Change Public Policy* (Chicago: Neighborhood Works and Center and Neighborhood Technology, 1991), 21.

40. Ibid., 22.

41. According to David Nasaw, big-city schools were centralized in the early years of the century, when progressive reforms aimed at taking control from ethnic politicians. This was achieved in Chicago at the time of World War I. See Nasaw, *Schooled to Order: A Social History of Public Schooling in the United States* (New York: Oxford University Press, 1979), chap. 7.

42. O'Connell, *School Reform Chicago Style,* 28.

43. John Camper, "Chicago School Reform Defies the Conventional Wisdom," *Illinois Issues,* January 1990, 36.

44. By 2009, Vallas had gone on to reform the Philadelphia and New Orleans school districts. Duncan became U.S. Secretary of Education in 2009 in the administration of President Barack Obama, also a Chicagoan.

45. As reported in "Separation Anxiety."

46. O'Leary Morgan and Morgan, *State Rankings 2008,* 134.

47. Ibid., 132, 134.

48. Harold L. Hodgkinson, *Illinois: The State and Its Educational System* (Washington, D.C.: Institute for Educational Leadership, 1989), 7.

49. "What Do People Think? Results from an Illinois Public Opinion Survey,"

Institute of Government and Public Affairs, University of Illinois, Urbana, June 24, 2008, 4–7.

50. "Current Enrollment Data, Fall 2005," Illinois Board of Higher Education, Springfield, 2005.

51. Ibid.

52. Michael Cheney and Christopher T. Erb, "Higher Education and Illinois' Future," in *The Illinois Report* (Urbana: Institute of Government and Public Affairs, University of Illinois 2007), 32–35.

53. "Financial Data: State Higher Education Operating Appropriations, FY 2003 to FY 2006," table X-1, Illinois Board of Higher Education, Springfield, 2007.

54. O'Leary Morgan and Morgan, *State Rankings 2009*, 145.

55. "State 'Exports' Too Many Students," *Bloomington Pantagraph*, March 10, 2007.

56. This background is taken from James D. Nowlan, *The Politics of Higher Education: Lawmakers and the Academy in Illinois* (Urbana: University of Illinois Press, 1976), chap. 1.

57. The five systems were the University of Illinois, Southern Illinois University, the Board of Regents (Northern Illinois, Illinois State, and Sangamon State universities), the Board of Governors (Western, Eastern, Northeastern, Governors' State, and Chicago State universities), and the Illinois Community College Board.

58. Northern Illinois University actually absorbed the private Lewis University College of Law in Joliet and moved it to the NIU campus at DeKalb.

59. The University of Illinois had a board that was elected statewide until 1992, when it became an appointed board.

60. As reported in Rich Miller's CapitolFax subscription service, various dates, May 2007.

61. Wagner made this personal observation in private conversation with James D. Nowlan, undated.

62. *Strengthening Private Higher Education in Illinois* (Springfield: Commission to Study Non-Public Higher Education in Illinois, 1969), 5.

63. From an Ameritech Foundation study, as reported in the *Bloomington Pantagraph*, January 18, 1990.

64. University of Illinois Development Office brochure, undated.

65. "Measuring Up 2008: The State Report Card on Higher Education—Illinois," National Center for Public Policy and Higher Education, San Jose, Calif., 2008, 8–9.

Chapter 10: Taxing and Spending

1. For a delightful, highly instructive essay about budgeting, see Robert Mandeville, "It's the Same Old Song," in *Illinois State Budget, Fiscal Year 1991* (Springfield: Illinois Bureau of the Budget, March 1990), 1–14.

2. *Illinois State Budget 2008* (Springfield: Governor's Office of Management and Budget, 2007). www.state.il.us.budget.

3. As reported in Charles Wheeler, "Ends and Means," *Illinois Issues*, November 2007, 37–38.

4. *Facing Facts: A Report of the Civic Committee's Task Force on Illinois State Finance* (Chicago: Civic Committee of the Commercial Club of Chicago, December 2006), 7.

5. Ibid., 9.

6. Ibid., 23.

7. Ibid., 49–50.

8. *Illinois Tax Handbook for Legislators,* 24th ed. (Springfield: Legislative Research Unit of the Illinois General Assembly, 2008).

9. *Fiscal Focus,* Illinois Comptroller's Office, May 2007.

10. *The Illinois State Budget and Tax Primer* (Chicago: Center for Tax and Budget Accountability, 2007).

11. *Illinois Tax Handbook,* 90–97.

12. "Tax Expenditure Report," Commission on Government Finance and Accountability, Springfield, Illinois, 2006.

13. *Illinois Tax Handbook,* 59.

14. Ibid., 69.

15. "Wagering in Illinois—2007 Update," Commission on Government Forecasting and Accountability, Springfield, October 2007.

16. Jack R. Van Der Slik, "Legalized Gamblers: Predatory Policy," *Illinois Issues,* March 1990, 30.

17. Mandeville, "It's the Same Old Song."

18. Illinois Constitution, 1970, art. 8, sec. 2 (a).

19. As observed by James D. Nowlan, who was a member of the 1976 transition team.

20. Mandeville, "It's the Same Old Song," 5.

21. As reported in James D. Nowlan, *New Game Plan for Illinois* (Chicago: Neltnor House, 1989), 113.

22. Raymond F. Coyne, "The Legislative Appropriations Process: Selective Use of Authority and Tools," in *Illinois: Political Processes and Governmental Performance,* ed. Edgar Crane (Dubuque: Kendall-Hunt, 1980), 287–305.

23. The Illinois Capital Budget, Governor's Office of Management and Budget, Springfield, 2007, http://www2.state.il.us/budget/FY08%20Capital%20Budget.pdf (accessed June 2008).

24. "Nearly $43 Million Diverted from General Revenue Fund in FY89," press release, Office of the Comptroller, Springfield, May 14, 1990.

25. "McPier Set to Tap Sales Tax for 1st Time," *Crain's Chicago Business,* May 14, 2007.

26. Commission on Government Forecasting and Accountability, "Pensions: Report on the Financial Condition of the State Retirement Systems," Springfield, February 2008.

27. "Federal Funds to State Agencies FY2007–2009," 18th ed., Legislative Research Unit, Springfield, May 2009, xiii.

28. Ibid.

29. Ibid.

30. Randy Erford, *Illinois State Spending: The Thompson Years* (Springfield: Taxpayers' Federation of Illinois, 1998), 9.

31. Illinois Department of Revenue, *Property Tax Statistics* (Springfield: Illinois Department of Revenue, 2008).

32. Kathleen O'Leary Morgan and Scott Morgan, eds., *State Rankings 2008* (Washington, D.C.: CQ Press, 2008). 311.

33. *The Illinois Poll, 1991* (DeKalb: Center for Governmental Studies, Northern Illinois University, 1991).

34. Illinois Department of Revenue, *Property Tax Statistics.*

35. Thomas Anton, *The Politics of State Expenditure in Illinois* (Urbana: University of Illinois Press, 1966).

36. Press release, Illinois State Board of Education, Springfield, January 19, 1989.

37. For an informative look at the Bureau of the Budget (retitled the Governor's Office of Management and Budget), see Craig Bazzani, "The Executive Budget Process," in *Inside State Government in Illinois,* ed. James Nowlan (Urbana: Institute of Government and Public Affairs, 1982). The quotation in the text is found on 42.

38. Coyne, "Legislative Appropriations Process," 144.

39. Michael D. Klemens, "An Overture to Overcome Overspending," *Budget Watch Reporter* no. 5 (June 1990): 1–8 (Springfield: Illinois Tax Foundation).

40. Michael D. Klemens, "Budget Crisis: The Seeds and the Harvest," *Illinois Issues,* August–September 1987, 46.

41. O'Leary Morgan and Morgan, *State Rankings 2008,* 311, 303.

Chapter 11: Illinois: Strong but not Achieving

1. James D. Nowlan, *A New Game Plan for Illinois* (Chicago: Neltnor House, 1985), 7.

2. James W. Fossett and J. Fred Giertz, "Money, Politics, and Regionalism: Allocating State Funds in Illinois," in *Diversity, Conflict and State Politics,* ed. Peter F. Nardulli (Urbana: University of Illinois Press, 1989), 244.

3. Ibid., 237.

4. Ibid., 244–45.

5. Illinois does have a beautiful state song, "Illinois," but it is seldom played.

6. Kent D. Redfield, "The Cost of Corruption: Political Corruption in Illinois and What to Do about It" (Springfield: Sunshine Project, 2006), emphasis in original. This is an eight-panel brochure, six thousand of which were distributed statewide. http://www.ilcampaign.org/PDF/BrochureCorruption.pdf.

7. Ibid.

8. Stephen Ohlemacher, "Early Presidential Primary States Are far from U.S. Average," Associated Press, Washington, D.C., May 17, 2007.

9. *State Rankings 2007* (Lawrence, Kans.: Morgan-Quitno, 2007).

Index

James D. Nowlan is a senior fellow in the Institute of Government and Public Affairs at the University of Illinois at Urbana-Champaign. He served as an Illinois state representative from 1969 to 1973 and as an aide to three Illinois governors.

Samuel K. Gove is director emeritus and professor emeritus of the Institute of Government and Public Affairs.

Richard J. Winkel Jr. is the director of the Office of Public Leadership in the Institute of Government and Public Affairs. He served in the Illinois House of Representatives from 1995 to 2003 and in the Illinois Senate from 2003 to 2007.

The University of Illinois Press
is a founding member of the
Association of American University Presses.

Composed in 10.5/13 Adobe Minion Pro
with Ariel and Bauer Bodoni display
by Celia Shapland
at the University of Illinois Press
Designed by Dennis Roberts
Manufactured by Thomson-Shore, Inc.

University of Illinois Press
1325 South Oak Street
Champaign, IL 61820-6903
www.press.uillinois.edu